LINDEN

ON THE SAUGUS BRANCH

Other Books by ELLIOT PAUL

THE LAST TIME I SAW PARIS
THE LIFE AND DEATH OF A SPANISH TOWN
THE STARS AND STRIPES FOREVER
CONCERT PITCH
THE GOVERNOR OF MASSACHUSETTS
LAVA ROCK
LOW RUN TIDE
THE AMAZON
IMPERTURBE
IMPROMPTU
INDELIBLE

Homer Evans Murder Mysteries

THE MYSTERIOUS MICKEY FINN
HUGGER-MUGGER IN THE LOUVRE
MAYHEM IN B-FLAT
FRACAS IN THE FOOTHILLS
SUMMER IN DECEMBER

LINDEN

ON THE SAUGUS BRANCH

By Elliot Paul

Random House · New York

To Mildred and Edwin Leslie Paul
of Harwood Street

The author wishes to thank Barbara Paul and Robert N. Linscott for editorial help and encouragement in connection with this volume.

Contents

Contents

LINDEN

ON THE SAUGUS BRANCH

CHAPTER ONE

A Name on the Snow

◆

LINDEN, in Massachusetts, at the turn of the twentieth century, was as obscure a little community as there was in the broad United States. It was neither backwoods, seashore, country, city or town, but only a detached precinct of the outermost ward of the suburban city of Malden, eight or nine miles distant from Boston, as the crow flies. It is almost incredible that such a neglected and isolated spot could exist in a section of New England that looks, on the map, thickly populated and devoid of open spaces.

To the north were miles and miles of virgin woods in which Indians had lived by hunting, not as vast as the wilderness of Maine, but extensive and mysterious enough so that there seemed to be no end to them. And in shocking contrast, to the east, lay the Lynn marshlands, all the way from Linden to the sea, flat, bleak, and containing beneath their drab camouflage all the wonders of the tidelands and the littoral. Southward lay more vacant miles. Gravestones in rows, acre after acre of Holy Cross Cemetery, one of the largest and least beautiful burying grounds in all the world. The view between Linden and the sunset, to the west, had in the foreground a winding creek bottom and a swamp, with the flat roof of rambling carbarns against the maples of nearby Maplewood and the jagged evergreens on the horizon.

Politically, Linden was the forgotten ward, the stepchild of

Malden, which in turn owed its existence to Boston. The Linden folks, who got nothing from their absentee government except tax bills for which few services were rendered, felt no civic connection with any other place at all. To all intents and purposes they were separate and autonomous.

Not far away, in Concord, just the other side of Boston, in 1776 the shot had been fired that had been heard around the world. I think it caused little stir in Linden. Five or six miles south by east was Bunker Hill, where local patriots had fought the British. None of those heroes, as far as the records indicate, had rushed over from Linden to join the affray. The first *Mayflower*, whose passengers are all catalogued and whose furniture has multiplied like the miraculous loaves and fishes, sailed into Plymouth, on the South Shore. *Mayflower* Number 2, of which too little has been said or written, landed in Salem, just north of Linden, in 1629, and the passengers, more resourceful and adventurous, if less pious than the Pilgrims, spread through the Mystic Valley, and down Cape Ann to the tip, at Pigeon Cove. For decades, all these hardy settlers overlooked what later became Linden.

There were never any fine old houses, examples of Colonial or European architecture, and none of the new houses were remarkable for their proportions or lines. The churches, or meeting houses, post-dated the period when clover blinds and white steeples made the houses of God in New England villages an expression of dignity and beauty. Linden's churches were aesthetic monstrosities, badly designed, jerry-built, and inexpertly painted.

No Linden pioneers had a conspicuous part in building up our nation. And if any of the nineteenth or twentieth century residents set the planet afire, in any field of endeavor, I have not been informed of the fact. F. P. A. and Erle Stanley Gardner were born in Malden, not in Linden. Harold Stearns, although he went to Malden High School, lived in Cliftondale. Alvan T. Fuller, the Massachusetts governor who sanctioned the official murders of Sacco and Vanzetti, taught Sunday School in Malden Center, but Linden knew nothing of him until he became top dog in state politics. Roland Tapley, reared and taught in Linden, became a member of the Boston Symphony Orchestra at an early age, playing in the violin section. That is about the size of Linden's contributions to the arts and sciences, and we produced no outstanding military figures or statesmen. No bankers or great criminals, either. The Linden men and women liked to think of themselves as slightly above the average Americans, not too smart, and certainly not stupid or provincial.

Our house was on Beach Street, the central thoroughfare to Linden Square, where the steam trains came in. Through the storm windows facing west, and the vivid winter sunsets, we could watch the horsecars and the struggling of beasts and drivers to get them up the hill to Salem Street. This Beach Street hill, today, is hardly noticeable, but in the late nineties it was a traffic hazard that offered much winter entertainment. The northeast blizzards, gathering momentum as they hurled themselves at Linden, across the marsh from the raging Atlantic, piled drifts against this hill, and biting frosts iced the streetcar rails and the bumpy path between them. So during and after a snowstorm the street railway company sent an extra pair of horses and an extra driver, red-whiskered young Ginger McSweeney, to help the horsecars up the hill.

When a horsecar passed our house, with slow rhythmic thuds of hoofbeats, jangling of harness, puffing of animals, thumping of gongs and shouts from the driver, it was possible to watch it through the north windows, to see who was aboard, then hurry to the west side of the house to see what happened on the hill.

The regular driver would wind the long brass handle of the brake, after transferring the reins to his left glove or mitten, making a din with the ratchet. Inside the car, which had red plush seats along the sides, and straps hanging down the middle, was a glowing wood stove from which sparks snapped out of the stovepipe. But the heat from this did not penetrate the front vestibule, on which the driver stood.

About the time the car came to a stop, just beyond Clapp Street, which faced Puffer's store, about a hundred yards from our windows, Ginger, cursing and blarneying his nags in a penetrating voice that no storm windows could keep out, would hitch them ahead of the regular pair. If he waited too long, the iron wheels of the car would freeze to the rails. As a matter of course, the railway superintendent sent his least-promising pair of extra horses to Linden, and none of the Bay State Street Railway's horses were prize-winning specimens. The best work horses in the region hauled brewery wagons in Boston and Chelsea, or delivery wagons from the Boston stores: S. S. Pierce, Jordan Marsh, Houghton and Dutton, or Stearns.

Ginger, himself, was sent to Linden, although he was one of the best drivers anywhere around, because his language, and his ways with women, had caused complaints elsewhere. The officials thought nothing mattered much in Linden. He lived in Edgeworth, the toughest neighborhood north of Boston, and at first had been assigned by the company to work near his home. There, among his fellow Irish, his language had caused little comment, but he had got into a fight, practically every day, and someone he had beaten up had sued the company. The liability of public service corporations for the acts of their employees was not in those days what it is now, but the Bay State Street Railway Company was not one to take chances.

In Linden, most of the men were working in Boston, daytimes, and came home tired nights. Furthermore, the women in Linden who lived along the street car tracks were Protestants.

Wherever he was, drunk or sober, Ginger was irrepressible and gay. He was not a tall man, but he was stocky. His eyes were agate-brown and crackled with malicious highlights, his hair was crisp and curly, and he wore luxuriant red moustaches that bristled at least four inches on either side of the part in the middle. Even as a young man, he had a magnificent start on a nose that promised to be an object of art and amazement. It was prominent, bulbous, in rose and crimson, pocked and veined with indigo. We were told that Ginger's nose was thus because he drank. Untactfully, I mentioned a number of others who drank with zeal and gusto, and whose noses were normal. Those, I was assured, had no more lining in their stomachs, but I could not see that they were the worse for the lack.

Throughout the years I lived in Linden, I had a chance to watch the progress of Ginger's nose.

When the horsecars gave way to electric cars, Ginger became a motorman. My friends and I used to stand on the front platform, watching him spin the brake handle, stamp on the gong, and hearing him bawl out teamsters or pedestrians who got in the way. When the first automobiles put in an appearance, Ginger was frankly contemptuous and used to race them with his trolley car, whenever they pulled alongside. Often this caused him to overrun his stops and brake the car abruptly, but most of the passengers, feeling as he did about the new machines, made no objection.

His nose slowly ripened and glowed. The early shades of rose and crimson deepened to russet and purple, and the once smooth and shiny surface was etched and stippled with veins, scrolls and tiny curlicues, with a texture like Moroccan leather.

It was in the dead of winter, while Linden was partially

7

snowbound, that we began to hear rumors that Ginger Mc-
Sweeney had written, in a way that became clearer as time
went on, the name of one of the Linden schoolteachers, Miss
Alice Townsend, in the snow, and that the consequences, to
Miss Townsend and many others, were grave and far-reaching,
indeed.

Miss Townsend, nicknamed irreverently by her third grade
pupils "Sweet Alice," on account of the song "Ben Bolt," was
then twenty-two years old, with a pale oval face, a little flat,
perhaps, honey-colored hair piled high on her head like that
of a Gibson Girl, slender, graceful, nervous hands, and a soft
and plaintive voice. She was far too timid to be a school teacher
and enjoy it, but very few occupations were then open to young
women, and Alice Townsend had a mother and an older sister
to support. As a matter of course, the Malden School Committee sent their least successful teachers to Linden. That is why
Miss Townsend was there.

Massachusetts children went to school at the age of five and
there must have been about twenty of them in the third grade,
between the ages of eight and ten. And the temptation was so
strong that most of them made life difficult for poor Miss
Townsend, who was so palpably afraid of them. Some of the
most susceptible dearly loved her and spared her what they
could, and on the days she suffered from "sick headaches," even
the most brutal boys and girls let up a bit. She never was cross,
or failed to promote anyone, having a horror of hurting the
children's feelings or antagonizing the parents, whom she seldom saw or heard from unless they were dissatisfied about
something.

The Townsends lived high up on Salem Street, in an old
wooden house badly in need of paint and repair. The front
porch was propped up on stilts, the back rested against the
steep slope of the northern hills. To reach their front door,

one had to climb a rickety flight of wooden steps, held up precariously by worm-eaten timbers. Mrs. Townsend was in poor health and liked to have anyone with whom she came in contact realize the fact. Her neck was scrawny, her hair a peppery gray, and while she showed some trace of former beauty that must have resembled Alice's, Mrs. Townsend had more of the manner and features of her older daughter, Elvira: the tight lips, onion eyes and stiff manners that made them both seem a little off the pattern.

Three or four times each week, Mrs. Townsend had to walk back and forth between her house and the stores in the Square, a distance of about a mile. She passed our house about halfway and on fine days, when Mother was out on the porch, she stopped to rest in one of the porch rockers a while and talk with Mother, who was always sympathetic. This, except for Mrs. Townsend's dealings with the tradesmen, was about the extent of her movements in Linden. She belonged to the Ladies' Social Circle of the Congregational Church and attended their afternoon meetings in the various homes of the members only when the weather, underfoot and overhead, was favorable to semi-invalids.

Elvira was never seen outside of the Townsends' roughly sloping yard except Sunday mornings, when she went with Alice and her mother to church, just beyond our house, at the corner of Beach and Lawrence Streets. Elvira walked with her head tilted to one side, and alternated between two expressions: one of resigned disapproval and the other, as if she were thinking of something very lovely that she she did not wish to share.

Linden people thought it was too bad Alice Townsend did not have a young man, she was so pretty and modest and good, but they also understood that she could not very well leave her mother and sister to their own devices. And no local young

9

man, with his way to make in the world, could take on the whole family and live with them, unless he were head over heels in love. Alice's timidity, her constant state of nervous exhaustion, and her virginal reserve and pride did not attract the young men.

Her pay as a teacher was about five hundred dollars a year. Food for three cost her about five dollars a week. That left two hundred and fifty, more or less, divided three ways, for clothes, fuel (a major item, about forty dollars), taxes, church contributions (about fifteen dollars a year at the Congregational), and entertainment. The Townsend women made their own clothes, the materials being used first by Alice, who had to keep up a neat appearance, then her mother, who had to show herself on the street to do the errands, and lastly by Elvira. Before the disastrous handwriting incident, they had never had to call a doctor. Their entertainment consisted of church sociables, horsecar rides which cost a nickel apiece, and free band concerts at Crescent Beach or Pine Banks Park.

Ginger's pay, as an extra horsecar driver, was about the same as Miss Townsend's—around ten dollars a week, three of which he paid his mother for board. The rest he blew merrily on drink, doxies, tobacco and Copenhagen snuff. Now and then, to pacify his old mother, he would go to Mass at St. Joseph's, in Maplewood.

"Everything but murder, Father, ten times," he would say to the priest, and not even the priest could be too severe with Ginger, who smiled and laughed his way in and out of everything.

Every day, after school, Miss Townsend walked home from the schoolhouse on Clapp Street. In cold weather she wore a neat fur hat, made over from one her father had left them, a woolen coat, overshoes, and gloves inside of mittens. She led, one with each hand, the two little Preston girls, who lived just at the top of the Beach Street hill, directly on her only passable route. Mrs. Preston always received the children at the door, and thanked Miss Townsend. Several of the older boys took the same way home, but they ran on ahead of the teacher.

Nearly always the boys stopped to watch Ginger and his horses, and talk with him. He got on well with boys.

On the day in question, Miss Townsend had a few papers to correct and other odd chores, so the Preston girls went up to her empty classroom to wait. The little girls looked forward to those days when Miss Townsend was delayed, because then they had a chance to look into a higher grade, where some day they would be, and which had different Perry pictures on the walls and problems beyond their knowledge on the blackboards.

It must have been four o'clock when Miss Townsend and the girls started out. The sun was sinking behind the carbarns and evergreens. Before sundown, the wind that searched the Linden streets all day was likely to calm down, and everything was still, except for the shouts of Ginger as he hooked his horses to the streetcar and urged them ahead.

As Miss Townsend approached and turned up Beach Street, the horsecar, with glowing stove and a dozen passengers, was being dragged up the hill. Everything was as usual except that Miss Townsend noticed five or six boys grouped outside the fence of Clapp's field, near the turnout. Her nerves responded with a faint tingling, and her heart beat faster, because she was wary of boys when they might throw snowballs. They probably would not try to hurt her with frozen ones, but their disrespect would emphasize to the neighbors that her pupils failed to take her seriously.

As she approached a little nearer, she saw that the boys were staring at something on the other side of the fence.

Jim Puffer, saluting her from his store window across the

street, distracted her attention a moment. When she looked back, the boys had vanished. This bewildered her and frightened her a little. They must be hiding somewhere. When Miss Townsend got frightened or excited her usually pale face got paler. The two little girls, aware that she was clinging to their hands very tightly, looked up to see what was the matter. She led them on, wishing they all were safe at home.

The drifts along Beach Street were deep, and the snowplow had heaped the snow shoulder high. On her left was the picket fence and a smooth glaze of crust dusted with fine, powdered snow. She heard the snickering and suppressed laughter of the boys, who were crouching out of sight in the frozen creek bed. She had been looking straight ahead, but now, startled, she glanced into the field and saw, in wavering letters, "Sweet Alice" on the surface of the snow. There was no mistaking the method by which the words had been written.

She did not stop, although she had to struggle to keep going. Her mind turned blank, her legs were leaden. As she got a few steps away, her pace began to quicken, until the bewildered little girls had to run to keep up. They felt that the teacher was stiffening and shuddering, her eyes staring ahead, her hands gripping theirs until it hurt.

From behind, the children heard the boys shouting with laughter. They saw Ginger at the top of the hill, pretending to dry off his panting horses with his mittens before he blanketed them. Ginger was watching Miss Townsend from the corner of his gleaming eye, pretending that he was not.

Mrs. Preston, opening her front door to thank Miss Townsend and greet the children, started to speak, then looked closer and asked anxiously, "What's the matter?" Miss Townsend stood there, tense with hysteria, unable to reply.

"Don't you feel well?" Mrs. Preston asked.

Miss Townsend's mouth opened, but no sound came out.

She dropped her muff, and when Mrs. Preston picked it up and handed it back, she fumbled it again. Then she swayed, and fell, but not in a faint. Her eyes were still open.

"Ginger," called Mrs. Preston. "Come here, quick!"

Ginger wrapped the reins around a hydrant, and came running over, vaulting the snow pile. He picked up Miss Townsend, dazed himself, and under Mrs. Preston's direction carried her inside the house and lowered her carefully to the couch.

"What ails her?" he asked.

They couldn't make Miss Townsend understand, so Mrs. Preston began questioning the children. Ginger was contrite and dumbfounded. He had foreseen no such results as these.

"When we got to the turnout," one little girl said, "she started walking faster and faster. She couldn't seem to talk."

"You'd better go for the doctor," Mrs. Preston said, and Ginger, leaving his horses hitched to the hydrant, started down the hill and toward the Square where the Linden doctor had his office.

The only telephone in Linden then was in the home of Norman Partridge, the richest man in town. The doctor had none, as yet. So Ginger had to run the length of Beach Street to call him.

On his way, Ginger had to pass all the houses, including ours, and run the gauntlet of astonished eyes. His gait and manner made it plain there was something the matter, some accident or emergency, and no such occurrence ever passed unnoticed in Linden, not even the least deviation from its everyday routine.

I had already, by the time he reached our sidewalk, started putting on my winter wraps and footgear—which meant sweater, jacket, overshoes, and mittens, with a loose overcoat outside and a corduroy cap with ear flaps. I was no Spartan, but I didn't mind the cold when it was not painful or uncomfortable.

"What are you up to?" asked my mother. But she knew. I was going on the trail of Ginger, to find out what was wrong. Some of the other boys with the same idea in mind appeared on the sidewalks and converged toward the Square, and several men and women followed a few minutes afterward, having thought of errands they could do. That was the best way to find out what was going on. Linden folks never felt ashamed of wanting to know. Perhaps they could be of service, and, if not, it would give them something extra to talk about.

When I saw that Ginger turned in at the doctor's house, just beyond the Saugus Branch railroad crossing, I quickened my pace. We all knew the accident, or whatever it was, must be serious, then.

CHAPTER TWO

The Doctor Rides at Twilight

AT THE turn of the century, medicine in Linden consisted mostly of home remedies passed on to their descendants by farmers, horse doctors and old wives. The discoveries of Lister and Pasteur were beginning to take hold, but in Linden Square there still stood a public drinking fountain with an iron ladle chained to it and the men who milked cows in Weeks' barn washed their hands before supper, but after milking the cows. Antitoxin against diphtheria came too late to save my brother Everett, who died of that dread children's disease at the age of four, six years before I was born. Folks in our neighborhood were either sickly or hardy, so that some were ailing most of the time and the others survived exposure to all kinds of contagion without knowing how lucky they were.

I can remember hearing in the barber shop an argument in which Luke Harrigan, head window dresser at Houghton and Dutton's, got the horselaugh from the whole crowd because the news had come through that, after Dr. Gorgas and General Leonard Wood had scrubbed up all the Cubans in Havana, the worst epidemic of yellow fever known to the island had broken out. Tuberculosis was called "consumption" and the general belief was that people caught it from sitting in a draft, smoking cigarettes, or being urged beyond their capacity by younger and insatiable wives.

But Linden was never consistently forward or backward

15

about anything. The only resident doctor was Dick Moody, a young man from the state of Maine who went through Harvard Medical School and hung out his shingle in our square when I was five years old. I remember because he vaccinated me for smallpox, unsuccessfully, just before I started going to school. "Doc" Moody said he had come to Linden because he liked duck-shooting and fishing and ours was the only community he could find that had no doctor handy, that was near enough Boston so he could keep in touch with his professors at Harvard and the doctors at the Massachusetts General, and had a big marsh for shooting ducks and trout streams in the woods, both practically at his doorstep. Doc had plenty of time for sport and study, because for the first few years very few of the Linden people called him, except in cases of great emergency. Then, usually, it was too late. The Catholics south of the railroad tracks patronized old Dr. Casey, in Maplewood, who was a pitiable drug-addict, and whenever a case was grave, insisted on consulting with another doctor from Malden Center. Most of the Protestant families had got accustomed to sending to Malden Center, too, and did not change their allegiance when Dr. Moody came to Linden Square, at least until after he had shown himself to be a good fellow, and as smart as they make them.

There were two other reasons why the Linden women, and the women were the ones who decided about doctors, did not warm up at first to Dr. Moody. Doc was under thirty, when he started practicing, although he grew a set of what were called "lilacs" to make himself look older. There were never less than ten or twelve Linden girls of marriageable age, mostly with anxious mothers coaching them, and while many young men left Linden for wider fields of endeavor, very few came into town with respectable professions, a hopeful future and no previous attachments. Doc Moody was soon one of the most

16

popular men in the vicinity, but he treated all the young girls
alike and hired as housekeeper a cousin of the fishman named
Mathilda Stowe.

Now the institution of housekeeper to an unmarried man
or a widower had long precedent and a firm standing in New
England. It provided homes and occupations for countless
worthy women who had been brought up as housekeepers and
knew no other way to make a living. It was a boon to men who
otherwise would have been lonesome and lived untidily.
Usually both the man and the housekeeper had reached an age
that made gossip rather pointless, or, at least, one of the parties
was safely over life's great divide. A housekeeper, in New England, was not a hired girl, in any sense of the word. She ran the
house, quite often high-handedly, and was likely to keep her
employer within bounds more strict than many wives established.

The catch about Mathilda was that she was under forty, well
formed, neat and handsome, with gray-blue eyes, brown curly
hair, small aristocratic hands and feet, and a sharp wit and
tongue, the latter of which she modified with respect and even
tenderness only when she was addressing the doctor. She was
as solicitous and protective as a mother hen and quite soon
after she had gone to work for Doc Moody, she had spoken out
plainly, in a meeting of the Ladies' Social Circle held at our
house, regarding her intentions.

"Just so's you all can quit worryin'," Mathilda said, in her
soft, tantalizing voice that took all the corners from her Cape
Ann vernacular, "I have not set my cap for the doctor. I won't
say I wouldn't, if I was ten years younger, but I ain't. When
the doctor is forty, I'll be fifty, and most o' you know what a
woman looks like and feels like when she's fifty."

This did not please many members of the Social Circle, who
were trying not to think about that, and with reason. The

Linden women of that epoch showed their age, and most of them, about ten years more. Mother, who was passing out cake, cookies and cocoa to her guests at the moment, was thirty-eight then, about Mathilda's age, and from outward appearances one would have said there was a generation between them, for Mother's hair was gray, her manner subdued, and her face was lined with sadness. Only her fine brown eyes, dark and responsive, remained of the flowerlike beauty she had had as a bride.

My Uncle Reuben, in speaking of Mathilda, in a conversation with Packard, the town lady-killer who clerked in the principal grocery store, said one day:

"I understand Mathilda won't clean Doc's shotguns for him."

"Well," said Packard dryly. "Can't a woman refuse a man something?"

"You've got an evil mind," my uncle said, but he added philosophically, "So've I, but it doesn't seem to get me much these days."

One thing was certain. The longer Mathilda kept house for Doc, the more content and easygoing he became, while she developed for him a consuming ambition. She was determined that he should make the most of his talents and go to the forefront of his profession. As Linden put it, "Mathilda kept him up to scratch." In those years, Doc handled very little money. Actually his income was just below those of Miss Townsend and Ginger McSweeney, and his expenses were higher because of his hobbies as a sportsman. Mathilda saved him more than she cost him, but neither of them would have been willing to reckon their relationship in terms of dollars and cents. She even took over the details of subscribing to the current medical periodicals and kept track of important lectures, meetings and conventions, and Doc, whatever his inclinations, could not avoid reading what he should, attending the lectures and such, and keeping abreast of all the medical developments.

"Doc'll have to get married to get a little freedom, one of these days," Packard said.

It was Mathilda who answered the bell when Ginger pulled at the knob the evening Miss Townsend collapsed. The day being Friday, she had a chowder on the fire, a basket of clams out in the ice chest, to be steamed as an appetizer, a fresh mackerel to be grilled, some homemade doughnuts spread on brown paper to take off the grease, and water boiling in the coffee pot. There was also in the icebox a case of Bass Ale, which S. S. Pierce delivered in a plain box, so that, in so far as the neighbors were concerned, it might have contained Moody and Sankey hymn books. Mathilda had decided that it was not good policy for a rising young doctor to let it be known that he had liquor in the house and drank it with his meals.

Doc was sitting in his shirt sleeves, chair tipped back, in the kitchen, enjoying the smell of the chowder. He could tell from the way the bell had rung that an urgent case was impending, and to him a case was always an adventure. He did not want to work himself to death, at all hours of day and night, but he wanted to prove that he knew what he was about and win the confidence of his chosen community and sociable neighbors. He got up, without breaking the back legs of the chair, slipped on his coat and came out of the kitchen to see what was up.

"It's the Townsend girl. The teacher," Mathilda said, helping him on with his overshoes, heavy bearskin coat and fur mittens. "She's had some kind of a spell."

"She's at Mrs. Preston's," Ginger said, and headed straight for the back yard to get the doctor's horse, Hippocrates, known as "Hip," harness him and hitch him to the sleigh.

Mathilda was glad in her heart that something had hap-

19

pened that might give Doc his big chance, and, characteristically concealed her deeper feelings with a complaint.

"Nobody calls the doctor unless he's fast asleep or the food's ready to go on the table," she said, before she closed the front door, to a small crowd of curious folks who wanted to know who was sick or had got hurt. Actually, suppertime was an hour away, but already in Mathilda's mind she pictured the pale schoolteacher in some kind of crisis that would keep the doctor at her bedside, watching every pulse beat and quiver of the girl's eyelashes, and in some masterly way no other doctor would have thought of, bringing the patient out of danger. Mathilda wished the patient was in some more influential family than the Townsends. Alice was a gracious, well-mannered young woman, without an ounce of spunk, according to Mathilda's point of view, but Alice's mother and her weird sister, Elvira, would not be likely to appreciate the doctor's work, no matter how brilliant it might be. Mathilda had all the stamina she needed, but she knew the Linden women, those who were known to be frail, might imagine all kinds of things wrong with them, or get dizzy spells because they laced themselves in so tightly. If Miss Townsend recovered before the doctor could get there, the whole affair would amount to nothing, in so far as building up his reputation was concerned.

"I'm thankful it isn't some young one, with the croup," Mathilda said to herself, as she went back to the kitchen to arrange things so the meal, if necessary, could wait without spoiling.

Some dread and acute form of what probably was bronchitis was known as "croup," and struck fear into the hearts of the mothers when any of the children showed signs of it. It came on suddenly, and for a few hours it was touch-and-go between life or death from strangulation. The best doctors, if called a little too late, were likely to lose the case, and that had happened once, within a month of his arrival in Linden, to Dr. Moody.

As the horse was being hitched in the back yard, Doc was trying to find out from Ginger what had happened, and Ginger, thoroughly rattled, could hardly make sense. He fastened one of the harness buckles wrong-side-out, a mistake he would not have normally made in his sleep.

"Get on to yourself," the doctor said, puzzled. "You might as well ride back with me."

Ginger agreed, more uneasily. Should he tell Doc all he knew, or would that do the teacher still more harm? He was in a hot sweat, not being accustomed to dealing with moral and ethical problems.

The crowd on the sidewalk parted as Doc drove out of the driveway and turned sharply up Beach Street. Doc always drove like a bat out of hell. Hip, nerved up by the tension, shied, snorted and reared when the railroad gates started coming down, with clanging of gongs, just ahead of him, to hold up traffic for the five o'clock express. Doc took a long chance and touched Hip with the whip. The gelding streaked ahead not a second too soon. The far gate just grazed the top of the sleigh.

"Sweet Mother of Christ," said Ginger, admiringly.

"He'll break his neck, and get me in trouble," Pat Finley, the crossing-tender grumbled.

The crowd in the Square watched the sleigh make record time up Beach Street, bells jangling, chunks of frozen snow flying. Everyone along both sides of the street was at the storm doors or in the windows, watching. At the corner of Clapp Street, just before the turnout on the hill, a horsecar had got stuck, blocking the way. Doc tried to swerve to the right and get around it, and the hard-packed snowpile upset him. Ginger, thrown clear, grabbed Hippocrates' bridle, and the gelding promptly started kicking the shafts and dashboard to pieces, while Doc rolled out on the other side. The passengers on the horsecar, jammed together with the conductor on the back platform, and a few customers from Puffer's store, started milling around.

The doctor, leaving Ginger to straighten out the jackpot, grabbed his bag and started on foot up the hill.

By the time Doc emerged from Mrs. Preston's house, looking for his rig, the horsecar had got started again. Seeing nothing of the sleigh or Ginger, Doc hailed it and the driver pulled up short.

"Give me a hand," Doc said to the conductor. "I've got to move Miss Townsend up to her house."

Obligingly, the driver held the horses, while the conductor and some of the passengers followed Doc into the house. The public conveyances, in those friendly years, were ready to be of service informally. And there were no ambulances, with sirens and stretchers and attendants in white coats to be summoned in an instant.

The teacher, fully dressed for outdoors, was lying face up, breathing so lightly it was imperceptible. Her fair face was so still and innocent, almost transparent. The shadows of her eyelashes shimmered because of the draft and the kerosene lamp.

"She ain't dead, is she?" asked Eddie George, the conductor, in horror.

"No. She'll be all right," the doctor said.

Under Doc's direction, the teacher's inert form was lifted and carried out to the waiting horsecar, where she was laid out on one of the brassy-smelling red plush cushions.

"Go easy, Mike," Eddie said to the driver and slowly, with

several of the neighbors aboard who had paid no fare, the car inched its way along Salem Street and stopped in front of the Townsend home. Mrs. Townsend, who had just been informed that Alice had "fainted" was on the sidewalk, distraught and wrapped in a shawl. Elvira was moaning on the porch, high above.

The doctor and three or four volunteers lifted the teacher tenderly and started up the long rickety steps. A board gave way and one man fell through, spraining his ankle; another caught at the railing to save himself and wrenched it loose, and, in the confusion, the doctor and the men carrying Miss Townsend lost their balance and fell down the steps to the sidewalk with their unconscious patient. Mrs. Townsend screamed, and set off Elvira. While the doctor leaned the teacher against a snow bank to ascertain if she had been injured, Eddie George, the kind-hearted conductor, tried to quiet the mother and older sister.

When at last the teacher, still in a coma, had been placed safely in her upstairs bedroom, the men, who had tracked snow all over the house, took their departure, all except the doctor. The horsecar moved on up Salem Street, toward the crossroads with the old Newburyport Turnpike.

"Has she had spells like this before?" the doctor asked.

"No. Never," said Mrs. Townsend.

"You and Elvira get her clothes off and put on her night dress," the doctor said. "Then I can examine her, and find out what's gone wrong."

Mrs. Townsend obeyed, in consternation. She and Elvira watched the doctor as he left the bedroom where no man had set foot before that day, and hysterically closed the door after him, fastening the wrought-iron latch and the hook and eyelet besides. They had not seen Alice or each other completely undressed for years, and the thought of a strange man about to look at her and perhaps lay hands on her, while she was exposed and senseless, demoralized them utterly.

Out in the hallway, the doctor was trying to decide what he should do. He had checked her heart, pulse and respiration. There were no symptoms of physical shock. She was not as rigid as an epileptic. He had little hopes of getting an accurate account of her history or heredity. The best he could do was to watch her, and wait, in the hope that she would regain consciousness and tell him what she could.

Of course, there was the thermometer, but already he had guessed that her temperature would be slightly subnormal. When, fearfully, Mrs. Townsend and Elvira opened the door just a crack, he opened it wider, stepped in, and went through a harmless bedroom routine, mostly for their benefit. He listened through the stethoscope again and said, "Mmmmm. Heart's stronger than mine." He slipped the thermometer under Alice's tongue and waited what seemed a long while. Then he took it over to the lamp light.

"Good. No fever," he said.

To keep the women busy, he asked them to prepare a hot water bottle or a soapstone for her feet, and cool compresses for her forehead. Now that they believed he was not going to peer beneath the bedclothes, they were calmer.

"Better make some broth," he said.

As he sat by the bedside, for what he feared would be a long and pointless vigil, he thought of the steamed clams, the fish chowder, the grilled mackerel, baked potatoes, fresh doughnuts and coffee, and Mathilda, waiting by the Square. And wondered when, if ever, he would get a case that matched some cases in his books.

CHAPTER THREE

Mene, Mene, Tekel, Upharsin

◆

SUNDAYS in Linden were different from other days. The men were all at home. No trains were running on the Saugus Branch, and the horsecar schedules were radically curtailed. For the purpose of visiting the sick, or giving the overworked housewives a little air, the folks who had horses could take a drive in the afternoon. Children were not allowed to play and could read only improving books, but they could take walks if they did not soil their Sunday clothes. Those who lived in strict families where the Sunday newspaper was taboo, managed to call on those with more liberal parents in order to see what the Katzenjammer Kids, Maude the Mule, Happy Hooligan, or the Hallroom Boys were doing. I used to do my reading of the funny papers at the Graydons'.

Early in the morning and intermittently until ten-thirty, the Catholics from the south side of Linden, mostly Irish, with a few Italians among them, walked past our house, in groups, in pairs, or singly, headed for Mass at St. Joseph's in Maplewood. There seemed to be enough of them to fill a church of their own, but none was built in Linden.

The Protestants had three churches, of different denominations. On Lynn Street, just south of the Square, where Eastern Avenue came in at an angle, stood St. Luke's Church, a dingy mauve conventional structure on a level triangular lot. The rector, the Reverend Doctor Danker, who in his robes looked as big as the back of a hack, wore *pince-nez* perched at a forbidding angle, spoke with a British accent that sounded as if he had a hot potato in his mouth, and made the ritual for his three dozen parishioners as High Church as he could. These Episcopalians, who did not relish the title "Church of England," were mostly born in England or one of the Dominions, or were first-generation Americans with an English influence at home.

The Methodist Church was on Oliver Street, near the western rim of Linden. Old Doctor Best, the minister, was nearly eighty, a kindly old man with white hair and a perpetual smile, but his memory was faulty and when, one Sunday, he preached the same sermon twice, with a hymn in between, and made the small congregation an hour late for Sunday dinner, quite a few of his flock decided to try the Congregational Church, at least for a while.

The largest and most influential church in the community was the Congregational, under the leadership of the Reverend K. Gregory Powys, a stocky, peppery little Welshman whose deep voice was like a clarion and who rolled his "r's" and stuttered when he got excited. He frequently got excited. On a good Sunday, his congregation numbered two hundred or more, including the children.

Because his wife was too feeble to get around much, and was too aloof to encourage confidences and gossip, and on account of his own fierce application to his subject between Friday and Sunday, the Reverend Powys (who would not permit his followers to call him "Doctor" although he was an authentic D.D.), had not heard the details of the Townsend incident. He was too busy putting the finishing touches on one of the favorite sermons about the feast of Belshazzar.

The bell in the square wooden tower of the Congregational

Church was the loudest and most clamorous in Linden, and since our house was only one hundred yards away, it clanged and reverberated in our ears so stridently that I usually had a dull headache before it subsided to let the church service go on. Its overtones were discordant and Deacon Parker, known to the boys as T.D., because he smoked the one-cent clay pipes of that name, liked to throw his weight on the bell rope and give his coreligionists their money's worth. Naturally, the other inhabitants within a three- or four-mile range had to take it, too.

Deacon Parker was a fixture around the Congregational Church. Not only did he ring the church bell, but he tended the furnace, a more troublesome task, and kept the large, ungainly structure as clean and free of snow tracks, mud and dust, inside, as possible. At no season in Linden was this an easy proposition. In spring the sidewalks were muddy and the crossings were pools and quagmires. The summer breezes wafted in dust, pollen and such a phenomenal variety of insects, featuring all kinds of flies and mosquitoes, that faith in God's unfailing wisdom was often sorely tried. The best season was the fall, with its gusts of wind, smoke and dead leaves. Winter meant for Deacon Parker a continual struggle.

Probably if the furnace of the Congregational Church were displayed today, it would be mistaken for some giant robot from Mars. It squatted obesely on the floor of the Sunday School room, just below the level of the ground outside, so that the ungainly zinc pipes, a foot in diameter, that fed smoke, powdered ashes and hot air into the registers of the main auditorium upstairs, were wired up against the Sunday-school ceiling, like tentacles of metallic sea monsters.

Most of the older members of the congregation, in point of membership, had pews near the registers, which were spotted along the aisles.

27

The Sunday morning after Miss Townsend's misfortune on Friday, was a cold and threatening one. The thermometer read five below zero at six o'clock, but as the wind increased its violence, the cold loosened its grip, and all the old sailors knew a blizzard was coming, and soon. By nine-thirty, when the first din from the church bell was sounded, the tones were torn from the steeple by the northeast wind and slapped against the houses nearby. My mother grimly got herself ready, and Leslie and I were obliged to do the same.

"We'll have hard work getting home," I said, but Mother knew I would do almost anything to stay home from church, and ignored the warning. As things turned out, I would not have missed the performance for the world.

The air was ominously still, and slate-colored stormclouds were crowding the eastern horizon beyond the marsh, in reefs and terraces, blue and black, when at quarter of eleven we started out. From our front porch we could see other church folks of the more rugged and faithful types converging toward the meeting house, down Beach Street, from Salem; up Beach Street from the Square. Spring Street and Revere Street, running south from Salem, and sloping downward, had been cleared by the snowplow, and were passable. So the Congregationalists were gathering from all directions, bundled up like Arctic explorers, all sizes, in groups and solitary figures, dark against the snow, their slow progress accentuated by the fixity of the stark, bare trees. Quite a few drove to church from the outskirts, in sleighs and pungs. Along the eastern wall of the church was a long shed with a roof and wide stalls, where the horses could be blanketed, hitched and left in shelter.

We always got to church ten minutes early because Mother had a horror of being late and distracting the attention of the worshippers after the services had got under way. We took off our rubbers, overcoats, mufflers and mittens and left them downstairs, near the furnace, as everybody did. Then we stood over the register, in the aisle near our pew upstairs until we were warm, and sat down, to watch the regulars come in and take their places. Some Sundays there were strangers, and everyone was eager to know who they were, and who knew them, and whether they were visiting or had come to Linden to live.

No strangers put in an appearance that Sunday morning.

My grandmother (Mother's mother), my mother, my brother Charles, then twenty-four years old, my brother Leslie, then eight, and I were in our pew. Norman Partridge, the richest man in Linden, lived right across from the church, at the corner of Lawrence and Beach Streets, and his support was another reason why the Congregationalists more or less dominated the community. Three of the four local grocers were members, also the druggist, the undertaker, the doctor's housekeeper, the tinker, the fishman, and many of the most prosperous commuters, an amazing number of widows, and three-quarters of the old maids.

The mixed quartet then consisted of Abbie Craven, daughter of the only grocer, who was an Episcopalian. She was paid a small fee because her voice was trained. Finding a contralto was always a problem, because the natural contraltos were as rare as white blackbirds. So some good-natured second soprano had to do the best she could, and whenever her part was supposed to be prominent, the other three eased up a bit to give her a chance. Will Crowell, the basso profundo, was one of Charles' friends, and president of the Wenepoykin Bicycle Club. Will could really get down there, and had such volume in his voice that he had to hold himself in unless he was the soloist, or his colleagues might as well not have been there at all. The tenor was a chipper young man, of the unathletic type, who wore nose glasses and a stand-up collar. On weekdays he was a floorwalker in a Boston shoe store. His name was Frank Horton, and he was vivacious and gay, with a repertoire of parlor jokes, conundrums and stories that were the despair of other young men at parties and socials.

Mrs. Ford, the comely little organist whose husband had consumption, started off with a processional on the large reed organ. This occupied a partly screened alcove to the right of the pulpit, across from the quartet who had a similar niche on the left. Mrs. Ford played fairly well, but she had to pump with her feet and the bellows of the organ were not strong enough for loud and dynamic effects. I felt myself straining the muscles of my arms and hands, trying to help her hit it with gusto when the piece cried for emphasis and majesty.

I shall not enumerate here all the people who came to church that day, but Mrs. Powys, the minister's wife, deserves a paragraph of her own. She was one of the most unsightly women, in an age and region where handsome females were the exception rather than the rule. Most of the vainer ones, when they got into their thirties, tried to conceal their years with false teeth, rats in their hair, bustles, pads, pleats, and ruffles. Make-up was not condoned, off the stage, and the stage was in ill repute with strict Congregationalists. The current styles revealed nothing of a woman's allure, and distorted what might have been attractive. But Mrs. Powys was in a class by herself. Compared with her full-blooded and virile husband, she looked like a moth-eaten Egyptian mummy rigged out in second-hand Victorian clothes. The material was shiny, the buttons grotesque, the small dabs of fur and lace pathetic. Her hands and neck were scrawny. Her hair was so scant that her yellow scalp showed through rifts in her absurd little bonnet. Her eyes were dull and bloodshot, her voice without timbre, her temples and cheeks were hollow, her ears had no lobes and stuck up too high and wide. Her nose was pinched and hooked like a beak.

Mrs. Powys sat in the second pew from the front, facing her husband, which must have made it harder for him to be eloquent. She was no good as a mixer, or a sitter with the sick. She had nothing to say, in a crowd, and would spill a drink of water if she tried to give it to a sufferer, because her hand shook with palsy.

"And, by Jesus," said my Uncle Reuben, "she hasn't got and never had a cent to her name, that I've heard about."

The men and women of Linden could figure out a lot of things, but never that particular marriage, and neither the minister nor Mrs. Powys ever said a word about it. It had happened years before, and in another country. Ministers were practically never chosen or received calls from on high to preach to men and women with whom they had played marbles and gone to school.

The lead-off hymn that Sunday morning was "Rock of Ages," and, as usual, I tried to figure out what sense it made, if any.

> *Rock of Ages*
> *Cleft for me.*
> *Let me hide*
> *Myself in Thee.*

I had heard the Deity referred to as a lamb, a loving shepherd, the Maker, the seven-day Creator, the Three-in-One, a king (somehow revered by republicans), the Cause of it all, a judge, the Holy Ghost, and the Holy Spirit. But a rock to me was either Gibraltar, which I saw on each year's issue of the Prudential Life Insurance Company's calendar, the Reef of Norman's Woe, the Natural Bridge of Virginia, or the enormous ledge near Black Ann's Corner, on the northeastern tip of Linden, where the granite quarry and stone crusher stood.

Everything went awry that day. Deacon Parker, who with his wife and son, William, sat in the pew directly behind ours, loved dearly to sing, but, like many other things, singing started him coughing. And Deacon Parker's cough, if it had flourished later, in the days of modern sound recording, would have been one of Linden's foremost claims to distinction. It is hard even to attempt to describe it. He started with a wheeze, inhaled and of incredible duration, then an exhaled hissing sound like a slow leak in a boiler, or the fuse of a pinwheel before it starts revolving. Then miraculously it ascended in a shrieking parabola that rasped as shrilly as the ungreased axle of a wagon wheel, and at the zenith broke up into gasps, yelps, groans and sneezes until it seemed that a gunnysack of ocelots had been slung over a clothesline.

The Deacon was built like Foxy Grandpa, being short, rotund and ruddy, with a bald head set off with a wisp of silver topknot. For such a small man to produce such prodigies of sound with only the normal respiratory organs was incredible and unforgettable. He shook and rattled while coughing, like a dried pod half-filled with seeds. And we all knew that nothing so completely disconcerted the Reverend K. Gregory Powys as to have the Deacon give one of his prime performances before the sermon was safely over. There was nothing the irate Welsh minister could do about it, except to boil and seethe inwardly and try to keep his face from swelling and turning beet-red.

While the Deacon was whooping, choking, yawping, yoiking, and puffing, the other voices scattered throughout the congregation continued dutifully, against the competition. The quartet stuck to its guns. The organ bleated and moaned. Deacon Parker tried to stuff a handkerchief in his mouth as he struggled convulsively for the nearest exit. He stumbled over a register, barked his shin on the corner of a pew, and finally made it, but when he opened the swinging door a blast of wind rushed in, and everybody knew that the storm would break before the meeting was finished.

After the hymn was over, the Reverend Powys led the congregation in prayer. At least, that was what they called it. Actually, nobody prayed but he, and for ten or twelve minutes he talked to God in a manner implying that if the Rock, or Ghost or Father did not answer the prayer, He would by no means have heard the last of it.

The selection by the quartet, which followed, was "Goodbye Sweet Day," a piece so well received that they frequently sang it in the morning. But their performance was marred by whinneying, thudding and squealing outside. A horse fight had got started in the sheds and three or four of the men who had horses down there had to scuttle up the aisles.

By that time, the minister could easily have bitten the head off a railroad spike. He sat in his high-backed chair, like a throne, glaring straight ahead and over the heads of his flock, while Mrs. Ford played "collection music," always rather vague and pianissimo. Four ushers passed the plates. The ushers were Deacon Puffer, the ineffectual grocer with silky mutton-chop whiskers, my brother Charles, who was running for the City Council, George Sampson, the most enterprising grocer, and Dud Shultz, the nervous little druggist.

Two ushers worked the pews on either side of one aisle, the other pair collected on the other side. Everybody knew who contributed and about how much, and that Norman Partridge, without ostentation, would make up the treasury deficit at the end of each fiscal year.

After the ushers had covered all the pews, they marched down the aisle to the table in front of the pulpit, each one counted the money in his plate, and handed it to the Reverend

Powys, two steps higher, on the pulpit. Dud Shultz, next to Deacon Puffer, was the prize fumbler in town. He could mix up what seemed impossible, on the face of it, to complicate. He had to check and re-check the prescriptions he put up four or five times, and then was likely to make a mistake, and come running after whoever had started away with the stuff.

That morning Dud dropped his plate and the coins rolled this way and that, some under the table, some under the front pews. Mrs. Ford, thrown off her base by the *contretemps,* accidentally pulled out the stop for the full organ, leaned on the swell and brought out a cluster of caterwauling discords before she could pull herself together. The druggist and my brother Charles got down on their knees, with what dignity they could, and retrieved what they could find, while the Reverend Powys stood up there, grinding his teeth.

The explosive possibilities of the minister's mood, what with the ominous wind outside, the sullen dimness of the light, and the series of mishaps, was communicating itself to the whole congregation, and developing a kind of mass hysteria. My own nerves were throbbing with anticipation.

At last the moment came when, all preliminaries having been disposed of, the Reverend K. Gregory Powys squared his shoulders, smoothed the lapels of his black frock-coat, took a sip of water from a glass nearby, and opened the enormous Bible on the podium before him. The place where the text would be found had been carefully marked, in advance, but K. Greg always made a dramatic gesture by taking one firm step forward, grasping the top cover of the Book with his left hand, sweeping the volume open, and pointing unerringly with his finger to the verse, he proceeded, simultaneously, to read.

"I take my text," he said that morning, "from Daniel, V; verses 5 and 25.

"In the same hour came forth fingers of a man's hand . . .

"And this is the writing that was written. *Mene, Mene, Tekel, Upharsin.*"

To heighten the effect, as he often did, the minister puffed himself up like a pouter pigeon, tapped the Book and repeated:

"In the same hour came forth fingers of a man's hand."

That was as far as he got before fat and jolly Mattie Freeman, oldest daughter of Deacon Clapp and wife of Dawson Freeman, the handsome young insurance man, threw back her head, gasped for breath, and let out a shrill, uncontrollable peal of laughter.

K. Gregory Powys stopped as if he had been hit with a snowball. The rest of the congregation, torn between horror and the feeling they were going to burst, held their breath and tried to decide where and where not to look, in order to preserve what was left of their decorum.

In Deacon Clapp's pew, consternation was growing, because Mattie, who weighed a good two hundred pounds, was laughing louder and louder, tears streaming from her eyes, mammoth breastworks heaving, limbs flopping helplessly. The dignified and shy old deacon, who looked like the left-hand Smith Brother, half stood up, as did his wife on the other side of Mattie. Charley Moore, the station agent, who was always ready and willing to help, got up and took Mattie by the arm. Mattie rose, shaking like jelly and letting out grace notes, demiquavers and appogiaturas, but some evil demon prompted her to look toward the pulpit and she nearly sank down again, her knees buckling under her.

Charley Moore and Deacon Clapp, the latter embarrassed almost to death, got the gasping and guffawing Mattie up the long aisle and out into the vestibule, between them. As the sounds died away, the members of the congregation tried to quiet themselves and to guess what the minister would do.

They had not long to wait. The peppery little Welshman stepped back from the podium, like David getting ready to take a shot at Goliath. This time, before he started reading, he glared at everyone who sat near enough the front, as if he were making mental notes of anyone who dared to find his text funny, or even who might laugh after he or she got home. He shook his right forefinger in the air, revolved it a few times, brought it down on the Book and started all over again.

"In the same hour. . . ." Unluckily for him, the Reverend Powys stuttered badly and rolled his "r's" more madly when he got too excited or lost his temper, or both.

"In the same hour came fu-fu-fu-fu-forrrrth fu-fu-fu-fu-fu. . . . fu-fu—fffffingerrrs of a mu, of a mu, of a mmmmmu-man's hand [he banged the Book flat-handed, gritted his teeth, and persisted] and wrrrrote."

Grace Dodge, the volunteer contralto, sitting in the choir loft at the minister's right, looked helplessly at the tenor, started shaking and shuddering, and to hide this from the congregation, dropped down on her knees, below the level of the green plush curtain, so that, from the auditorium she was completely out of sight. From where the minister stood, he could see her very well, and turned like a bantam. The tenor swallowed a cough drop whole, it got stuck in his throat, and he started to throttle and gag. The paroxysm got worse and worse, so Frank had to stagger down the stairs, with Will Crowell, who was glad of a pretext to escape, pounding the tenor on his narrow and unsubstantial back.

I was having one of the best times of my childhood, watching everyone in front and listening hard for indicative sounds from behind. My grandmother, who had no use for the Reverend Powys, looked serene and frankly triumphant. My brother Charles, who had a sense of humor, was keeping a straight face on account of Mother. My brother Leslie was gleeful. My mother looked as saintlike as she could, and most certainly was deeply regretting the minister's predicament, but her eyes had a characteristic expression that showed she wanted to laugh and knew she ought not.

There was a lull, and Mr. Powys succeeded in getting past the text, with the cryptic words I always confused with Eenie, Meenie, Minie, Mo. For a while I got quite interested in what the minister was saying. He had a flair for the dramatic and descriptive when he let himself go, and drew such a word picture of the great hall of Nebuchadnezzar and the magnificence of ancient Babylon that I was carried away. Each comment on the old city's wickedness, abandon and extravagance endeared it to me. I loved the sound of the names of great rivers, the Araxes, the Tigris, the Euphrates. I liked to try to visualize the Medes, Chaldeans, Assyrians, and the great monarchs: Tiglath Pileser, Assur-bani-pal, Shalmaneser, Sennacherib, Sargon, Darius. I could not identify them with colorless types like Norman Partridge or tradesmen like J. J. Markham.

I tried to picture the Hanging Gardens, blooming and rising, terrace upon terrace, through languorous days and nights; the great reservoir fed by the Euphrates; the ponderous drawbridge between the great palaces, the Gate of the Gods and the Admiration of Mankind. The Reverend Powys evoked the colored half-pillars, glistening in the sun and shimmering by moonlight; the Tower of Babel that confounded men's tongues; canals and pyramids; the great universities of Erech and Borsippa, which must have been marvellous in comparison to Harvard and Yale, which then I thought of purely in terms of husky young men in turtleneck sweaters, who let their hair grow thick and long.

Nebuchadnezzar had ruled the world from Babylon, for forty-three years. He had left his son, Belshazzar, a mighty heritage, with all the captive Jews. Where had the great king failed? He worshipped the Moon Goddess and a lot of idols, instead of the God of Hosts, Jehovah.

The Reverend K. Greg Powys, after the gardens and palaces, the lakes and pyramids, the golden bulls and bronze lions, the battles won, the power and the glory, got down to the scene in the banquet hall. Belshazzar was feasting. Around the walls were bas-reliefs depicting the triumphs of his ancestors, slaves served the choicest fruits and meats and game. Already I had noticed that in the Bible stories there was little said about vegetables. Little birds, larks and thrushes, were served in pies; on golden platters from the Temple of Jerusalem were roast wild boar, gazelles, lambs and calves. And what impressed me most was the minister's tale of how, crawling on their knees and begging, in chains and halters, their hands and feet having been chopped off to humiliate them to the utmost, were the captive kings the Chaldeans had overthrown. With the palace hounds, they had to scramble as best they could for the scraps thrown from the table. Detestable sportsmanship.

The Jews, God's chosen people? They were menials. Belshazzar's lackeys flogged the hide off their backs, and worked them, laying bricks and drawing water, till they died.

The One and Only God? Belshazzar mocked at Him, too. The proud king was surfeited with the richest of foods, and it wearied him. He tried to lose himself in wine, from golden goblets, and the wine turned bitter in his mouth. The dancing-girls failed to please him. He had them sewed into sacks in pairs, and drowned in the Euphrates, while drunken rioters looked on and watched the bubbles rise. There was nothing vile or cruel that the king did not do. And still he was ruler of the temporal world. Men trembled at the mention of his name. And then . . . in the middle of the feast. . . .

Mr. Powys dropped his voice and I was frankly shiver-

ing. The minister paused for effect, extended his right arm
and revolved his forefinger again, pointing to the empty wall
between stained-glass windows. He would have been all right
had not the blizzard, at just the wrong moment, hurled its
first blast of sharp sleet against the windows. That caused the
slip that broke up the meeting.

"In the middle of the feast, inflamed with meat and wine,
Belshazzar looked and saw, being written by the fingers of a
ghostly hand, on the *snow . . . Mene, Mene, Tekel, Upharsin.*"

The last mysterious words were drowned in laughter,
nervous at first, then swelling into a ragged chorus. No one
in the congregation meant to laugh, but those who did could
not help it. A few of those led off, and this broke the reserve
of others. I was far too busy looking around to laugh. Deacon
Parker got to coughing again. And through it all, Mathilda
Stowe sat calmly facing the apoplectic Reverend Powys as
if nothing unusual were happening.

The Reverend Powys at first was the personification of
outraged dignity, then he cut loose. The members of his congregation who scoffed at divine warnings and had lost their
respect for God's House would share the fate of Belshazzar,
he roared. They would be weighed and found wanting. Which
ones among them could call themselves Christians? Did they
imagine he did not know of the sins and shame that were
countenanced in Linden, by men and women who pretended
to be worshippers? Did they think they could bluff their way
into Heaven, or buy their way? Did they believe, in their folly
and pride, that the God of Hosts, who saw a sparrow fall, would
overlook and fail to visit His vengeance on their small sink of
iniquity, because in great cities the sinners were like the sands
of the sea in number?

The outraged little preacher had tossed aside his manuscript

3 9

and started singling out, by references everyone could not fail to grasp, those who had been disrespectful. He was a vain man, as men go, and had a formidable temper, and before he got through he had bruised the feelings of half the most faithful members of the congregation, but they, aware that he did not know what they had been laughing about, took the tirade in good part and did not hold it against him.

One day not long afterward, my Uncle Reuben was seen entering the minister's house, an unprecedented occurrence, and soon thereafter, a passerby was startled to hear the two men's hearty voices in uncontrolled laughter. My uncle was anything but pious, but he was a sport, and what took place in the privacy of the minister's study he never revealed, not even to his closest cronies at the Massasoit bar.

CHAPTER FOUR

The Massasoit House

AMONG the many paradoxes and contradictions that added savour to life in Linden was the happy situation concerning strong drink and good cheer. The commonwealth had for decades extended to its cities and towns local option on the question of the sale of intoxicating liquors, and regularly, at every election, the Malden Protestant Republicans had voted "No," outnumbering the license advocates at least three to one. Wherever Malden led, hapless Linden had to follow, but as a matter of fact, in this instance, Precinct Two of Ward Six voted just about the same as the city at large. The Linden women who were most active in the churches were zealous temperance workers, and no boy or girl could get through a Sunday School class without signing a pledge, on a neatly embossed card with gilt lettering, renouncing alcohol forever.

Actually, Linden had some very accomplished drinkers, men who could hold their own in almost any seaport on or off the map. They did not have to worry about companionship or thirst because of the Massasoit House. This famous old inn was technically across the line in the town of Revere, although the nearest house in Revere, the fine rambling farmhouse belonging to John P. Squire, was a mile and a half distant, with bleak marshland between, while Linden Square was less than two hundred yards away. As long as the Massasoit was geographically and socially a part of Linden, little did any of its patrons care that, in reaching its hospitable doorways, it was necessary for them to pass over an imaginary boundary between the city of Malden and the town of Revere. And Spike Dodge, the Linden cop, as well as the rest of the Malden force, was without authority to interfere with Admiral Quimby's conduct of his barroom, restaurant and hotel. The Revere police, put into office and kept there by saloon politicians, were not likely to journey miles and miles across primeval swamplands to harass a saloon-keeper who served another town, although his place happened to stand a few yards inside the limits of Revere.

So on his five-acre lot, fronting on the extension of Beach Street, Linden, the Admiral reigned supreme, and always with distinction. I have said that there were no examples of the best early-American architecture in Linden, but the Massasoit House, just a stone's throw eastward, built in 1750 by an anonymous ship's carpenter, had the simple and pleasing proportions of the best New England houses, the easy sloping roof, just steep enough to clear itself of heavy loads of snow, the tightly-fitted windows with detachable green blinds, so that the building had contrasting aspects for summer and winter. The main building, about forty feet by eighty (but not exactly), and two and a half stories high, contained an attic where the help could be accommodated, hotel bedrooms upstairs, and the ground floor was given over to a dining room known and praised far and wide, with a private banquet hall behind, on one wall of which was a balcony for musicians. All the public rooms had broad stone fireplaces.

There was a spacious wing extending toward Linden, but lower than the main building. The peak of the roof of the wing was on the level with the base of the larger roof. Then, from the wing, a shed extended farther, still lower and of similar construction.

Every element in the design was balanced, but not too obviously. The chimneys of the main hotel were squat and broad, the chimney of the wing rose high and was topped with glazed bricks. Rising to twice the height of the chimneys, a grove of horse-chestnut trees overshadowed the gray roofs and white walls, stark black and white in winter, in summer shimmering green, with the white showing through. The outbuildings included carriage sheds for customers, ice house, a stable with a smart gold-plated weathervane aloft, and two backhouses, one staunch and roomy to accommodate six males, the other more dainty, where four females and/or children could sit, side by side. In the year 1895, the Admiral had three bathrooms and toilets of the then modern style the Linden men called "society crap-houses" installed inside the hotel. With the help of the Linden carpenter, Swede Carlson, and the plumber from Revere, he managed to make room for these radical improvements without spoiling the interior of his hotel. Nevertheless, for reasons of prudence and sentimentality, and on aesthetic grounds, since the buildings as originally planned formed such an harmonious group, the Admiral left the outdoor backhouses as they were. One was neatly labelled "Men" and the other "Ladies." Both had their entrances and exits well screened with green latticework on which were twining grapevines.

Sam Quimby was not really an Admiral. He had worked as steward a few summers, years before, on the Bangor boat. His Uncle Ebenezer had left him the hotel and Sam was an ideal host. He wanted his guests to feel welcome when they arrived, comfortable and carefree while they were there, and satisfied when they departed. He enjoyed the company of those who patronized his bar, and never was moody or bored. I remember him as a man of about sixty, a forceful, hearty and picturesque figure, although he ran the Massasoit thirty consecutive years,

and must have formerly been younger, but never more mischievous.

I have described the restful beauty of Linden's one hotel
from the outside. From within, it had a more intimate charm.
The barroom and back room were in the wing, broadside to
Beach Street, and well back from the sidewalk. Neither Linden
nor Revere did anything about the mud in that vicinity where
the street was on the level of the marshes, and sometimes was
inundated by the high-run tides. But within the boundaries
of the Admiral's land, there were flagstone walks, and scrapers
near the doorways. The bar was of mahogany, about eighteen
feet long, with a firm brass rail and a mirror behind it. Above
the mirror, in the center, was an oil painting of Adam, Eve,
the tree and a very rakish serpent. Adam was a small man,
relatively insignificant, and wore a leafy garment around his
loins. Eve was on a larger scale, voluptuous and nude. Her head
was at such an angle, with her eyes looking downward, that
her gaze seemed to follow the drinkers in a tantalizing way
as they shifted from one end of the bar to the other. She looked
a bit like the Venus de Milo, in the face, with a suggestion
of Mrs. Leslie Carter, because of her auburn hair.

The lighting in the Massasoit bar was dim, but never dingy.
The floor was of chestnut planks, the rafters of oak, the walls
were panelled in mahogany. Kerosene bracket lamps and
chandeliers were used there until 1910, when electricity was
available. The Admiral might have used gas, five years before
he made the change, but so many country people had died in
Boston hotels from blowing out the gas lights that he did not
want to take the chance. His guests were not hayseeds, as a
rule, but most of them drank and might forget themselves, and
revert to former fixed habits.

Admiral Quimby was not merely concerned with the comfort of his paying customers. He wanted life around him to be

merry and in movement. He liked to have everybody except a temperance crank get what he desired, whether or not it happened to be good for him. His Massasoit House, while it was practically immune from interference by the law, and because of Linden's "no license" ordinance was free from competition, was exposed to the weather on a grand scale, in keeping with the host's princely personality. There stood no protecting barriers between his snug establishment and the raging sweep of the Atlantic that bred and sped the northeasters. The salt ice that formed on the marsh was broken into fragments and displaced by every rising tide, and when the waters receded they left behind an area of glacial wreckage that was forbidding by day and ghostly at night. To protect the Massasoit, its outbuildings and fenced grounds, the Admiral had set up snowbreaks ten feet high, to catch the drifts before they overwhelmed his place, and to add to the joy of young and old, he had walled in a low, flat area which could be flooded with fresh water and serve as a skating pond. At his own expense, the Admiral kept the pond swept clean of snow, on days and evenings when the weather was cold and clear, had put up shelters with benches, in which the skaters could put on their skates and take them off, and nearby a large warm fire was kept burning, so the skaters could thaw themselves out when the wind was too cold to be ignored, even by young folks in violent motion.

In winter the Admiral's public skating rink was called "Massasoit Pond." In spring, he had it drained and planted with clover, so that it would swarm with bees and butterflies instead of mosquitoes.

So, in Linden, the influence of K. Gregory Powys and the Congregational Church was balanced by that of Admiral Quimby and the Massasoit House.

"A town should be like Caesar's wife," the Admiral said. "All things to all men."

He loved to quote Bobby Burns and Shakespeare as well as the ministers loved quoting from the Bible, but the Admiral was less restrained by the need of accuracy than the leaders of the respectable element.

There was a group of men, and one mannish woman, who used to make the barroom of the Massasoit their headquarters, and used the place as a sort of club. Two or more of them were likely to be found there, drinking as gentlemen should, conversing on a variety of topics that ranged from the personal to the esoteric, with sporting topics and political comment in between. The Admiral would be leaning against the bar or seated near them. Sometimes they preferred to group themselves at the bar, each with one well-shod foot on the rail. Again it would please their whim of the hour to sit in the solid and comfortable barroom Windsors around the circular oak tables, which had been scrubbed as smooth as satin.

Foremost among the regulars was my Uncle Reuben, a stocky, broad-shouldered man of medium height, with disarmingly candid blue eyes, sandy hair and long drooping moustaches that showed faintly red and gold in the sunlight, a hearty voice, the slightly rolling gait of an experienced sailor, and a vocabulary like all the fleet. He was a link between the two foremost strata of society, being not only one of the most convivial habitués of the Massasoit, but also a deacon of the Congregational Church. He drank to please himself, and went to church to pacify his wife, my patient Aunt Carrie.

The third member of what was really the triumvirate of the Massasoit was Mr. Wing. His full name was Christopher Van Volkenburgh Wing, and he came to Linden from New York, nobody knew why. He owned the only apartment house in town, a triangular building at the intersection of Oliver and Beach Streets, one hundred yards from the Saugus Branch crossing and the Square, but everyone understood that he had other properties and investments more important than the one in which he occupied a bachelor apartment and rented five others to families without small children. Boys, he liked and understood, when they were ten years old or older. Before that, he held them in mild horror and said more than once that they should be seen and, on rare occasions, heard, but not by him.

Mr. Wing's admirers or his critics never claimed that he was as rich as Norman Partridge, but he was the richest man in Linden who did no work whatsoever, on principle.

"Gad, sir," he would demand, on occasion. "Is there an instance in recorded history in which a nation has been brought to grief by idle men of substance? Cite me one, and, by Jove, I will blister these hands on yon woodpile, depriving the good Irv Walker of a day's subsistence. No, my friends. It has always been the industrious blighters who have proven themselves the scourges of mankind."

He spoke with an accent and a choice of words strange to Linden, and therefore fascinating to me. It was neither the Harvard manner, nor the Oxford, nor that of the vaudeville dude. Furthermore, Mr. Wing departed farther from what was usually condoned in nineteenth-century Linden. He employed a valet. Not a hired man, or a cook, or a janitor. A valet.

"Pfeiffer," he would say. "The whale-bone stick, if you please. This Malacca is a trifle too garish for today. I am not at my best. . . ."

Pfeiffer, the valet, a gaunt Dane whose eyes sometimes glittered like those of the Ancient Mariner, and whose manners, as a trained servant from birth, in high New York society, were as perfect as his master's, in another way, would bow and almost shudder.

"I am sincerely sorry, sir," he would say, knowing exactly what was the matter. The pair of eggs he had served Mr. Wing that morning had matched in color. That is, they both had pale yellow yolks. It would have been just as bad if they had both had deep orange yolks. What Mr. Wing required was one light and one dark one.

In the light of the best practices in the high-class New England restaurants of the period, that was not as far-fetched as it seems today, when breakfasts are snatched on the fly. The best places, when they served a pair of eggs, saw to it that the yolks contrasted in color, and therefore, subtly, in flavor, providing a nuance for discriminating egg-eaters that put the latter in the best of humor.

"I should not like to have you think I was remiss, sir," Pfeiffer would continue, head still inclined. "All the eggs delivered yesterday were light in color, and either I had to delay. . . ."

"Quite all right," said Mr. Wing, expansively. "Speak to Packard about it. . . . Emphatically."

Actually, Pfeiffer had, in preparing the breakfast, broken a dozen eggs, one after the other, in search of a dark one, and had considered carefully whether he should hurry out to the store, and keep Mr Wing waiting, or serve the eggs matched that day.

Of course, Mr. Wing knew that Linden relished, behind his back, the comedies he played with Pfeiffer, and I am sure the valet understood and responded by being a little more meticulous than was humanly possible, when he was sober. That was the rub with Pfeiffer, and made the relationship between him and Mr. Wing a touching and continuous performance that raised them both in local esteem, and heightened the neighborly interest in their quaint duet through the years.

Pfeiffer, about every six weeks or so, retired to his attic bedroom for several days, during which Mr. Wing rolled up his fashionable shirt sleeves and did his own housework, and took his meals at the Massasoit. As many times as were necessary each day, the fat and jolly man-about-town, weighing two hundred and sixty-five pounds, would mount three flights of back stairs, with provisions, some solid, but mostly liquid, the remedies and antidotes for alcohol then believed efficacious, and if more complicated medicines were needed, Mr. Wing would consult the doctor privately and call at Dud Shultz's drug store with a prescription.

There was never a suggestion from Mr. Wing that Pfeiffer should reform. That was manifestly impracticable and unlikely. What he insisted upon, and Pfeiffer, in his wildest deliriums never contravened, was that the valet, when he felt it best to go on a bender, either stay in his room or leave Linden and vicinity until he was ready to resume his work again. Also, he would not permit Pfeiffer to apologize, or swelter in remorse.

"My man, you follow the dictates of your nature, as I pander to mine. What is there to moan about? Because of your occasional excursions into the realm of the spirit and imagination, by the only method within your means and suitable to your station, you serve me better between-times. More important. You cause me to demonstrate to myself, periodically, that I am not dependent upon you, or anyone, and that a bachelor's existence, with its admitted drawbacks, is the lesser of two evils, as I have always maintained." With words like those, Mr. Wing would receive the faithful Pfeiffer, when he returned from one of his bouts with the D.T.'s.

Mr. Wing came nearer than any man in Linden to doing at all times exactly as he pleased, or so it seemed to me. We were drawn together when I was at an early age by our mutual passion for music, of the informal and spirited kind. He had in his bachelor's living room, so richly and tastefully furnished, a Chickering grand piano on which he played, with amazing dexterity, all the reels, jigs, pigeonwings, moriscos, sarabands, fandangos, flings, hoedowns, polkas, gavottes, quadrilles, horn-pipes, minuets, mazurkas, schottisches and cancans known to the Old World taverns and greenswards or to the surging American frontiers.

I never heard Mr. Wing play any other type of music, and I never asked him to. I knew by instinct that when anyone is playing, from the heart, he should not be prompted in his selection of tunes. Often Mr. Wing would tell me of the origin of the folk dances he was playing. Some were English, French, Scandinavian, Gaelic, Belgian, Dutch. Rightly or wrongly, he avoided the Italian and German music, complaining that the operas of Verdi and Wagner had helped drive him from New York. I felt happy and welcome in Mr. Wing's ornately fur-nished flat, knowing that by listening as I did, I was helping him play.

Now and again, at the Massasoit, Mr. Wing, Bill Daley's father, Uncle Reuben and Jeff Lee, the only Negro in Linden, would go into the otherwise empty banquet room, in the main part of the Massasoit, and play together, Mr. Wing and Mr. Daley following the printed music with miraculous ease, Uncle Reuben and Black Jeff doing quite as well without notes of any kind. There in a corner would I be found, trying to appear invisible, because no one else was encouraged to enter. Now and again, on public occasions, when professionals could not fill the bill, the Massasoit ensemble, with Mr. Wing at the piano, Mr. Daley, first fiddle, Uncle Reuben, second fiddle, and

Jeff Lee, picking the guitar (which he pronounced *"guie*-tar"), would oblige.

The fourth member of the group that represented the senior or postgraduate tosspots of the Massasoit was Ruth Coffee, a Junoesque and powerful woman with a deep, booming voice, muscles much harder than those of the Linden blacksmith, who was rather slight, and a hale and hearty manner with everyone, man, woman or beast. She dressed like a man. That is, with a man's coat and collar and a felt hat, but to her sex she made the concession of wearing a sensible skirt and whatever went with it underneath.

Most of the comment on Ruth's unwomanly behavior must have spent itself before I knew her, because she was born in Linden, had always lived there in her neat little cottage on Salem Street where her father had lived and died, and had established herself, as she was, and become an accepted phenomenon in Linden before she reached mature womanhood. She had liked to go hunting and fishing with her father, so later she liked to go hunting and fishing with the men with the kind of tact and understanding he had had. They were not hard to find or to select: the Admiral, Uncle Reuben, and Christopher Van Volkenburgh Wing. Mr. Wing went so far as to address Ruth by her last name, to make her doubly certain she was within the inner circle of their friendship on her own peculiar terms.

"Coffee, drink up, damn it," he would say. "You're worse than an old woman, lately."

"Here goes," Ruth would respond, raising her glass and taking its contents without a chaser. "And when you say that, smile."

Offhand, one would never expect that Mr. Wing dearly loved to stalk and shoot game birds, at some ungodly hour of the morning, but when he set his mind to it he could tramp as far, as fast and as long as any of his companions. He was a fair shot, but never tried to excel.

"Nothing too much," he would say. "Don't you think it's a trifle vulgar to hit too many of them?"

Mr. Wing could reduce almost any question to a matter of taste.

As far as I could ever find out, nothing happened in Linden that was not known and discussed at the Massasoit bar, and nearly everything was talked about at the weekly meetings of the Ladies' Social Circle. The church women were not so blunt or direct in their language, but little escaped their notice and the primmest of them seemed to be able to follow, however disapprovingly, the items that were brought to their attention.

The evening after Miss Townsend had shown such an unexpected and disturbing reaction to Ginger's thoughtless prank, after Ginger had stowed away the doctor's damaged sleigh and led Hip back to his stall off the Square, Ginger had thought first of the Massasoit. He found it prudent, however, to hurry back to Clapp's field, by a circuitous route, in order to erase the evidence from the surface of the snow. He was not sure that the school boys, or anyone excepting Miss Townsend, the victim, had seen the words "Sweet Alice," and hoped that she would recover promptly and be too modest to mention the inscription, either to the doctor or her family.

When he entered the Massasoit, a little later, his bottle companions were gathered, as usual, in the back room. The younger Linden drinking set found the tone of the conversation at the Admiral's table somewhat over their heads, and too formal as a rule, and each evening sat around a long oblong table in the room adjacent to the spacious barroom. It was possible to get into the back room two ways, either by entering the wing of the Massasoit from the Beach Street side and passing through the barroom to the rear, or taking the flagstone walk around the back way to the door marked "Family Entrance."

In the back room the dean of the regular customers was Hal Kingsland who for some years had been promised the next appointment as fireman in Malden, a job for which he was superbly suited by temperament and gifts. Hal was an easy-going, good-natured man, with such a flair for women that, according to my Uncle Reuben, he could not walk under a pair of drawers hung on a clothesline without an instant physiological acknowledgment taking place, noticeable from a considerable distance. Hal was a fine horseman, and had a dare-devil courage that got him into quick and efficient action whenever the occasion arose. Then he would relax for weeks, or months, to think it over.

Hal Kingsland sat at the head of the table, facing the swinging door that led into the bar. The potbellied stove was at his back and the waiter, a former sailor with a peg leg named Gimp Crich, tended the stove, the kerosene lamps, the mixed company of customers, and kept fresh sawdust on the floor as spryly as any man could who had both of his legs.

Gimp's conversation was confined to "Yea, yea," and "Nay, nay," and everybody knew that no matter what happened in the back room, short of mayhem or theft, it would never, on Gimp's account, go farther than the oak-panelled walls.

The men at Hal Kingsland's table included Ginger Mc-Sweeney, during the hours he was off duty at the Beach Street turnout; Dick Lanier, who worked as a house carpenter's helper or house painter in season, spent the winters hunting in the woods and on the marsh, or fishing through the ice, and was waiting for the next appointment to the city fire department after Hal Kingsland got his. Ordinarily, Linden would not have been given consideration for such a large share of city employment, even though the employment was not yet in existence, but there had been talk of building a branch fire station in Linden, and it was understood by the local active Republicans and their perpetually unsuccessful opponents, the Democrats, that Linden men would be favored for Linden jobs, if they were qualified to fill them. Dick Lanier was only a first-generation resident of Linden, having been brought there by his French-Canadian parents when Dick was four years old. In nineteen hundred, he must have been about twenty-eight. When he worked, he kept up a swift pace and gave whoever hired him his money's worth. That was his reputation. When out of work, which was at least half the time, and mostly in winter, Dick did not fret. He was light-hearted and affable, and second only to Markham's clerk, Packard, as a squire of Linden females, and others in neighboring towns. His Canuck brogue, in contrast with the Irish inflections of Hal Kingsland and Ginger, the Finnish lilt of the two stone-cutters and masons, Pehr and Paavo Wallenius, and the New York lingo straight from the Four Hundred delivered by Mr. Wing, gave the Massasoit a mildly cosmopolitan atmosphere, or what politicians then referred to as the vapours of the "Melting Pot."

Directing a friend as to how to get from Malden Center to the Saugus Branch depot, Dick said, without meaning to be irreverent, "When you get off the car at Ferry Street, you put your ass to the First Baptist Church and miss on the left with your face to the High *School,* and go straight like hell downhill from there."

Two cockney twins, George and Ernie Hobart, who played left and right ends, respectively, on the football team, and worked in a shipyard in Chelsea, were often present, toward the first of the week. Like most of the Linden young men who worked for wages, they found themselves short between

Wednesday, the traditional night on which they were supposed
to take out their girls, and Saturday, which was the almost
universal payday. The Hobart boys were short in stature, as
tough as tripe, but they paid whenever their turn came round,
and when they had no money they hauled in their belts and
worked up a yeomanly weekend thirst.

The Admiral followed a number of salutary rules in running
his place, but never too strictly. There were always exceptions, that made sense. Women were not supposed to sit in the
barroom, for instance, but Ruth Coffee invariably did, and
was welcome. Unescorted women, theoretically, were not admitted through the "Family Entrance," but good Irish housewives who came to rush the can were always accommodated
and asked to sit down while the bartender, Nick Spratt, was
drawing the beer for them. Also, there was a group of neighboring young women, between twenty and thirty, who dropped
in when they felt like it, and if no man came in with them,
they found a few to talk with when they got inside, or seldom
had too long to wait for company. They were described by
Uncle Reuben, affectionately, as "the roguish kind" and never
caused any trouble.

Big Julie Goan, who lived on the Square, was one of them.
In summer she worked as a waitress in one of the restaurants in
Crescent Beach before the big state bathhouse was built and
the beach became a New England Coney Island. She was ami-
able and rangy, with a gift for repartee, and no man got fresh
with her unless she took a fancy to him. That was often enough
to keep her in tiptop condition, and quite well content with
life.

A shapely Italian girl named Palmira Di Brazzio came in
now and then. She had a flair for bright colors that set off her
large and expressive brown eyes, and had to be careful that
her father, a section-gang foreman on the Boston and Maine,

was either away or safely snoring in bed before she could leave.

Young Gertie Walker, one of the six daughters of Irv Walker, the poorest family man in town, was a favorite of Ginger's but, luckily, neither Gertie nor Ginger was jealous or possessive and did not expect more fidelity than was natural to either of them.

Letty Ledbetter, of Canadian parentage, worked as hired girl for a family in Maplewood, but she roomed in Linden, with Julie's family, and preferred the good cheer at the Massasoit to the more elaborate distractions in Boston or Lynn.

Maive Bagley was the sister of Tom Bagley, an Irishman who ran a small express business which took little of his time. He was said by the Admiral to "have a soft hand under a hen." But at home he was, until a few things happened, the heavy husband and brother and his womenfolk had no leeway until, unexpectedly, one night, Maive appeared at the Massasoit with her suitcase and a few bundles and asked the Admiral for a room.

"What will your brother say?" asked the Admiral, who had little use for Tom, but wanted no complications.

"Just let him open his trap," said Maive, her dark blue eyes flashing.

The Admiral shrugged, and showed Maive to a small hall bedroom for which he asked a very small rate. A little later, he gave Maive a job as chambermaid, and waitress in the main dining room, and from that day on, Maive was as much a part of the Massasoit entourage as the tall horse-chestnut trees that shaded the inn formed a part of the scenery. Evenings, after her work was done in the dining room, Maive joined the group in the back room and spent a good part of her pay. Tom did not speak to her after she had left his roof, and she ignored him, but she bought useful presents for his wife and two children, all of whom were fond of her, when Tom was not looking.

The evening that Ginger came in, after his harrowing experience involving Miss Townsend, he chose to enter the front way. The door was propped open, for the moment, between the bar and the back room where at Hal Kingsland's table and the others nearby, Jack, Dick Lanier, the Cockney twins, Big Julie, Young Gertie and Letty Ledbetter were sitting, expectantly.

At the bar, among others, were the Admiral, Mr. Wing, Pehr the Finnish mason, and Ruth Coffee. My Uncle Reuben was sitting at a table nearby, with pen in hand and paper before him, pretending to write. They all said "Good evening" to Ginger, who greeted them somewhat self-consciously, but they seemed to pay him no further attention. From his point of view, their attitude was a little too aloof, or studied.

Just as Ginger got abreast of my uncle's table, my uncle's stub pen slipped, spluttered and scattered blots all over the paper.

"Confound it," said Uncle Reuben, looking up at the Admiral, "It's a wonder the House wouldn't supply some decent materials in here."

Ginger was trying to slip by, but my uncle detained him.

"Ginger," he said, in a voice loud enough for everyone in the kitchen and back room to hear. "Lend me your pencil, like a good fellow. I want to write a *billy do*."

The driver turned every shade of scarlet and crimson, and the chorus of guffaws that arose dispelled his last prayerful hope that his part in the day's main event had not been traced to him. It was well known to one and all that Ginger had no use for an ordinary pencil and never was known to carry one.

"Well. What do you say?" persisted Uncle Reuben.

Ginger sighed ruefully, and turned toward the bar.

"I guess the drinks are on me," he said, and Nick Spratt reached for two handfuls of glasses as Ginger went on, into the back room, where he was met with a fresh burst of laughter, in which the girls all joined.

"A man has no Goddamn privacy in this town," he said. "Every Tom, Dick and Harry reads his mail."

"You're getting pretty stuck-up about who you write to," Big Julie said. "There's plenty of your friends who wouldn't mind a postcard now and then."

CHAPTER FIVE

Morning Mood

THE first man up each morning in Linden was Alexander Graydon, namesake and direct descendant of the financier and diplomat who was a colleague of Alexander Hamilton. All that heredity and history meant nothing to Alec. He did not get up so early because he was enterprising and energetic. Alec took life easier than almost anyone in town.

Alec's house was on Oliver Street, diagonally opposite the old grammar school. His back yard, with a barbed-wire fence, touched the railroad right-of-way, so that the firemen of the Saugus Branch trains, eastbound, began to pull the rope and clang the bell and start slowing down for the depot about the time they passed his place, from the rear. His old barn was patched and sagged a little, but the roof was tight, the loft was roomy, there were nails on which to hang the harnesses and garden tools on the unpainted walls, and there was a stall for his fat and cranky old mare, Daisy, whom Alec treated like a beloved but troublesome old female relative who seemed to blame him for the ravages and inconveniences of age.

None of the space in Alec's yard was wasted, and none of it used to the best advantage. There was a small orchard to the right of his house, a few very old and gnarled apple trees and some stunted pear trees. On the other side of the house was a tomato patch, a few rows of corn, including the purple variety that the Indians had liked best, shell beans climbing on poles that were never exactly straight or plumb, some squash and pumpkin vines, and trellises of Concord grapes.

Alec took care of the mare, Daisy, and what time was left over he devoted to odd chores and outside jobs, so that no day passed when he could not have found many things to do. Instead of forcing himself, he put things off as long as possible and when he finally started working on them, he took his own time, and proceeded according to his own ideas. He did only the jobs one man could manage, alone, and never had a boss. Most Linden men, even the idlest and most shiftless of them, followed some perceptible routine. Whatever Alec did was suitable to the season, and seasonal regulation was the only kind to which he ever submitted. Within seasonal limits, his existence was an impromptu.

The checker games at the Massasoit, and later at the Linden Fire Station, took up lots of his time, and he played very shrewdly, letting his opponent do the talking, the boasting, and deliver the apostrophes to fate. Alec would sit in his shirt sleeves, puffing at his acrid briar pipe, and when the pattern was working out in his favor the crow's feet would deepen around his dark eyes that seemed to contain in their depths so much native tolerance and wisdom. Alec laughed very often, and heartily, without much noise, till the tears came into his eyes, but he seldom laughed at any man directly. He would wait until he was out of sight, then lean against a post or tree and laugh till he was satisfied. As he was jogging along in his wagon, behind old Daisy, his face would light up, he would smile, then grow pensive, enjoying his shifting moods as the surface of a woodland pond reflects the light and shadow when the sun is screened, then revealed by cirrus clouds.

In summertime, Alec would cut the grass from strips of

railroad right-of-way or vacant lots, spread it to dry in the sun, stack it, and cart it into his hayloft, with the volunteer aid of the boys. A little later, he picked elderberries along the edges of the lanes in the woods, and the old Newburyport Turnpike. With these he made a thick liqueur, of royal purple, that he called "elderberry wine." He counted votes for the Democratic party, on election day, being one of the few Yankee Democrats, and holding a sort of Olympian disdain for the McKinley and Teddy Roosevelt administration. McKinley did nothing quietly, while Teddy did even less with a lot of noise, Alec would say. He was for Bryan first, last, and all the time, but he did not expect the Commoner to win. Alec did not think the general electorate had sense enough for that.

Alec Graydon was the sole owner, operator and proprietor of a small carpet-cleaning establishment way over in Melrose, so that two or three times a week, if the weather was right and he felt like it, he would drive over in the morning, with his lunch in a pail, clean carpets in a cloud of dust that would have choked an ordinary man until three or four in the afternoon, then drive back to Linden. Naturally, he spent more time on the road than he did in his shop, but he enjoyed the drives. The budding shrubs, or the changing colors in the leaves, the birds and chipmunks and garter snakes and humming insects, dancing butterflies, clouds, all registered gently with him, as he sat on his seat, and Daisy jogged along. The smell of alder catkins, of damp springs by the roadside, of hay, of tansy, wild honeysuckle, drying codfish or tan bark, hollyhocks, peonies, he would inhale and recognize as the minutes and hours and days passed by. Peonies were Alec's favorite flower. There was something about them—their presentation, their perispherical freedom from nonsense, their confidence and unique perfume—that kindled Alec's admiration. I have seen him stand, leaning on a rake or a hoe, looking at his peonies, or one particular peony, as if from all the universe, and God-possible plants and blossoms, he, Alec, had set apart that peony, or cluster of peonies, for contemplation. Concerning this he never said a word.

Once in every two or three years, at the instigation of his wife, who was of one of the best Salem families, Alec would get into his boiled shirt, dress suit and wear the stovepipe hat he wore habitually at the time she fell in love with him. I never saw a more distinguished-looking man; not even Mr. Wing or the Admiral could hold a candle to him. Perhaps that was because they were always dressed well, and Alec, day after day, wore an old shirt and patched pants and shoes that Mr. Laws, the cobbler, had put more thread and leather into than the original manufacturers had. He smelled of horse, beer or wine, the crudest tobacco extant, of old carpets, and new-mown hay.

One of Alec's trivial jobs was to drive each morning, about four o'clock, to Maplewood, a couple of miles distant, to get the roll of Boston morning newspapers intended for Linden. The paper train left North Station in Boston a little after 3:00 a.m. and in due course, depending on the weather, arrived in Maplewood. Unluckily for Linden, this first morning train was an "express," and passed through Broadway, Linden, and one or two other little stations without stopping, as so many of the more useful trains seemed to do. It would appear to have been easy for the baggage-man to toss off the roll of Linden papers when the train was passing through Linden, to be received directly by Seymour Batt, the nearsighted dry-goods dealer who superintended the newspapers' distribution and collected from the subscribers. No Saugus Branch train moved much faster than the average buggy horse. Nevertheless, some technicality cooked up between the Express Company, the Boston and Maine, and the newspaper owners, required that an agent be on hand to receive and sign for the bundle of papers, and that could not be done in Linden, on the fly.

Therefore, Alec Graydon drove to Maplewood each morning, signed for the Linden papers on receiving them from the baggage-man, then drove back to Linden Square to turn them over to Seymour Batt, whose two newsboys, Jerry Dineen and Frigger Bacigalupo, were by that time on hand to start out on their routes.

Puffing on his short-stemmed pipe, and with one small boy for company, Alec would sit contentedly on the blanketed front seat, so covered because of the faulty upholstery. Alec's wagon was held together by straps, brads and haywire, and the harness was patched up with parts of other discarded harnesses. Daisy maintained a pace a little faster than a walk, and whenever Alec let his mind wander, she would get the reins under her tail. In the stall, when he was off guard, the mare would nip Alec or step on his foot, never very hard. She liked to be annoying, in small ways.

There was a real feud between Mrs. Graydon and the mare, Daisy. Mrs. Graydon fussed and fumed because Alec "spent all summer cutting hay" and drove all the way to Melrose when the carpet-cleaning apparatus could easily have been set up somewhere handy, in Linden, where small vacant lots could be had for a song. Alec listened, and frequently agreed in principle, but he never did anything about it.

Mrs. Graydon was an exceptionally capable and energetic woman, with a good social background and high ambitions for their two children. In no way could she influence Alec. She was one of the Methodists who, when old Dr. Best tottered into senility and the church standing committee would not turn him out of the pulpit he had occupied fifty years, went over to the Congregational Church and became one of the most active members of the Social Circle. It had been a long time since she had found an outlet for her administrative urge, and she was thereafter as busy and bustling as her husband was indolent and calm.

After he had delivered the papers each morning to Seymour Batt, Alec drove over to the Massasoit for what he called "a snifter." I hitched Daisy in one of the stalls of the customers' shed, and went to the kitchen where Jeff Lee always passed out some pie or doughnuts, with a glass of milk or Linden blossom tea.

At that hour of the morning, neither the Admiral nor the regulars were likely to be around, and Jeff doubled as cook and bartender. One of Alec's oldest friends, and also one of the few Spanish War veterans in Linden, Tim Curtin by name, had had his nerves unstrung by malaria and one arm cut off above the elbow because of a shrapnel wound. Tim was the principal reason why the Linden Democrats had plenty of arguments to use against the majority Republicans who were jubilant about the election of Teddy Roosevelt as Vice President. Whenever anyone would listen, Tim would tell by the hour of his baptism of fire in the jungle between El Pozo and San Juan Hill.

Tim had enlisted, in a patriotic fervor that Alec Graydon had done his best to quench before it was too late. Being a poultry dealer by trade, Tim had found himself in the Signal Corps, one of the buck privates who held a rope attached to the U. S. Army's first and only observation balloon.

"I felt like a kid at the county fair," Tim said, "until the shrapnel and bullets began to fly around."

He had waited at El Pozo with his unit on the historic morning of the battle of San Juan Hill. The American batteries had started firing, but they had no smokeless powder, and while their shells did not bother the Spaniards much, the Spaniards used the smoke as a target; artillery men and some of what Tim called "those bloody stupid Rough Riders" began to fall, and the American artillery was ordered to cease firing.

Some New York infantry were sent into the jungle, toward San Juan Hill, but when they got half-way, and could not find their direction, they were shoved off the swampy trail, into the jungle, to let the Rough Riders go through. Tim's balloon followed the Rough Riders, and when everybody got mixed up, cavalry and infantry alike, in the swamp holes and thickets, the balloon was held up, so the major aloft just sat there and waited, while the Spaniards found the range. Tim was hit in the arm, and another man grabbed the rope he had been holding, but as Tim fell, and before the medical corps men could get around to him, a long thin green snake dropped down on a New York sergeant from a palmetto and stampeded the whole squad of National Guardsmen who were lying in the puddles and weeds Goddamning the day that Roosevelt and his cowboys ever were born. More than ten hobnailed soldiers, fleeing the snake in a panic, trampled over Tim, so aggravating the fracture of the humerus he had sustained in line of duty that the arm had to come off above the elbow.

The hospital in which Tim was bedded while his arm was healing was not adequately screened, so he was bitten by mosquitoes and came down with malaria. At that time, the army doctors did not connect the cause and effect, and Tim thought of the mosquitoes and the malaria as separate discomforts. Either one would have been enough to dampen the zeal he formerly had felt for United States imperial expansion.

After Tim had been evacuated a few miles to the rear, his outfit had been shot up, halfway up the slope of San Juan, by American artillery. Before that, the Spanish marksmen who had been aiming at the balloon and decimating the troops around and below it, punctured the bag and reconnaissance from the air was over, for the duration.

"It was like a Jesusly burlesque show, without any women, until men started getting killed," Tim said. "And for what?"

Alec never said "I told you so," but he smiled his wonderful smile, and the crow's feet showed around his eyes.

Tim used the adjective "Jesusly" as a term of disdain, and "un-Jesusly" as a word of high praise. So he spoke of the Jesusly war, and the un-Jesusly good beer.

I have already made it clear that Alec Graydon was sparing of his energy and effort, but he had one characteristic in common with so many Linden men who otherwise were not given to Spartan endeavor. He would not let the weather get the best of him. In the fiercest blizzards and the bitterest cold, he kept his rendezvous in Maplewood with the early morning train, and on days when the Saugus Branch tracks were blocked—of course, they were the last on the Boston and Maine system to be cleared—he would wait in the Maplewood depot, sometimes until twilight, and carry out his part of the bargain.

The Admiral depended on Alec to keep the skating pond clear of snow, and to haul for the bonfire a supply of oak and birch logs. Alec had rigged up a scraper and a sweeper that Daisy could haul back and forth over the ice, and spent many a winter hour driving slowly but steadily, first westward, then eastward, in his contemplative way. The logs he cut from a lot over by the piggery, just south of the Irish part of town, by arrangement with the officials of the Catholic cemetery who owned the land and trees and wanted to clear the area and blast out the stumps to make room for more graves. Alec drew the line at blasting. He had kept out of war and never had fired a gun. Explosives in any form were not for him. Alec believed firmly that the manufacture of gunpowder or dynamite was a mistake, and when he was told by Mary Stoddard, Linden's most vehement pacifist, that the Chinese had invented powder hundreds of years before, and had never used it for killing, but only for amusement, Alec was taken aback. It made him quite thoughtful for a while, and he looked more closely and with what seemed to be greater respect at the local Chinese laundryman thereafter.

There were not more than three hundred morning newspapers delivered in Linden, and they cost, retail, only two cents apiece, of which at least one cent went to the publishers. That left three dollars each morning, from the newspaper distribution, to be divided between Alec, who brought them down from Maplewood; Seymour Batt, who hired the newsboys, solicited the subscriptions, kept the accounts and returned titles torn from the front pages to get credit for those left unsold; and the two newsboys.

Before either of them were out of short pants and long stockings, everyone in town was sure that the newsboys would make their marks in life, and they did, Jerry becoming a pioneer dealer in automobiles and Frigger doing so well for himself during Prohibition that he wore silk shirts, nifty suits and ties, elaborate shoes, and paid for music lessons for at least twenty of his young relatives. Frigger loved music, but could not play a note himself, never having had time to learn, or an instrument to play on.

The Boston morning newspapers then circulating in Linden were the *Boston Herald, Globe, Post* and *Advertiser*. Each had definite and separate characteristics, and placed their purchasers in distinct groups well recognized in Linden.

The *Herald* was conservative, Republican, with a Protestant slant and a moderate style, the natural choice of the ministers, Protestant tradesmen and solid citizens. To see Norman Partridge or Deacon Clapp reading the *Post,* instead of the *Herald,* would have been as startling as seeing the Reverend K. Gregory Powys scorching through the Square on a racing bicycle with low-slung handlebars and an enormous sprocket.

Around the Massasoit bar, and in sporting circles, the lively, sensational *Post* was the favorite. Nearly all the Irish families took the *Post,* which never ran lengthy stories, gave the Catholic news the preference, and spared no expense or trouble with its sporting page.

A few Linden people favored the staid old *Globe* (Democratic), which let the stories run, column after column, and avoided the spectacular make-up affected by the *Post.* Those in our town who read the *Globe* did so because it covered carefully local news north of Boston, as far as the Canadian border, and south to the tip of Cape Cod. There were pages of small-town items, not significant individually, but collectively giving quite a picture of New England. Also, the *Globe* was scrupulously accurate in its market tabulations and sporting page, where the accounts of horse races and ball games were written in a florid, dignified style like political and commercial news.

Only five men in Linden read the *Advertiser,* which contained little else than shipping, commercial and financial news. These were Norman Partridge, for the market quotations; Dawson Freeman, for insurance news; J. J. Markham and George Sampson, who had to watch the wholesale prices of meat and produce in Faneuil Hall; and the fishman, Ezra Stowe, who had to know what fishing vessels were coming in to Gloucester and Boston.

Jerry Dineen had the harder of the newsboys' assignments. He covered the area north of the Saugus Branch tracks, and had to be careful which paper he left on the various doorsteps. Frigger had mostly *Posts,* with a very few *Globes,* to distribute on the south side of the tracks. Jerry was held up to all Linden boys as an example. He never was late. He never made mistakes. He saved the pennies he earned. In bad weather, he never left the papers exposed to the rain, sleet or snow. He was not very smart in school, but he was tenacious, and never missed a grade. His various odd jobs kept him busy outside of school hours, and all day Saturdays, so he was not an athlete, although he was healthy and strong. Jerry was considered by everyone as the boy most likely to succeed. Linden folks knew that when Jerry went into Sampson's store, as clerk, he would soon go into business for himself.

I was then, and always since then have been a little in awe of men, young or old, who were hustlers and whose career was clear to them and could be built, step by step, according to a plan. My brother Charles was one of those. He was a good student, deliberate and thorough, with a leaning toward practical science. From the time he entered school it was a foregone conclusion that he would go to Boston Tech (the Massachusetts Institute of Technology) which was known to be the toughest scientific school in the world. He chose civil engineering, for which he was ideally equipped, and never failed or faltered. He accepted his responsibilities, discharged his duties, overcame his obstacles, all in a quiet, steady and determined way.

My younger brother, Leslie, was placid and easygoing, had no ambition except to shun effort and responsibility, did badly in school, took care not to rise too rapidly in any field of endeavor, was kind and considerate, courageous and unassuming, and preferred to be inconspicuous. He has never left New England for any length of time, except to serve in the artillery in France in World War I. All the worrying he ever has done could be accomplished by the average citizen in less than half an hour.

I, born of the same parents, and brought up in the same environment, turned out to be a wanderer, without direction or governing philosophy, with no stabiiity or purpose, no achievements which did not come to me easily, impulsive, reckless, impractical and inconsistent, receptive to almost any kind of experience, with limitless curiosity and no standards at all.

This diversity of temperaments in families is characteristic of New England, where any attempt at standardization has led to rebellion, confusion, and has resulted, backhandedly, in progress or disaster. It is partly responsible for the reticence that, to outsiders, is a New Englander's most baffling characteristic. They talk very little, and if at all, indirectly, about what means most to them. A large proportion of their inner or their outer life they keep to themselves.

For instance, there was the Old Saugus Race Track, on the edge of the marsh in Cliftondale. My mother, having to count every penny to keep us all going, had a horror of gambling, and disapproved of racing on that account. So did my pious aunts and uncles, and the other Linden people who took the *Herald* and went regularly to church. But my cousin Ella's husband, from Amesbury, owned a trotter named Waldo which now and then was entered in the gig races at Old Saugus and was driven by Lawyer Perkins, himself. My mother's cousin, Survina, had a husband named Luther Morrill, one of the best of the Faneuil Hall restaurateurs (a competitor of the famous Durgin and Parks), who had two race horses, Molly and Maisy, one or both of which was frequently in the money.

On the days when Lawyer Perkins' Waldo was running, on the Saugus track, just a couple of miles from our house, Cousin Ella used to come to spend the day with Mother. Cousin Ella, with her gray hair (at the age of thirty) and soft gray-blue eyes, was the most beautiful and exotic of our family connections, and the daughter of adventurous Great-Aunt Lucy, one of the first New England women to get a divorce. Cousin Ella and my mother would talk all day, mostly about various relatives

one had seen lately and the other had not, but no mention of
the races at Old Saugus would be made. Late in the afternoon,
Lawyer Perkins would show up, smelling of bay rum and the
stable, and would stay to dinner, but he never talked about
the race.

The same was true when "Uncle" Luther Morrill and
"Aunt" Vine appeared. "Aunt" Vine came first and spent the
day, "Uncle" Luther would come to fetch her late in the day,
and would stay for supper. Naturally, I had seen the races,
either as guest of my uncles, through a knothole in the fence,
or from a high water tower that commanded a view of the
track. That was not mentioned, either.

Some summer mornings, when the clouds along the horizon
were gray and a peculiar fragrance was in the air that meant
the day would be fair, instead of riding to Maplewood with
Alec Graydon to get the papers, I would go alone into the
woods, before the birds awoke. I knew every step of the pathways and trails, in the thinning darkness, and would seat myself on a rock on the edge of a feather-grass meadow festooned
with damp cobwebs, near Elephant's Back.

First I would hear faint clicks, as drops of dew fell down
on dried leaves, and sometimes the soft, unstealthy tread of a
woodchuck among the stones and fallen branches. Then would
come the barely audible murmurings of thrushes as they stirred
sleepily in the bushes, at the level of my ear. My hearing was
sharpened by the morning dampness. The thrushes' whispering would spread and slowly become general, a rustle from
which a liquid note would escape. Then from the grass, and
between the trees, the clear-weather song of the robin would
confirm my guess about the weather. A jay would scream. Another. Woodpeckers would start drumming, song sparrows
would scatter notes in clusters, as, one by one, the trees would
take shape in the dimness—birches with the evergreens, groves

of oaks and maples, pine, fir, spruce, cedar and hemlock. Willows grew in the damp places, alder almost anywhere. There were walnut trees, beechnuts, sumach, and berry bushes.

The chorus of birds would swell from its tentative beginnings to a moderate stage, then all of them would let themselves go, until the sound was overwhelming. Miles of woodland, acres of shrubs and fields, all eloquent with birds. Along the streets of Linden, far below, the orioles in their swinging nests along Elm Street burst into song. Sparrows chattered along Beach Street. In the meadows and reeds the red-winged blackbird and the bobolink clung to swaying stalks and cat-o'-nine-tails, reflected in the pools. Around me, in the woods, now the tanagers and flickers, the rose-breasted grosbeaks and the bluebirds joined the demonstration. No one bird seemed to be listening to the others. Each sang at the top of its voice, which was swept into the joyous ensemble.

I did not go to the woods to study wild life. That was farthest from my mind. I wanted to hear the performance, alone, to be in the midst of it, trying to penetrate its quivering volume for component sounds, for broader effects, to hear melody tossed and scrambled in profusion, rhythm complicated beyond analysis, until it began to throb and beat with hidden rumblings, chants, deliriums and ecstasy. I liked to hear the chorus race like fire, flow like the tide, flap like pennons on a thousand spars, roar, mount, blur, then, note by note, subside.

CHAPTER SIX

Linden Square and Packard's Powders

THE retail trade in Linden, which years ago was so friendly, so intimate and unhurried, and so personal, was centered in Linden Square. It goes without saying that Linden would not have a Square that was shaped like one. The south side of Beach Street, and both sides of Lynn Street coming in from the direction of Everett, had room for all the stores and shops. The Saugus Branch depot was fifty yards north of the grade crossing and between it and Beach Street, bordering on Lynn Street, was a triangular lot on which stood a few elm trees, spaced evenly, so that it passed for a park, only there were no benches, no flower beds, and the grass did not grow very well.

The depot was painted a dingy railroad red, with dark green blinds, dark green trimmings and a shingle roof so old that it was flecked with moss. A broad macadam walk stretched all the way from the Beach Street sidewalk, which was of mud or dust, to the unguarded grade crossing where Lynn Street cut across the tracks from behind the depot, at an angle. Probably the Beach Street grade crossing would have had no tender if the horsecar tracks had not intersected the steam car tracks there. Inside the depot, front and center, was Charley Moore's office. He was the station agent, who checked the trains in and out, tended the clicking telegraph that brought in mostly bad news and condolences in those days, loaded the outgoing trunks and boxes into the baggage cars, after trundling them along the macadam from the baggage room to the far end of the walk, either way, where the baggage cars stopped.

Between crossings in Linden, there was just room for an ordinary Saugus Branch train. If the engine nosed the sidewalk of Lynn Street, the baggage car would be touching the sidewalk along Beach Street, and vice versa. Two extra cars would block traffic on both sides and cut Linden in two, at its narrowest and most vulnerable point.

The American Express Company maintained a service along the Saugus Branch, but it was efficacious only if goods were coming from, or destined for, the north of Boston. Any shipments that had to pass from the South Station to the North Station in Boston were delayed anywhere from ten days to a fortnight, so perishable goods could not be sent that way.

Charley Moore, the station agent, was a loose-jointed, good-natured man, just under thirty, who bent his knees when he walked and wore thick-lensed glasses. He could afford neither liquor nor tobacco, but was always chewing gum. Charley was studying to be a lawyer, and always between trains, his nose was buried deep in his books, so that one hesitated at the grilled window before disturbing him to buy a ticket. Charley had been studying law several years, and after he passed the bar examinations and hung out his shingle and built up a practice, he intended to marry Rena Carberry, to whom he had been engaged five years, in 1900. When the dispute as to whether the turn of the century should be celebrated January 1, 1900, or January 1, 1901, Charley had sent a letter to the *Boston Globe,* in favor of the even date. There were arguments, and even fist-fights, all over America on account of that mathematical riddle, some insisting that on January 1, 1900, only ninety-nine years of the century had been endured, and that the hundredth year lay between January 1 and December 31 of the year numbered 1900. I do not remember any fights in

Linden on account of the century-turning problem, but there were quite a few headaches, and I did not ask my brother Charles for fear that, if he did not know the answer, it would make him feel badly to admit it, since he had been an honor student at the Massachusetts Institute of Technology.

Pat Finley, the crossing tender, who let down and raised the gates across Beach Street before and after the trains had crossed, lived in a square little shanty so near the track that the whoosh of the eastbound "express" trains stirred all the cinders and dust with which his tiny room was coated. He had a wooden bunk with blankets, nails on which to hang his lanterns, a soap box stood on end for a bed table, another, with a basin, for a washstand. His water he got from an outside faucet in Dr. Moody's back yard. When his socks got too stiff and his towels too grimy, Pat tossed them away. He read dime novels nearly all the time he was awake—Nick Carter, Frank Merriwell, and the like—and loaned them to the boys he could trust to return them. Pat was a real critic of the dime novel, and was so tensely involved in Frank Merriwell's romance that he would grind his teeth and mutter under his breath when he saw a dark-complexioned, dark-eyed woman go by.

Frank Merriwell, it will be remembered by those who followed his career in their youth, was loved to distraction by two girls, one named Elsie, a white-skinned, blue-eyed blonde of the clinging kind, the other, Inza Burrage, a brunette with an olive skin, black hair and luminous dark eyes. Actually, Frank was not indecisive. That would not have been consistent with his sterling character and unimpeachable judgment. It seemed that Frank was not quite sure that Elsie could love him, in the ordinary way. She was so frail and pure and ethereal. Inza left no doubt in anyone's mind. She loved Frank so passionately that Pat Finley was disgusted that any woman should so far forget herself and her modesty. Inza knew she was going to lose out to the fragile blonde, and she tried not to embarrass Frank, but Frank knew. He knew everything, and could not bear to hurt Inza.

This went on, volume after volume, as long as the average soap-opera lasts today.

"Those black-eyed floozies have hearts just as black. Don't trust 'em, or let one of 'em near you," Pat would say. "You'll rue the day, if you do."

When the author and publishers of the Frank Merriwell series brought out another, centering around Dick Merriwell, Frank's younger brother, Pat was furious. He engendered a dislike for the younger brother that kept him muttering and pacing his cabin.

"That young whippersnapper," he would say, shaking his fist at Dick's picture on the paper cover of the book. "He's not the man his brother was, and I can lick the man who says so."

Naturally, knowing what rise we could get out of Pat, we would let him overhear us say that maybe Dick, after all, was a better pitcher or scrapper than Frank. For us to suggest that Frank might be getting too old put Pat into a rage, and he would, in extreme cases, refuse to let such young lunkheads as ourselves read his books. That only lasted through the day. On the morrow, Pat would forgive and forget, and tell the boys all the high points of the stories before they had a chance to read them.

When a train was approaching Linden, a bell started ringing in Pat's little shack, giving him warning in time to clear the crossing of traffic and get the gates down. Very infrequently freights would be routed our way, because of congestion on the main lines, or deliveries of coal to J. J. Markham, the local dealer. Those would annoy Pat, who liked everything according to schedule. There were no toilet facilities in Pat's shanty, so in daylight he would ask one of us to stay in his place on the chance that a freight might come through while he was at the depot "for purposes of nature," as he expressed it. I could not hope to reproduce Pat's rich Irish brogue.

In the depot were two waiting rooms, with potbellied stoves, giant size, resting on metal mats large enough to accommodate large coal hods. Each waiting room had a toilet, of the "society" brand, equipped with overhead tank that spattered, and a handle and chain. The "Gents" toilet was kept locked, and Charley Moore had the key, which was attached to an inch board, a foot long and three inches across, so absentminded patrons would not stick it in their pockets. The "Ladies" toilet was left unlocked while the depot was open, so that the women would not have to reveal to Charley when they felt the urge to relieve themselves. Most women of that period would have risked almost anything rather than show such immodesty. Some of the most ladylike and lovely of them built up such an illusion that a Linden bridegroom, after the Spanish-American War, burst into tears and went on a ten-day drunk when by accident he pulled the backhouse door open and saw his bride seated there.

Charley Moore's office had two grilled windows, one opening into the men's waiting room, the other into the ladies', so there was no enforced mingling of the sexes in Linden's small station. The melodramas involving the innocent country girl and the city slicker with the black moustaches were still vivid and meaningful north of Boston, so much so that unescorted girls, if they made a journey that passed without adventure, began to feel a little doubtful of their attractions.

Starting eastward from Pat Finley's shanty, the next building, two stories with an unfinished attic, was rented by Doc Moody, who used the front rooms for an office and waiting room and the others as living quarters.

"Doc sure is an optimist," Uncle Reuben said, to plague

Mathilda. "He's fitted himself out to handle three or four patients at a crack, when it's all he can do to get hold of one."

"That one's enough trouble for half a dozen doctors," Mathilda said, referring to Alice Townsend, who, after she had come out of her first coma, had started acting strangely and kept relapsing every day or two, until Doc was at his wit's end and the sentiment in Linden had veered from sympathy with the modest teacher to open impatience with her state of nerves.

"I got an idea about the right kind of treatment . . ." Uncle Reuben said.

"You aren't the only one," Mathilda agreed.

Seymour Batt's little dry-goods store was wedged in between Doc's driveway and the tailor shop. There were innumerable odd-sized shelves and drawers in Seymour's place, and broad counters on which material was cut and measured by the yard or the width of his outstretched hand. He kept thread, buttons, hand-made and machine-made laces; socks, shirts, underwear and neckties for men; bustles, corsets, ruffled drawers and petticoats for women. The sales he made were almost always small, and he had to hunt from one end of the store to the other in order to find what was wanted, so he added to his income from dry goods, which could not have exceeded three hundred dollars a year, by handling newspapers, magazines, and paper-covered novels, the dime novels for boys, and the twenty-five cent kind for women who liked romantic stories. The favorite writer among the last named was Laura Jean Libbey. Seymour was tall, stoop-shouldered and very nearsighted, so he had to peer and lean over like a crane in search of spools of thread, hooks and eyes, and spare whalebone strips for busted stays. He carried an enormous bunch of keys, unmarked, and when he tried to open up his place or lock it after closing time, he would spend five or ten minutes, trying one key. fumbling for the keyhole, then trying another.

"Why don't you paste some hair around that thing? You'd find it then, fast enough," Packard, the lady-killing clerk at J. J. Markham's nearby grocery, would say.

Seymour would pretend that he had not heard, and continue trying keys, one after another. What the other keys were for, no one knew. There were only two doors, front and back, to the dry-goods store, and two to Batt's little house on Oliver Street, where his daughter, Minnie, kept house for him. That was all Minnie ever did. She was slow in school and did not graduate until she was fifteen. She had to wear glasses, like her father's, and they made her look odd and undermined her confidence so that she moved awkwardly. Her natural inaptitude made the housework last all day, so she had no time in which to be discontented. Once in a while, when Seymour had to make a trip into Boston, to replenish his stock or get some new novelties his customers had begun pestering him for, Minnie kept store, and on those occasions the customer and Minnie might have to spend an hour or more rummaging through pigeonholes and cabinets for a yard of ribbon that would retail for eight cents.

Moe Selib, who kept the tailor shop next door, was the only Jew in town, and as such, was a fine ambassador for his race. He worked hard when there was a rush of trade, took it easy when he could, was witty and resourceful, and accepted the role of comedian that seemed to be expected of him: frock coat, flat derby, sagging knees with toes spread outward, and eloquent shrugs and gestures.

The next little shop on the Square was the cobbler's, where the brisk little Lancashireman, Henry Laws, toiled prodigiously, up to his waist in old misshapen shoes he turned out like new, or as nearly as was possible. Shoes then, and especially children's shoes, were worn until there was little left of the original leather. They were soled and half-soled, sewn at the seams, patched, repatched and mended. Like so many men who learned their trades in England, Mr. Laws was thorough and proud of his workmanship. If he could not fix a boot or a shoe, it could not be fixed. That was all there was to it. He could make a pair of shoes by hand, starting from scratch. He could start farther back than that, and shape a last, after measuring and studying a foot. Mr. Wing, who liked to have everybody happy, once ordered a pair of hand-made shoes from Mr. Laws, to let the little Englishman show the town what he could do, and the result was more than satisfactory. The only trouble was that Mr. Laws put in so much time on the custom-job that his little shop was piled high with shoes to be repaired and dozens of customers had to wait, while the cobbler was doing fancy stitching and holding his work to the light, in an ecstasy of pardonable self-approbation. And when the custom-shoes were finished, Mr. Laws would only charge eight dollars, having used at least eighty dollars' worth of time. A few more orders like that, and the cobbler would have gone out of business, but those shoes for Mr. Wing were the high spot in Mr. Laws' stay in America. He and his wife were so homesick that it was painful to see them, and in the end, they went back, with, let us hope, enough money earned and saved to see them through a comfortable English old age.

The horse trough and public drinking fountain, with its metal cup on a chain, stood on the northwest corner of the crossroads, next to the little railroad "park." Across Lynn Street, on the northeast corner, stood the big house, with the enormous horse-chestnut tree in the yard, where Big Julie Goan's mother kept a rooming house. The roomers were Big Julie, who paid her room-rent and chipped in more, when it was needed; Letty Ledbetter, the Canadian girl who worked in Maplewood; Packard, J. J. Markham's clerk who never passed up a skirt, regardless of age, looks, status, or previous condition of servitude; a huge grass widow named Martha Loomis, who stayed in bed most of the time to keep herself from eating, and every few weeks broke her self-imposed bonds and went on an eating jag that became legendary all over the countryside. When she could control herself, she went as far as Young's Hotel in Boston before she started stuffing, but sometimes she could make it only as far as the Massasoit House, and after two or three days, during which Jeff Lee, eyes bulging with wonder and hands trembling for fear she would die on his hands, waited on her, hand and foot, and in the end, persuaded her to send to Doc Moody who, in extreme cases, had to pump her out.

Mrs. Loomis was dearly loved by her fellow roomers and the men and women around the Square and the Massasoit House. She was serene, fat, good-natured to an incredible degree, and as psychic as any clairvoyant or professional medium could be. Serious-minded Christian business men, like George Sampson, the second grocer, sat at her bedside and took her advice on commodity investments. Mrs. Goan insisted that whenever George Sampson called, after he was gone Mrs. Loomis cried as if her heart would break, but the fat seeress would never explain. Years later, when Sampson's only daughter died suddenly of pneumonia, and Mr. and Mrs. Sampson were so paralyzed with grief that it looked for a while as if neither could recover, Mrs. Loomis broke down and admitted that whenever she had seen George Sampson she had seen a shadowy figure of a dead young girl behind him. I submit this for what it is worth. I know that Mrs. Loomis predicted that a terrible disaster at sea was impending, before the *Portland* went down. I know that she said, categorically, that Susie Lowe, of Rockport, who came to us to keep house while Mother was recovering from blood poisoning, and who had been stone-deaf for thirty years, would one day suddenly recover her hearing again. That Susie did, on falling downstairs at the age of sixty, is a matter of record.

Sometimes I thought Mrs. Loomis was one of the most beautiful women I had ever seen, in spite of her bulk. She had lovely dark-blue eyes, skin as white as a baby's, and a low and well-modulated voice. She spoke of her absent daughters with affection and understanding, and of her eating habits, which made it necessary for them to maintain her at a distance, where she would not hinder their chances for good marriages. I think she would not have had things otherwise. She loved her companions of the rooming house, and the Linden folks who trusted her visions and relied on her advice. She accepted the worship of Jeff Lee, as a queen might receive it, and permitted him to remonstrate when he served her a whole keg of live oysters, as a starter on one of her tremendous meals.

That her love life was not neglected was due to the warm-hearted Packard, who was likely, on occasion, to be found in any room, including Mrs. Goan's, from top to bottom of the large rooming house. Anyway, that was what everybody said, and Packard never denied it.

"Any man who's able, and refuses a lady, is no gent," Packard said. "He's sure to wish, some day, that he hadn't been so mean."

On the southeast corner of the Square, Dud Shultz pottered around his dim little drug store, like a white mouse in a cage. Next door was George Sampson's grocery, and set apart on a small unfenced lot was the Chinese laundry.

The southwest corner, with an extensive frontage on Beach Street and at right-angles on Lynn Street, also, was J. J. Markham's grocery, the largest in Linden, and farther south, adjacent to it, were the hay scales and the wood and coal yard, with storehouses for baled hay and sacks of grain.

Beyond the coal yard was the Linden barber shop, Webb Higginson, proprietor.

Before the year 1900, at which time J. J. Markham had a telephone installed in his store, the second phone in Linden, the first being in the residence of Norman Partridge, the different ways the four Linden grocers conducted their business was the subject of much comment. Two or three times a week, the grocers had to drive their wagons to Boston, for meat, poultry, butter, cheese and eggs, fresh vegetables and other perishable produce. Their staples were ordered from the wholesale houses and delivered by wagon or freight.

The first up in the morning was George Sampson, who, before he went into business for himself, had been head clerk at Markham's. George was a large solemn-faced man who took himself and his work seriously. Before sunup in winter, and not later than five o'clock in the morning in summer, George would hitch up his two horses to the wagon or pung and start out across the marsh toward Revere. He would pass through Chelsea, and was prudent enough to look up the tides in the Old Farmer's Almanac so he would not be likely to be delayed by open drawbridges in Charlestown. Thus he would reach Faneuil Hall, Boston's superb central market place, in time to get the pick of the provisions.

Often he would have his wagon loaded aand be almost back in Linden when he met Jim Puffer, his shiftless competitor, on his way in, past midmorning. That was one reason why Sampson succeeded and Puffer periodically failed and had to be rescued by his wife's brother, Norman Partridge.

J. J. Markham, a chipper little man who handled the bulk of Linden's trade in groceries, provisions, coal, wood, hay and grain, could afford to stay in bed until nearly six o'clock, and started off about seven, the days he drove to market. J. J. wore a white linen duster down to his ankles, and a straw hat in his store, the year round. He had a word to say to everybody, addressing all men as "Charley" and all the women as "Ma'am." His manner was breezy, and while taking an order, filling it, or totaling up bills, kept up a running fire of chatter, all inconsequential, almost like a barker in a county fair. Being the only one who sold feed and fuel in town, nearly everyone traded with him to that extent, but he did not like having Sampson take away any of his grocery trade, and sometimes cut prices on meat, or fresh vegetables. His special pride was his large, commodious icebox, as big as the gate-tender's shack. He liked to handle meat and was a skillful butcher. When he got back from Boston with a load of meat, J. J. would peel off his overcoat and hat, get back into his duster and straw, and help unload the carcasses of lamb and sides of beef, resting them on his straw hat and holding the ankles in his hands. If his hat got bloody, he would look at it fondly, and wipe the blood off on a gunnysack of spuds or meal.

Like the other grocers, J. J. used small spuds as stoppers over the spigots of the kerosene cans, so the kids would not spill the kerosene on the way home and cause him to be accused of giving short measure.

The weights and measures in a grocery store of that epoch were a sight to behold. Potatoes, turnips, parsnips, dried peas and cracked corn, numerous articles that were fairly durable and dry, were sold by the peck and half-peck. Cylindrical boxes without tops were used for dry measure, graded in size from the smallest, not six inches in diameter, to the bushel, as big around as a military drum. Spring balances were used for meat, platform scales for sacks of meal. It was several years later that the Commonwealth of Massachusetts started taking an interest in weights and measures, and sent inspectors to the local stores, and up to the time of the first World War, this interference with local business was resented deeply by the tradesmen, and most of their Linden customers agreed with them. The farther away a seat of government was situated, the more the pre-war New Englanders distrusted it, when any of its representatives stuck their noses in local affairs.

Just after J. J. installed his telephone, the story got started around Linden about Packard's powders, and never completely died down.

Packard, Markham's best clerk, as I have suggested, was known far and wide as a ladies' man. Whenever a woman came near him, Pack began to get a mischievous gleam in his eye. It was quite clear what was foremost in his mind, but he said or did nothing tangible to which any of them could take exception. In the mornings he stayed in the store, taking orders, wrapping up the stuff he sold, or packing it in wooden boxes for delivery in the afternoon. There were three kinds of women in Linden. The larger group consisted of wives who were faithful, and single women who were either unattractive or unapproachable. Then there were several—some married, some single, some in their teens, others middle-aged and gray —who, everyone knew, were amenable to improper suggestions. Most of these were attractive, with a merry zest for life and a healthy disregard of consequences.

It was in the middle zone, between the two extremes, that Packard seemed to be most active, among those housewives and working girls who looked tempting but that the men were never quite sure about. Packard never said a word about his conquests or rebuffs. He enjoyed being noncommunicative, and that helped him in his lusty avocation. Everybody in Linden kidded Packard, but they never found out anything definite from him.

No one was sure how the story got started about Packard's powders. The nature of them, the source of supply, the method of application and the results were discussed, both facetiously and in earnest, for years. One of the tales was to the effect that the secret came from an old Indian squaw, Ann Welcome, for whom Black Ann's Corner was named. Black Ann's Corner, where Lynn Street ran into Salem Street, near the stone quarry and the Cliftondale line, was always a sinister spot because a man named Herty had killed his housekeeper there with a hatchet, in 1764. That was after Ann Welcome had lived there. How the formula for the love powders was handed down through nearly one hundred and fifty years to Packard, was never clearly explained. No Indians had lived in Linden since that time.

Hen Richards, who gathered herbs and simples in the woods, brewing them occasionally to keep himself healthy, was also charged with having given the secret to Packard, in exchange for a cigar box full of fishhooks.

Others insisted that Packard had a prescription, from some doctor in Bangor, and that Dud Shultz filled it, secretly, in the middle of the night.

The story I first heard was that Packard's powders were white and tasteless, and that, while he was making his afternoon deliveries, he sifted a few grains into the flour or sugar. This tiny dose was said to make any woman so eager for a man that the lightest touch would cause her to fall over backwards.

Packard's first stop, as he drove Markham's grocery wagon up Beach Street from the Square was at Mr. Wing's apartment house on the corner of Oliver Street. There he stopped and chatted a long while with Mrs. Thole and Milly, mother and youngest daughter, respectively, in a theatrical family whose other members were nearly always on the road with their famous puppets which had earned them an international reputation. Mother and daughter were a handsome, lively pair who might have passed for sisters. Milly was about fifteen, but extraordinarily well-developed for her age, and her mother, who must have been over forty, was at the height of her beauty and, at least ten months of the year, away from her husband. All the time Packard was in there, and his horse and wagon hitched outside, tongues were wagging, but neither the Tholes nor Packard did anything to stop them. The local women, and young girls, were somewhat in awe of Mrs. Thole and Milly because they had been on the stage and Milly, in the last grades of the Linden Grammar School, had a provocative, well-rounded physique and assured manner that set her apart from her schoolmates and put most of the teachers in the shade.

One of the Linden women on Packard's route was a good friend of my mother's named Daisy Hoyt. Daisy was large and buxom, with an hourglass figure, hair that was naturally curly, and a complexion almost as clear as Mrs. Loomis'. She was a widow, and a gay one, and contrived to have a pot of tea on the stove when Packard came around. She always invited him in, and he accepted. And when Mother would reproach her mildly for giving people such a chance to gossip about her, Daisy's eyes would light up and she would throw back her head and laugh so heartily that Mother would be forced to smile. On every street through which he drove, Packard was welcomed by three or four otherwise lonely women.

It was Mrs. Hoyt who told my mother what she had heard about Packard's powders, and admitted, in order to aggravate Mother, that sometimes after eating biscuits made from flour that Packard had delivered, Daisy felt so kittenish that she put on her best lace nightgown and waltzed with her pillow in the moonlight.

Packard used to go to Dud Shultz's drugstore for his cigars and pipe tobacco. When he noticed that the nervous little druggist seemed to be uneasy whenever he showed up there, Packard, always ready to be the instrument of harmless malice, contrived to go in when no other customers were in the store.

That made little Dud tremble and stutter. He miscounted the change, grabbed for the wrong brands, and otherwise acted as if he were on the verge of a nervous breakdown. This condition was aggravated if, as usually happened, once the word got round, other men, mostly those from the Massasoit brotherhood, would glance in at the windows while Packard was making his purchases, find excuses to linger in the vicinity, would nod, grimace and talk slyly with other passersby, making it plain to the timorous Dud that his actions were under close observation and were the source of subversive comment.

Packard, meanwhile, would take his time, bringing up all odds and ends of conversation, pretending not to notice that Dud was ready to cry or fly, acting as sociable and leisurely as you please.

One evening, when a popular and free-spending travelling man for Blackstone whiskey and assorted Crosse and Blackwell relishes was at the Massasoit, a course of action was suggested and agreed upon, the results of which came close to putting poor Dud Shultz in hospital. Walt Robbins was the drummer's name, and he was an old friend of my Uncle Reuben and the Admiral. He made Linden about twice in three months, driving in from Chelsea, in the late afternoon, to give himself time to make his calls and take Admiral Quimby's order, have one of Jeff's famous suppers, tell stories around the bar or in the back room after supper was over, and then settle down with my incorrigible uncle, the proprietor, Mr. Wing, Dawson Freeman and Doc Moody for a social game of poker that often lasted until dawn, or later. That was a game in which, according to Doc, everybody lost and nobody won. Any of the players, if asked how he came out, would say that he lost a little, in the long run, or that he was about even. In the case of my Uncle Reuben and Dawson Freeman, the insurance man who had married Deacon Clapp's oldest daughter, that resumé of their luck was in the nature of mild boasting. Doc, himself, did manage to keep almost even. Admiral Quimby, as host, did not like to take large amounts away from his guests. The game was table stakes, with a quarter ante, Jacks or better to open, and a dollar limit for a raise at one time.

Walt Robbins, although his losses could have been absorbed in his expense account (the "swindle sheet" as he called it), usually came out ahead, and Mr. Wing seldom won less than ten or fifteen dollars, and sometimes collected as high as fifty dollars a sitting. No one resented that, or let drop the faintest suspicion that a gentleman of Mr. Wing's presence would have cheated. He was competent and lucky, besides.

"Some men hold cards and others don't," my Uncle Reuben said. And he added, with a rueful smile: "I'm one who don't."

"You could find better uses for your money than paying for those other rounders' rum and loose women," said my Great-Uncle Lije.

Aunt Carrie, who never had any accurate idea of the family finances, accepted the fiction that the men did not play for money, but she thought it was wicked to play cards at all, that there was something inherently evil in pasteboards covered with hearts, spades, diamonds, clubs, kings, aces, queens and jacks. Like most of the stricter Congregationalists, she would not have a pack of cards in her house. My own mother relented concerning cards, for harmless nongambling games like Casino or Hearts, a year or two before I graduated from high school.

It was one of those cool, invigorating evenings in the fall, when the air was crisp, the smell of burning leaves hung faintly in the air, when Jeff felt most like cooking and his steady customers felt most like eating, that it was decided at the Massasoit to postpone the poker game and utilize the presence of Walt Robbins for a practical joke on Dud Shultz. Whether Packard, himself, was in on it or not is a question that never can be determined. Packard's inner life was a closed book to everybody. So was his outer life, except those phases of it that could be observed from the Linden sidewalks.

It was a fact, nevertheless, that on the afternoon before Walt and his fellow-conspirators called on Dud, Packard had gone into the drugstore and had asked Dud for some memory pills, which he swore he had seen among the Humphrey's Specifics, somewhere between Numbers 1 and 80.

"I've had a hard time rememberin' who wants Pettijohn's and who asks for Force, over that dratted telephone," Packard said. "Not once, since I was a boy, have I forgot an order when somebody gave it to me, face-to-face. The minute I pick up that darn machine, all the wits go out of my head. They tell me a few of them memory pills will fix all that."

"I assure you, Mr. Packard, I never heard of any pills like that," Dud answered nervously. Little by little, in spite of himself, Packard was edging him nearer the prescription shelves and counter.

"You got Humphrey's Specifics, haven't you?" Packard asked.

In desperation, the jittery little druggist started taking bottles of pills from their compartments in the case containing the famous specifics, glancing at the labels, and shaking his head. His fingers grew moist and his hands began to tremble, so that he dropped pills on the floor, and put them back in the wrong compartments. Outside, on the sidewalk, watching and nodding wisely, were Hal Kingsland, Gimp Crich, the old sailor, Ruth Coffee, young Frigger Bacigalupo, and Spike Dodge, the Linden cop.

To add to Dud's consternation, Packard offered to go around behind the counter and help the druggist look for what was wanted. This was against the rules, and the last thing

Dud wanted at the time, but Packard suited the action to the word and soon was scrutinizing the mysteriously labelled jars, bottles and drawers, as if his life depended on it. Finally, Packard found something he said he wanted, and the watchers on the sidewalk saw Dud wrap up a package and saw Packard shove it into his pocket, paying for it with coins from his leather purse. Packard emerged from the drugstore, not seeming to pay attention to the men assembled on the sidewalk, and, with a casual nod to them collectively, went about his business in the grocery store.

Hal Kingsland and Gimp Crich, after giving Dud a little time to get more excited and rattled, went into the drugstore, and headed straight for the prescription counter.

"What was that you just sold Packard?" asked Kingsland.

Dud was in a panic. "I don't know. I don't remember," he said.

"Come out of it," said Hal, still good-naturedly. "Ain't this pharmacy a public place?"

"Can't any citizen get service here?" Crich asked. "I've been to more'n half the seaports all over the world, an' I ain't never seen nothing like that. A store that sells to one man, and not to another."

"I'll sell you anything you ask for, if the law allows it," Dud began.

"Ah," said Hal Kingsland. "Is Packard a privileged character, who gets stuff here that's unlawful?"

The door opened, causing a rusty bell to jangle in the back room, and my Uncle Reuben came in, ostensibly to buy me some candy. When he was flush, he was always doing that. When he was broke, he charged it, with a grand, irresistible air.

"Reuben. Did you ever hear tell of anything like that? Packard, next door, comes in and buys some powders, or whatever it is he gets here. Gimp and me come in, right after, and Dud, here, won't sell us none," Hal asked and stated, in an injured tone of voice.

"That don't sound like the Dud I've known all these years," Uncle Reuben said. "He's always been on the level, as far as I'm concerned, and I don't like to have anybody say anything to the contrary."

"Mr. Paul, I really don't remember. Mr. Packard came in here for something—something about his memory—we looked for what he wanted, couldn't find it, then he saw something else he wanted, handed it over to me, I saw the price on it, accepted the money and wrapped it up. I was so confused, with him behind the counter, which is against the rules of the State Board, that I didn't notice what I was doing." The little druggist addressed this, appealingly, to my Uncle Reuben.

"Do I get what I asked for, or don't I?" Hal Kingsland persisted, eyeing Dud as a tomcat looks at a cornered mouse.

"If Packard'll tell you what it is," Dud Shultz said earnestly.

"Fat chance a fellow's got of getting anything out of Packard," Hal said disgustedly.

"He don't volunteer no information. Never has," said the sailor, Gimp Crich. He turned and beckoned to Hal. "Come on. We're wasting our time in here. We got to go higher up."

"Gentlemen," implored Shultz. "I'm doing the best I can. No one has ever entered a complaint."

"Think it over, why don't you? Give Dud another chance," my Uncle Reuben said. He turned to Dud, and grew confidential. "You know, Dud. A lot of the men with restless wives and growin' daughters have been gettin' good and scared. They say that Packard has been feedin' the womenfolk some kind of medicine that makes 'em itch where it's risky to scratch. And some folks say you put the stuff up for him. Mr. Weeks told the cop that it was getting so he couldn't figure on more than half a crop from his best hayfields, the grass gets flattened so."

"I don't know a thing about any such medicine," Dud said, plaintively.

"Then you think it may be somebody else who's peddling this Spanish fly, or whatever it is?" my uncle asked.

"I've heard nothing about it," Dud said, uneasily.

"Got your doctor's book handy?" my uncle asked.

Reluctantly, the druggist got out his worn *Pharmacopoeia*. My uncle frowned and pawed the leaves, turning them slowly over and peering at the contents. This time, Admiral Quimby, Harry Weeks, Charley Clapp, Big Julie Goan and Ginger Mc-Sweeney peered in, then winked at one another significantly.

"Mmmmm. Aphro . . . Aphrodisiacs. Isn't that what you call 'em?" asked Uncle Reuben.

"I don't know. I've never had call for them. Of course, some of the drugs may be in stock. I don't know." Dud reached anxiously for the book.

"You know pretty well what's in stock," my Uncle Reuben said. Then, to me. "Come on, nephew." He stocked me generously with candy, then asked me to stop in on my way home to tell his wife, Aunt Carrie, that he had some business to talk over that night, at the hotel, and wouldn't be home to supper. As we left the store, I knowing that Aunt Carrie would receive the message resignedly but sadly, Uncle Reuben took a parting shot at the already demoralized Dud.

"I'd be extra careful, if I were you," my uncle said.

Poor Dud was already wringing his hands and was ready to cry. He knew of what activities, from one end of town to the other, Packard was suspected. Nothing could be farther outside Dud's range of character than to have a part in such projects. It was never clear in his mind whether Packard's magic compound or elixir worked only in Packard's favor, or had a general effect on womankind. As a graduate pharmacist, he felt sure the whole story was based on myths and hearsay, with no foundation in chemistry, physiology or fact. Psychology was a study no serious or practical man had any time or use for. It was plain common sense, applied to human nature, and he was afraid he had very little of either. He felt insecure and almost nonexistent, with no margin, physically, financially or socially. If his store became unpopular, and people in Linden suspected him, he was finished. He had no hope of being able to establish himself elsewhere, or to get work in a busy city pharmacy, where the pace already was too swift for him. Druggists, lately, were expected to deal with all kinds of innovations, such as developing and printing plates and prints for camera enthusiasts.

Just before closing time, which was eight o'clock, Dud was informed by another of Markham's clerks, a serious-minded owl-like young man named Evans, that he was "wanted" on the phone. This method of communicating with the druggist was very rare, and Dud had never got used to it. If the glib and progressive Packard had trouble with his memory, when a telephone was brought into play, Dud became quite hysterical. In case a doctor was giving him an emergency prescription, Dud checked and rechecked each item and amount until he was blue in the face.

"This is Inspector Chatham, of the State Board," said a gruff and pompous male voice.

"Yes. Yes. Inspector, you said," mumbled Shultz, before he let the receiver slip from his hands. When he had retrieved it and held it again to his ear, teeth chattering, the Voice said:

"You won't be leaving town this evening, will you, Mr. Shultz?"

"No. I'll be home," Dud promised. He felt sick and dizzy, too frightened to react.

"I'd like to have a talk with you, and look around," the Voice said.

The little druggist could not answer. He still clutched the receiver, looking fearfully to see whether the late clerk, Evans, was hearing what had been said. A harsh click grated in Dud's ear. He held on a moment longer, fearfully, then replaced the receiver on the hook. Evans, who was sweeping in a distant corner, having locked the doors for the night, came over and let Dud out into the air, where the little man gasped.

"Somebody sick?" asked Evans.

"No . . . That is . . . I don't know," stammered Dud and fled into his drugstore. He turned down the lamps and blew them out, shuddering in the darkness, and crawled up the back stairs to his quarters above. There, without supper, or light, he waited, his mind fluttering back over everything he had done or failed to do in recent years, in some instances as far back as his childhood.

There had been a few occasions when men, and a very few women, had confided in him that some friend, never anyone with whom they were directly concerned, was "in trouble" and had begged him for something that would save the unlucky ones from disaster and their families from disgrace. Invariably Dud had told them he knew nothing about such remedies, that he could give out nothing without a doctor's prescription, and that he knew of no doctor who would handle such a case. All of these statements were true, but to be approached in such a way left him uneasy for weeks. His accounts he kept as best he could, but he was so inept that they were seldom, if ever, in order. No one had questioned his conduct of his little business before. He knew of no one he could ask for comfort or advice.

He did not know that a delegation from the Massasoit had watched him from the waiting room in the depot as he had scurried into Markham's store, in response to the summons to the telephone, had seen him return, douse the lamps in his drugstore, and had noticed, with amused satisfaction, that he had not lighted the lamp in his quarters upstairs.

At the same time, at the Massasoit bar, Walt Robbins was being rigged out as "Inspector Chatham." He was equipped with an official-looking notebook, and wrapped in a black Inverness cape which would have qualified him for the role of villain in any melodrama. On his upper lip had been glued a pair of black handlebar moustaches. Hal Kingsland had lent Walt a silver badge which had been issued to Hal as deputy fireman.

About nine o'clock, "Inspector Chatham" appeared in Linden Square, descending from a horsecar which he had boarded only two hundred yards away, in front of the Massasoit. He stood under the street lamp in the Square, one of the few of which Linden then boasted, took ostentatiously from under his cape a scroll of paper on which was a ribbon and a seal, peered at the signs on the various shops and stores, located the drugstore, and crossed the Square to Dud Shultz' doorway, where he pressed the night bell. All this, Dud had seen, cowering inside his unlighted window.

After a pause, the "Inspector" pressed the bell again, more peremptorily. Dud, more dead than alive, pushed up one of his windows.

"Who's there?" he croaked.

"Ah. Mr. Shultz. It's the Inspector. Could you come down and let me in?"

Dud descended, and took in the ominous details of the big man's cloaked figure. The "Inspector" was affable in the extreme.

"Sorry to intrude at this time of night. Pressure of official business, you understand," he said.

"Wwwhat can I do for you, sir?" Dud answered.

"I'll just take a look around," the "Inspector" said. "A routine matter."

He had to help Dud unlock the door of the drugstore, but he stepped back with exaggerated politeness and insisted that the little man precede him into the store.

"Shall we have a light?" the "Inspector" suggested. He had to help with the sulphur matches and the lampshade. Once the lamp was lighted, and the kerosene flame began to penetrate the dimness, the "Inspector" seemed to forget that Dud was there. He made himself at home, going straight to the prescription counter and the shelves containing drugs and solutions. Every now and then, as he peered at a label, he let out a learned "Hmmmmm" or an "Ahhhh." He looked behind the jars and bottles, took up the prescription record book, and in his own notebook made notations.

Dud hovered around, expecting to be denounced or handcuffed at any moment, but nothing happened except that the preoccupied "Inspector" looked at him sharply, from under his heavy eyebrows and stroked carefully the handlebar moustaches.

"Is anything wrong?" asked Dud, unable to bear the strain any longer.

"A mere formality," the "Inspector" said. "There's been quite a lot of illicit traffic in aphrodisiacs. Indeed, sir, what amounts to a veritable crime wave. The Board is taking steps. . . ."

Disarmingly, the "Inspector" turned on Dud and fixed him with a fishy eye, made colder by a rather twisted smile. "By the way, Mr. Shultz. Did you happen to know a young man called Packard or Pickhard hereabouts?"

"You mean Packard?" asked Dud, his heart beating so hard he could not swallow.

"Ah! Precisely. . . ." The "Inspector" fixed Dud with his piercing eye again, his head cocked on one side, like a macaw's. "A customer of yours?"

"He comes in now and then . . . For tobacco and cigars. Quincy cigars and Mayo's cut plug," said Dud.

"Was he here today?"

"I think so. Yes. This afternoon."

"For cigars and tobacco?"

"No. He wanted some . . . memory pills . . . I think he called them," Dud said. "I assure you, sir, I had never heard of them."

"So he went away empty-handed?" persisted the "Inspector."

"No. He took a box of pills. I . . . I'm not sure what they were."

"He stole an unspecified box of pills, am I to understand? Come, sir. You must be candid."

"That isn't what I mean. He paid for them. One of Humphrey's Specifics, I believe. They're all priced the same, so I didn't notice the number," Dud said, trying to keep his knees from knocking.

At that moment, Admiral Quimby, my Uncle Reuben, Hal Kingsland and Mr. Wing appeared. They tried the door. It was unlocked. All four of them came in.

"Good-evening, Dud. What keeps you so late. . . ." the Admiral asked. Then he seemed to notice the "Inspector" for the first time and mumbled, "I beg your pardon."

"I'm Inspector Chatham, gentlemen. Of the State Board," the big man said.

"Maybe we ought to come back another time," Hal Kingsland said.

"By no means. By no means. I'm about finished with my inspection," but as the four customers edged Dud toward the cigar counter and started looking over the familiar brands, the "Inspector" went over to the case of Humphrey's Specifics, closed the glass door, latched it, and took the whole case under his arm.

"I shall have to take these for analysis. You'll hear from me again," he said, and strode from the store.

The four conspirators were all sympathy and curiosity.

"Nothing wrong, I hope?" asked my Uncle Reuben.

"What was that he took away? Did he give you a receipt?"

"Who is he?" Mr. Wing asked.

"Did he ask about anyone in particular?" inquired the Admiral.

Dud Shultz, at the end of his feeble endurance, sank down into a cane-seated chair and began to cry, almost soundlessly. The others looked at one another, a little shamefacedly, and started away.

"Don't let these officers push you around," Mr. Wing said. "We'll all stand by you."

"But I haven't done a thing," Dud quavered.

"We none of us are perfect. Buck up, and let us know if there's anything we can do to square you. The courts go easy on a first offense," said the Admiral. And leaving Dud to dry his eyes and try to pull himself together, they left the drug-store.

Two days later, the case of Humphrey's Specifics was received at the Linden depot, from Boston, addressed to Mr. Dudley R. Shultz, without a word of explanation.

A fortnight later, Ginger McSweeney appeared in the drugstore, on a Saturday evening just before closing time, when the store, except for Ginger and the proprietor, was empty, took Dud cautiously aside, pulled out a ten-dollar bill, and said:

"Look, Dud. We're all wise to you. I'll give you ten bucks,

no questions asked, for just one shot of that stuff you furnished Packard, to stir up the women. I swear by all the Holy Saints I'll never tell a soul."

For two days afterward, Dud stayed upstairs in bed, without opening the store.

CHAPTER SEVEN

The Passing of the Balm of Gilead Tree

LINDEN, before the days of the Puritans, was a sheltered and isolated area in the hunting-grounds of some Indian tribes who found protection from depredations by the powerful Five Nations in the rigors of the coastal climate and the natural advantages of a location where forest, meadowlands, and teeming marshes joined together. Soon after the white settlers came, in the early part of the seventeenth century, most of the native Indians died of measles, to which they had built up no resistance, and the others migrated north, to the dense wilderness of Maine, for a few years more of grace.

Those original inhabitants, if they could have returned to peer over the rim of northern hills at the turn of the twentieth century, would have recognized the fields sloping downward from the woods to the winding creek bed, the higher ground, comparatively flat, on which the town was built, and two great natural landmarks, the granite ledge that stood like Gibraltar to shield Black Ann's Corner, at the northeastern extremity of Linden, and the giant Balm of Gilead tree in the shade of which our house had been built.

There had been an intermediate stage in Linden's development, between the epoch of the redskins and the settlement of commuters from Boston and Lynn, small tradesmen and shopkeepers, and day laborers who liked to raise their families away from noisy city streets, and were described collectively

101

as Ward 6, Precinct 2, of Malden. Between 1630 and 1830, what later became Linden was covered by three or four large truck and dairy farms. One of these, the homestead of which stood on the site of the old Clapp mansion, included all the central part of Linden, and the Balm of Gilead tree, and when at noon, or during light showers, the farm hands and teamsters gathered together they found shade beneath its branches and lint for their wounds.

The first and only industry in Linden came a little later, when a Boston firm of contractors started working Black Ann's quarry for building and foundation stone.

When Newburyport, about twenty miles northeast of Linden, developed a flourishing commerce by sea, and needed a connection with Boston, the Newburyport Turnpike, one of the first toll roads in New England, cut back of Linden, through the woods, emerging at the clearing where later the Broadway carbarns were put up, and continuing through Everett to Boston. The Everett section of the Turnpike, when that municipality was ready to take it over, was given the impressive title of "Broadway." The Turnpike always marked Linden's western border.

While Clapp's farm on one side, and Squire's broad acres in Revere, were still undivided, the grove of horse chestnuts and poplars on the high land that bordered the marsh attracted the builder of the Massasoit House.

All the Linden streets, as they were laid out later, had reference to these three landmarks, the granite ledge, the Balm of Gilead, and the grove below the Square. The horsecar tracks followed Salem Street down from Malden, and cut through Beach Street toward Crescent Beach and southward to Boston, and Beach Street had been a lane that was shaded by the Balm of Gilead tree. When the Saugus Branch of the

Boston and Maine brought steam trains through Linden, the right-of-way was chosen because it then was the southern and eastern boundaries of the community; but the railroad was obliged to swerve and cut off Linden Square from the rest of the town in order to avoid the swampland and quicksand of the marsh, or else to purchase the land on which the stores and shops stood and which, therefore, was the most expensive.

It may appear that in all this planning from without, Linden's convenience was little considered, but someone, or some group of men, did Linden a service that almost to this day has set it apart from other suburban communities. Along all the principal streets, when they were first surveyed or broadened from primitive lanes, shade trees in double files were set out, and these trees gave Linden its scenic distinction, unifying and blending the effect of the houses, haphazardly matched, budding with new life in the spring, shimmering and whispering in summer, in the autumn all colors from buff and pale yellow to the richest crimson and purple, in winter asserting darkly all their fundamental grace and patterns against the sleet and snow.

East and west on Beach Street were perfect linden trees, spaced in a way that was dignified and orderly, but not unpleasantly symmetrical. Maples lined Lawrence and Oliver Streets. Elms marked the course of Elm Street, and sturdy horse chestnuts guarded Clapp Street.

Most of the men and women who lived in Linden fifty years ago are now elsewhere. Quite a few of the trees have remained. What is known as "Greater Boston" has leaked out over the area; broad traffic arteries have spread tentacles this way and that. The streetcar tracks have been abandoned, making way for buses. I assume that Linden still gets the old damaged ones and they seldom run on time. The Saugus

103

Branch is used no more for passengers, and only in emergencies for freight. Heavy trucks have made it obsolete.

The granite quarry is still in use, busier than ever, and shows no signs that its boundless supply of rock will be exhausted in another long century. The eruption that hurled its molten mass through the crust of the continent antedates the Indians by millions of years.

Since in 1900 the Balm of Gilead tree was twelve feet in diameter, with a spread of more than two hundred feet, it was then at least four hundred years old, and probably more, and must have stood between what later became Beach Street and our own front yard when Columbus set out from Spain.

Linden, between Revolutionary days and 1900, had passed through what has been rarest in American history, and what promises to be rarer still, a century of easy, uninterrupted development where changes grew imperceptibly, like trees, maintaining the community's form and shape on a slowly expanding scale. The horse had helped do the work and furnish the transportation, and still was predominant. Men who did not like to work for wages had small businesses of their own, and got along fairly well. Great fortunes had been made, the names of J. Pierpont Morgan, John D. Rockefeller, and John Jacob Astor were bandied about in the newspapers and magazines, and there were a few Massachusetts millionaires not well known locally. The trusts were talked of as a bugaboo, but Linden men were mostly conservative, and believed that the smart successful men knew what they were doing and that the country was safe in their hands.

The disappearance of sailing vessels from the seas and New England shipyards hit many of the coastal cities very hard, but navigation from the Atlantic to Linden was so difficult that not more than a half-dozen Linden men would attempt it, and then only in small craft that drew four feet or less of water.

Chain stores had not yet stifled competition in Linden, although there was talk about them. Electricity was not in general use for light and power. The daily life of a Linden man was not essentially different than it had been at the time of the War of 1812, and while a few Linden men had fought on the Union side in the Civil War, and the feeling against the Rebels was practically unanimous, the community had suffered little, and had gone on through the war years almost as if the struggle were taking place in another country. In our family, the Civil War brought about one of the series of misfortunes that made my mother's life so sad. Her brother, George W. Dowsett, contracted tuberculosis in an army camp, and died later out West as a result.

The Spanish-American War had been accepted in Linden without much understanding, had been soon over and America's part in it had been served up to the inhabitants and school children of Linden with such a patriotic gloss that it was considered a minor triumph, the consequences of which in Cuba and the Philippines were turning out to be a nuisance. Much more interest was shown in the fight the Boers were making against the British, and the dozen English families in Linden, including those of the cobbler, the Hobart twins, and Tom Craven, proprietor of Associate Hall, had a hard time trying to defend the British policy against their neighbors who, without wishing to hurt them, rejoiced openly in every British setback. That, no doubt, was a result of the extremely anti-British text of the school books from which the Linden folks had learned what little most of them knew about history.

I was born and lived nine years in the shade of Linden's Balm of Gilead tree, which was the most remarkable tree in a community which, without its trees and life-loving individualists, would have had nothing whatever to set it apart. I thought of our house and the giant tree as a unit, of which the

105

Balm of Gilead was by far the most important part. I waited for the snow to thaw and expose its great roots that sprawled across the sidewalk and tripped unwary passers-by. I could smell the fragrance as the sap began to stir and the buds appeared, to lengthen into catkins which carpeted the whole area, more than six thousand square feet, beneath its branches. That they also clogged the gutters of our house and covered the roof and porch roof and front lawn did not trouble me at all, although it seemed to bother my mother and my older brother, Charles.

From the ground, it was impossible to climb the trunk of the tree, but I had a way of getting up among the boughs and branches by letting myself out of a front bedroom window on the second story, sliding cautiously down the porch roof, and swinging my body over the nearest bough. In this way, I spent much time concealed by the foliage as I watched the traffic up and down Beach Street and in and out of our neighbors' yards and houses.

Hour after hour I watched the shadow of that tree over dust and leaves, and puddles after rain, as it revolved and turned and changed its shape, extent, and details. I was excited by the polished new green of the leaves in May, how they developed and expanded, and the hues of green grew more mature and deeper, to turn buff and brown and yellow and the color of eggshells and ashes in the fall.

The first rumor that I heard to the effect that "the city of Malden" intended to cut the Balm of Gilead down was while men were putting up poles at regular intervals along Beach Street that were to support guy-wires for an overhead trolley, so that the horsecars could be replaced by electric cars. I knew what electric cars were, and how badly they smelled of brass and oxides, having ridden on them in Boston. Most of the communities around Linden had been served by electric cars a few years before the company got around to converting the

Linden lines. I did not believe what I had heard until I asked my family about it, and by doing so threw my grandmother, Mrs. Sarah J. Dowsett, into such a temper that she had a heart attack and almost died. This distracted our attention for a while, until the doctor came and quieted the staunch old lady with sedatives and pronounced her out of immediate danger.

As soon as my grandmother was able to talk, she began protesting and remonstrating again, and insisted that Charles, who was running for the Malden City Council, do something to stop the outrage. My mother, mild and tactful, tried to point out the advantages that would result if the tree were removed. No more leaking roof and clogged gutters, no more raking catkins from the yard or having carpets ruined by sticky fallen buds tracked inside. My grandmother's dark eyes flashed, her stern eyebrows were knit and her jaw was set. Everybody in the family knew what that meant. Grandmother did not set her will against all comers very often, but when she did, nothing in heaven or on earth could move her. She reduced my timid but courageous mother to the status of a child again. Charles, who as head of the family, the student, breadwinner, youngest candidate for the Malden City Council, never argued with our grandmother. She was well read, up-to-date and educated, too, and had seen more of life.

Strange to say, of one with such a vacillating nature, I, from boyhood, have shown streaks of determination, or obstinacy, if you wish, at variance with everything that was expected of me. Always such a tendency in me would be traced to Grandmother Dowsett, and through her to her father, referred to in the family as "Pa Tarr."

I had been badly shaken by the news that predatory interests had designs on my tree, for I thought of that Balm of Gilead not only as my own, but standing for everything in America's development and Linden's history that I could ad-mire. To find that I had an ally in Grandmother Dowsett gave me a little hope, and our household was split into two camps, with Mother and Charles quite reconciled to the loss of the Balm of Gilead, and Grandmother and I implacable.

Uncle Reuben, when the affair came to his attention, put up quite a lot of money at the Massasoit bar.

"If Sarah Dowsett says no, that tree will stand there just as long as she lives," my uncle said.

"What do individuals amount to now?" asked the Admiral. "The big railroads and streetcar lines and trusts ride rough-shod over all of us."

"Not Sarah Dowsett, they don't," Uncle Reuben said.

It was not long before my grandmother had plenty of sup-porters. I can hardly remember any question that arose on which Linden was so sharply divided. Mary Stoddard, the old maid who lived with her mother in the little house across the street from us, went to the Mayor's office in Malden Center, shook her fist in his face and said that he, or any man who would touch that tree, should be drawn and quartered.

The Mayor, of course, pretended to know nothing of the matter, and promised to get in touch with the officials of the streetcar company. Meanwhile, Mary Stoddard tramped from one end of Linden to the other with a petition to the board of aldermen and city council, demanding that they take action to prevent the destruction of Linden's most remarkable land-mark and natural monument.

Dawson Freeman, the young insurance man who had mar-ried Mattie Clapp and moved to Linden from the city, drama-tizing that nine-mile migration as a return to the land and sound American values (although he took the steam train back and forth each day to continue his insurance business), warmed to the conflict with his customary vigor, eloquence and energy. He put the proposition so forcefully that the Partridges, Clapps and several of his immediate and well-to-do neighbors donated enough money to hire Associate Hall for a mass meeting.

To all the initial protests the street railway company was indifferent. The city had given the company a franchise. In order to string poles and wires along the streets where the cars were to pass, it was necessary to clear the way. Wherever it was feasible, trees, branches and foliage were spared. The Balm of Gilead on Beach Street was an obstacle to traffic and progress that, in the interest of modern transportation, must be sacrificed.

The Malden politicians and editors were against the big tree, on the ground that it had no definite historical or literary associations, like the Washington Elm in Cambridge, or Long-fellow's "spreading chestnut tree." It was merely a big tree, and of little public benefit to Linden as a whole, since it shaded only one of the houses.

Associate Hall was crowded on the evening of the protest meeting and, disregarding the doctor's warnings, my grand-mother sat with the rest of us on the hard wooden settee, nod-ding and grunting agreement with the speakers on our side (hers and mine) and showing signs of contempt and disgust when the opposition had the floor. For the first time she was pleased with the Reverend K. Gregory Powys, who came out flat-footedly in favor of retaining the tree. The Reverend Powys quoted Thoreau, who had warned his countrymen against worship of material improvements and astounding in-ventions, without regard to their possible effect upon the spirit. Luckily for all of us, that detestable jingle setting forth that only God could make trees had not then been written. Never-theless, the Reverend Powys pleaded that it was a pity, after one of God's majestic creations had stood as a symbol of Linden for a longer time than the Republic had then endured, to destroy it in the interests of a company that was chartered by the cities and towns and allowed to make money for its stockholders by using the public thoroughfares without charge. The course of Beach Street, the Reverend Powys said, had been determined by man alone, and who was to say that it could not be turned to the right or the left, to leave intact a thing of beauty and a joy for centuries.

Admiral Quimby said he was pleased to find himself for once on the side of the cloth.

"Should any man come to me and ask, 'Admiral, which do you value highest, your chestnut trees or your hostelry?', I should answer: 'Which, kind sir, could you replace in my lifetime?' "

Dawson Freeman brought tears to the eyes of many of the women when he arose, and throwing back his proudly shaped head, let his voice out, then dropped it low.

"I defer in this matter," he said, "to the mother of my children."

With a sweep of his hand he indicated the astonished Mattie, née Clapp, who had already produced Lincoln, Walcott and Marian, and was well started on a fourth whose name was to be Gladstone.

"While men are in the marts of toil, the patient women they leave behind, at home, each morning, have much to do and little to distract them. Is there one of these, our mothers, wives, sisters, daughters, sweethearts, who has not paused in reverence to behold that tree, or rested in its shade? Whose is Linden? Is it the property of the men who return to it evenings, or of those who spend their days and years within its borders? We try to beautify our homes. There is none so poor among us who has not made some effort to relieve the monotony of his humble walls, and none so rich that he has not halted by the roadside to pick a wild rose from a crumbling stone wall and look at it with gratitude and wonder.

"Strip Linden of its noblest tree? Demolish what is most ancient in Linden and by more generations than we can count has been beloved? For whom? To relieve a soulless corporation of a little expense. Cannot electric wires be protected by insulation? I move, Mr. Chairman, that a resolution be adopted and copies of the same be forwarded to the members of our city government, to the effect that it is the wish of a majority of the residents and voters of Ward 6, Precinct 2, that the Balm of Gilead tree near Number 63 Beach Street, be preserved in its present condition and that the street railway company be required to find other ways and means, without removing the said tree, to install trolley wires!"

The prudent members of the community were always the same, and included the richest man in Linden—Norman Partridge, Deacons Harper, Plummer and Clapp of the Congregational Church, Mr. Weeks, the milkman, my Great-Uncle Elijah, and my brother Charles. There were many more who nodded and clucked in their favor but seldom spoke. The conservatives had most of their strength in the newly formed Linden Improvement Association, whose president, Francis Newcomb, was one of Charles' most influential supporters. I could see that Charles was suffering, in a quiet way, what with Grandmother Dowsett sitting at his right, erect and stern, feet planted firmly on the splintered floor, and everywhere throughout the Hall the quiet, careful men who looked to him for their kind of leadership in the rising generation.

Mr. Newcomb said a few words in praise of Dawson Freeman's resolution and Dawson's good intention, and complimented the Reverend Powys on his civic spirit, but he asked that a committee be appointed, with representatives of the new association among the members, to confer with the city government and the street railway officials and report in the public press. To my surprise and dismay, Dawson Freeman's resolution was tabled and Mr. Newcomb's motion carried, with a safe majority. I slowly realized that everyone had come to the meeting with his or her mind made up, and that all the oratory, while relished as such, did not sway the vote one way or the other.

Bryan's "Cross of Gold" speech was only four years old then, and how many times I had heard the Admiral quote it, with local variations:

"The man who is employed for wages is as much a business-man as his employer; the attorney in a country town is as much a businessman as the corporation counsel in a great metropolis; the merchant in Linden Square is as much a busi-nessman as the frenzied financier on State Street. . . ."

Bryan had lost in 1896 and was losing again in 1900. And most of the men I liked best in Linden had been heart and soul for Bryan. I began to suspect that most of the causes for which I felt strongly would not prevail, and it bewildered me.

My grandmother was indignant because of the action of the mass meeting, but not depressed.

"Those men think they can whisper anything to death," she said. "We'll see."

The local paper began printing editorials about progress, of how fortunate the community was to be served with modern conveniences for the same five-cent fare that hitherto pur-chased a ride at a snail's pace behind a pair of spavined and sway-backed nags. When the Linden committee's report was published, it was what I had expected. The tree, according to tree experts, was very old and could not stand forever. The century, with its electrical wonders, was young. The expense of curving Beach Street around it would be prohibi-tive, since it would necessitate filling in a part of Weeks' field to a depth of four to six feet. In time of storm, if the highly charged wires were broken by swaying branches, danger and death might result. And if the street railway company was required to change its plans and estimates according to the whim of each property owner along the right-of-way, it would not be possible to operate on a five-cent fare, and still pay dividends to the stockholders, many of whom were widows and orphans with no other security than the investments of their dear-departed.

My grandmother read the paper grimly, and did not rant or collapse. Instead, while Mother watched with misgivings, the old lady went straight to the writing desk in the sitting room, took her pen in hand, and wrote a letter. She did not tell Mother to whom she was writing, nor let Mother see the address. Later, when Grandmother had retired in her upstairs room, she tapped on the floor with her cane, the signal for me to go up and see what she wanted. It was part of Grandmother's eccentricity that she was extremely partial to me, while other members of the family and all the neighbors found Leslie and Charles more sympathetic and predictable.

"If you'll drop this in the Lawrence Street box . . . There's a collection in fifteen minutes," she said, handing me the letter she had written. Although her movements were restricted, even in the house, Grandmother Dowsett knew in detail whatever was happening in Linden, and elsewhere.

The letter was addressed to Frederick H. Tarr, attorney at law, in Rockport, Mass. Fred Tarr, one of my first cousins about Charles' age, was starting to practice in Gloucester, and already had a good reputation and was taking part in Essex County politics. Fred had always handled Grandmother's affairs, such as they were. My grandmother had been a widow twenty-five years, and had been left enough money so she could pay her own way, but she had always been active in family affairs, throughout the wide network of our family connections. On several occasions she had supported various minority members in rebellion against fate, to such an extent that she risked running out of money before the end of her lifetime. Actually, when she died and the funeral expenses had been paid, there were about three hundred dollars left, and some very quaint, lavender-scented, old-fashioned clothes, some silks and satins, that once had been in style. My grandmother had been one of the most striking beauties on Cape Ann.

Fred Tarr had taken over the management of Grandmother's money when he was admitted to the bar, and always had admired her courage. (Later he represented the district in Congress with distinction many years.) First, Grandmother had insisted that her youngest sister, Lucy, get a divorce, for which she had practically all the grounds then extant. It was a truly revolutionary move, in our family and region. When my father's sister, Elizabeth, found herself a bitter and frustrated old maid chained to the occupation of teaching school, which she detested, my grandmother persuaded her to drop her school work and go into training as a nurse. Aunt Elizabeth followed Grandmother's advice, accepted her aid, and became happy and successful. It was Grandmother Dowsett who finally told Charles to pack up and get out of Linden, where the only civil engineering was a political football and his field was hopelessly constrained. He had not been able to believe that he could leave Mother and the rest of us "without a man in the house." Mother turned faint at the mention of the prospect. Grandmother said "Go" and Charles went, and from that moment on began to rise to the height of his profession, until few large projects of hydraulic engineering in America were undertaken without his advice.

The next few days were ominously peaceful in our house.

Grandmother did not thump with her cane, but read quietly, ate carefully, and slept more soundly than usual.

"She's up to something," my mother said, uneasily, to Charles. Both looked at me, but I said nothing about the address on that letter, and, both being honorable to a degree that was almost painful, they could not ask me to betray a confidence.

Sunday, about dinnertime, Fred Tarr and his wife drove up and hitched their tired span of horses in the driveway. They had started from Rockport early that morning, and the thirty-mile distance, along the North Shore, was about all the horses could do that day. I knew they would stay all night, and start back early Monday morning.

While Angie, Fred's wife, another very progressive and intelligent woman, talked with Mother and Charles, Fred was with Grandmother, upstairs. Before midafternoon, I was sent across the street for Mary Stoddard, and down to the Square for Dr. Moody.

"Doc" Moody and his housekeeper, Mathilda, were staunch defenders of the Balm of Gilead tree.

I don't know what was said, or how Grandmother found out the date on which the tree was due to come down. Probably that was through Dick Lanier, who had a temporary job with the company that kept him climbing trees and poles. I only remember that, a few days before the showdown, my grandmother called me to her bedside. She was no female Polonius, but on very few occasions gave me good counsel.

"Elliot," she said. "This pesky heart of mine has been a nuisance all these years. If I try to get some good out of it, don't worry. Do you understand?"

I didn't, quite, but nodded, feeling sure I would understand later.

Two evenings before the men were coming to cut down

115

the tree, Grandmother Dowsett had one of the worst "spells" with her heart she had suffered in years. Dr. Moody was summoned on the hotfoot from the Square, and Fred Tarr happened to come into town on the evening train from Lynn. We were up all night, those who were useful attending Grandmother, the others sitting fearfully, drinking coffee or hot milk, and hoping for the best. I am sure that what Grandmother had said to me about not worrying flitted in and out of my head, but I had seen her heart attacks before, and could not convince myself that this was not the real thing. She was enduring the excruciating pain that, in those days, could not be relieved; she was holding on to life in her shapely and regal old head, on which to the day of her death there was not a gray hair. Early in the morning, Fred and Dr. Moody drove to Malden, and a half hour after the courthouse opened, came forth with a paper that I suppose was an injunction.

Fred and Charles both were expert at whittling. As boys they had made models of full-rigged ships and schooners, in every detail. Charles was urged to go to work, and reluctantly did. Fred made two wooden signs, with sharp stakes. They read: "Sickness. Quiet." One was driven into the sidewalk west of the big tree, the other several yards east of our house.

The men with huge saws and axes, ropes and tackle, arrived from Malden, and were met by Fred Tarr and Spike Dodge, and the all-powerful injunction.

Lawyers from the company called at our house the next day. Fred and the doctor conferred with them. The patient was not out of danger. There was no saying when she would be. And she could not be moved. Excitement might prove fatal, and, added Fred Tarr, in his slow, pleasant voice, the company would be liable.

Two doctors from the company came down to Linden the next day, and asked permission to see my grandmother. Dr.

Moody acquiesced, and after fifteen minutes in the sick room, they all three came downstairs, nodding gravely. The company doctors were convinced she would not last through the night. That frightened my mother so badly that Fred and I broke down, and told her that, while Grandmother Dowsett had a bad heart, as she well knew, it was no worse than it had been for years. All of a sudden, Mother began putting two and two together, and relapsed into that silent, reproachful attitude that had a smile quite near the surface.

"I might have known," she said, and sighed.

Uncle Reuben bought himself a topcoat, a derby and six new neckties on the strength of his winnings at the Massasoit bar.

Meanwhile, men, women and horses trod softly along our sidewalk between the warning signs, and Ginger and the other drivers did not use their gongs within a hundred yards of the house. It seemed to me that the Admiral and Dawson Freeman smoked more cigars than usual during that period, and enjoyed them well. Miss Stoddard was so triumphantly happy that she talked and sang to herself.

Then, after more consultations, the company tree-climbers and electricians clipped off a few small branches, nailed some heavy insulators on various stout boughs, and the big Balm of Gilead, without loss of majesty, helped sustain the guy-wires and the trolley, so the work of electrification went on through Linden and the electric cars were dappled, in passing beneath its shade.

The next onslaught against the old tree came from another direction. In the dead of winter, one afternoon as I started home from the old wooden grammar school at Oliver and Clapp Streets, I saw smoke coming from the back of our house, white and black, pouring upward in great volume. I ran quickly, to find a crowd gathering across the street. My mother and my grandmother, wrapped in shawls, were standing in Miss Stoddard's front yard. I saw, against the flames in our smashed upper windows, Jim Puffer and Dick Lanier throwing articles out, presumably to save them. In emergencies as well as through the humdrum days, old Jim Puffer was destined to make a mess of things. I saw Lanier stop and remonstrate with him after Jim, ignoring things, no doubt, of higher value, had tossed a chamber-pot onto the cluttered front lawn. Lanier himself was tossing out some of my grandmother's books, in such a way that they would land in a soft snowbank. Unfortunately the snowbank melted in the heat of the raging fire, so that the books ever afterward had stained leaves and swollen bindings. My brother Charles' engineering library, in the back of the house, was lost. Practically everything we had was lost, and as the years' accumulation of household goods and souvenirs was burning, I remember how well-meaning members of the church and neighborhood tried to comfort my mother by saying how lucky it was that the house and furnishings were insured. That I did not understand at all. I was worried first about my grandmother's heart. Actually, my grandmother was the calmest individual around there. She watched the blaze, and the comings and goings of the crowd, in a reserved and dignified way, smiling with quiet irony when someone acted particularly absurd or futile. Once I saw that Grandmother was going to bear up all right, I was worried about the cat. We had a gray and white cat, Mopsy, and everybody remembered, too late, that for two days and nights before the fire, she had been uneasy, had refused food, and roamed from place to place, all over the house, switching her tail impatiently, bristling, sniffing and growling at times. The fire, according to the experts who viewed the ashes, must have been burning inside the walls for two or three days.

When the roof caved in, the heat rose so intensely that half the Balm of Gilead's branches and limbs caught fire.

"Never mind," my grandmother said, with a toss of her head. "Those barbarians will never get a chance at it, now."

There was nothing left of the house but a small section of the sitting room floor on which stood, almost unharmed, the old Vose square piano, and when nothing was blazing but the tree, the crowd began to cheer and catcall wildly as the Malden fire engines finally careened down the hill, stopped, hauled out ladders and hose, and tried vainly to throw a stream to the topmost branches of the burning tree.

When all was over, the charred trunk was standing, and the branches over the street were intact, but the tree was maimed and crippled. I could not bear to look at it for a long time.

One of the results of the fire that destroyed our house was a vote and appropriation by the Malden city government for a fire station to be built in Linden, and before many years the work was begun. Not, however, until the old wooden schoolhouse had gone up like a strawberry box in the middle of one night, without loss of life, or anything but its obsolete books and equipment. A new schoolhouse was built of brick, a block away, and the site of the old one was used for the firehouse.

Soon after my grandmother died, in 1902, a windstorm broke off the largest remaining limb of the Balm of Gilead, so that in falling it tore down the trolley for a hundred yards. That time, the company succeeded in demolishing the rest of the tree, but I had been prepared for this in stages. Still, I never forgave the men who completed its destruction. Luckily, they all were strangers. The huge trunk was sawed through, and fell; the roots were dug up, the branches stripped of boughs, and the wood sawed up and carted away. I saw it hauled, load by load, in wagons up Beach Street hill and out of sight, and was glad, for the moment, that Grandmother Dowsett was not present. I thought of her, not as dead, with a fly walking unheeded across her waxen face as she lay in a satin-lined casket, but absent. Never have I believed in the existence of a Biblical Heaven, but if I chance to be wrong, and there is one, I feel certain who is running it.

The nineteenth century, for what it was worth, went out of Linden in wagonloads, with that Balm of Gilead tree.

I had made such a fuss about the tree that when we moved back to Beach Street, into the second house, my brother Charles, on a visit home from Philadelphia, borrowed a wagon from Deacon Clapp, drove to the woods without letting me know why, and came back with a well-formed little linden tree about ten feet high. The roots had been dug up with plenty of soil, and the tree began to grow, not on the sidewalk, but on our lawn just left of the driveway, between our house and the double house next door. I was assured that it would grow, and in time become as big as I could wish.

"Then some men will come down from Malden and saw it down," I said.

That has not happened yet. When I last saw the house and the tree, forty-six years after the latter was planted and the former built, the tree was tall and stately, and towered above the rooftop by a good ten feet. It was spreading with impunity, because the trolley wires that doomed the Balm of Gilead have outlived their usefulness and also have been superseded.

CHAPTER EIGHT

An Evening Not Soon to Be Forgotten

BEFORE Alice's collapse, the Townsend women had lived a secluded life, and inside their ungainly house against the hillside had shared one another's existence very intimately. Every detail of their small affairs had been discussed, gently and somewhat fearfully, by the mother and two daughters. Each expenditure had been considered, and was weighed to the last odd cent.

Nearly all the Linden families got along on small incomes and earnings, and before the incident that cost Alice her job, it was felt among the neighbors and tradesmen that the Townsends had almost no margin at all. Callers who came to solicit for church funds, and deliverymen from the various stores, knew that Mrs. Townsend, when she paid for anything, reached into a hand-painted vase that stood on the dining-room mantelpiece and counted out what was needed from a small handful of greenbacks and coins. It had flashed through the minds of many of the kind-hearted people that, under the circumstances, with nothing coming in, the savings in that faded old vase could not last forever. That quiet, semidesperate kind of finance was understood by many residents of old Linden, and struck responsive chords in their hearts.

Dr. Moody said little about Alice's condition, but he was naturally too candid and honest to put on an act. He was worried, more worried as each day and week and month passed by. Alice would recover consciousness for a while, would be sweet and obedient, taking her medicine and light nourishment as the doctor prescribed, then, when the slightest shadow of a practical problem passed over her pillow, she would close her eyes again and go back into deep sleep that was practically a coma.

All Linden knew, before the meeting had adjourned, when, in August, before the schools opened again, the Malden School Committee, which included Linden's Norman Partridge in its membership, voted reluctantly to replace Miss Townsend.

Dr. Moody had never sent a bill to Mrs. Townsend, and did not intend to, at least not until his patient was on her feet and able to earn money again. But the women of the Social Circle, including my mother and two of my aunts who talked freely in my presence when I pretended not to be listening or interested, were aware that increasing friction between Mrs. Townsend and Elvira, on the one hand, and the doctor, was developing. Mrs. Townsend had remarked that Dr. Moody was not her regular doctor, and someone remembered that fifteen years before, when Mr. Townsend had died, he had been attended by Dr. Goodenough, from Malden Center. Since then, the Townsends had called no doctor at all, and Dr. Moody had arrived at their house with Alice.

When Mrs. Townsend's remarks came to the ears of Mathilda Stowe, and thus reached Dr. Moody, he insisted that old Dr. Goodenough, who was on the verge of his dotage, be called into consultation.

The folks along Salem Street saw Dr. Goodenough's buggy drive down from Malden way, and Dr. Moody's buggy arrive from the opposite direction. The two doctors, the younger helping the older and feeble one, went up the long flight of outside steps, and disappeared inside. When they came out, old Dr. Goodenough was driven right back to Malden, but everyone in Linden who saw Dr. Moody knew that the old man's opinion had been contrary to his own, and profoundly disturbing to him. Mrs. Townsend told my mother, with lips set tight and a hard glint in her eyes, that Dr. Moody had been wrong from the start.

"My daughter has *dementia praecox*," Mrs. Townsend said. Mrs. Townsend did not know exactly what that meant, but several others did, and believed it was incurable and meant that Alice would probably end up in an asylum.

That evening Doc Moody quietly overruled Mathilda and dropped in at the Massasoit bar. Most of the regulars were there, and also Ginger McSweeney, but the gravity of the new development caused the drinkers to refer to the case discreetly and not to persecute Ginger, who was heartsick and depressed. Seated across the table from Ginger was big Ruth Coffee, who was comforting him. Dr. Moody, after nodding to the others, walked over and took a seat between Ginger and Ruth.

Ruth turned to the doctor. "Ginger, here, is worrying his fool head off," she said.

"Who isn't?" asked the doctor dismally.

"I've just told him," Ruth continued, "that nobody throws a fit, all of a sudden, about a little thing like . . . well, you know."

"Go on," said the doctor. "You've got some sense. What do you think is wrong with the girl?"

"Mother of God," said Ginger. "Sometimes I'd like to cut the damn thing off."

"Shut up, Ginger," said the doctor. "Let's hear what Ruth has to say. Then you can go ahead."

"Alice wasn't built for teaching school," said Ruth. "The kids rode hell out of her, and made her nervous all the time. She was afraid of 'em, and they knew it, and took advantage.

123

She knew she was slipping, that some day she'd lose her job. . . ."

"She's already lost it," moaned Ginger.

The doctor was paying no mind to Ginger, but was listening attentively to Ruth.

"You mean," he said, "that she'd been worrying for years—with reason—and that little by little the headaches got worse, the kids got noisier, and any shock at all would have broken her down."

"That's what I mean," Ruth said. "Would that have anything to do with *dementia praecox,* or whatever the old gazabo from Malden said she had?"

"I don't agree with Dr. Goodenough, if that's what you're driving at. I think she's got a chance. . . . " He looked appraisingly at Ruth. "That is, if you'll help me out."

"Who? Me?" asked Ruth, bewildered.

"It's not good for her, having only her mother and that odd stick of a sister around. They mutter and whisper. They're more fidgety than she is. That state of mind is contagious, I tell you. Now if you'd sit with Alice, and inject a little common sense into that household?"

"Sure I will," Ruth said. "I'm pretty heavy-handed for a nurse, but I'll sure give it a try."

"You may have trouble with those women," the doctor said. "They hate to have outsiders in the house."

"Leave it to me," said Ruth.

So the doctor had a talk with Mrs. Townsend, and told her what had to be done. And soon it became part of Linden's routine to see big Ruth, in her shirt sleeves, raking leaves from the Townsend's steeply sloping yard, or striding down Beach Street, shoulders swinging like those of a sailor ashore, to do the errands for the Townsend household. When Ruth entered Alice's bedroom, however, she seemed to shed her brusque and vigorous ways. She dressed more daintily, and was quite soft-spoken. Alice responded and seemed to improve. The doctor and all the neighbors praised Ruth for her devotion. And slowly the Junoesque young woman, who had always seemed to be at sixes and sevens, found a place in life and her warm personality expanded.

The more Alice depended on Ruth and enjoyed her company and faithful attentions, the more Mrs. Townsend and Elvira froze. Especially the sister. Her eyes gleamed with jealous, almost frantic, resentment, as it became evident that Ruth, and Ruth only, was acquiring over Alice a sort of control, exactly what the sick girl needed. Ruth ignored Mrs. Townsend's unfriendly words and actions, and soon Elvira had worked up such an antipathy that she avoided any contact with Ruth, day after day.

In Alice's dainty bedroom, the windows of which looked out over the tops of the elms, Ruth spent many happy hours, her shirt open at the neck, her sturdy legs crossed carelessly. She relayed the town gossip, such of it as she thought fit for Alice's ears, talked about life and mankind in general, and solved, one by one, a number of the Townsends' practical problems. Alice, on her best days, fairly glowed, and rested her frail, slender hand in Ruth's strong, capable ones. Then, suddenly, a change came over Alice and she acted as if she were afraid. She clung to Ruth more tightly, but the least sound outside, like a creak on the stairway, sent fear welling into her eyes, so that she trembled and slipped into a coma again. When Ruth or the doctor tried, gently, to find out the reason, Alice receded like a ghost beyond their control. Mrs. Townsend and Elvira grew more furtive and hostile, reluctant to admit either Ruth or the doctor; but Ruth, now bound to Alice in a way she had never experienced with regard to any human being, would not be brushed aside. Mrs. Townsend sat with Alice in the afternoon, and at dusk Ruth took over for the long night hours. Elvira, while Ruth was in the house, remained in hiding, usually in her downstairs bedroom, with the latch firmly fastened inside.

Late one afternoon, before Ruth arrived, Mrs. Townsend left Alice alone and went downstairs to make some tea. She was in the kitchen half an hour, slicing and buttering bread, opening a jar of barberry jam that Deacon Plummer's wife had left, shaking the grate to let the ashes from the fire sift down in the range. Elvira was in the sitting room running the sewing machine. When Mrs. Townsend went back upstairs with the tray, she opened Alice's bedroom door, entered without noticing anything peculiar, and, with her back to the bed, set the tray down on a table by a window. Then she turned, saw the bed was empty, and called, "Alice."

There was no reply. Alice was not in bed, or elsewhere in the room. Mrs. Townsend pulled open the clothes-closet door. Alice was not there, either, but some of her clothes were missing. Elvira, hearing her mother calling, came running upstairs. She had not seen Alice come down. The sewing machine had been making the usual noise, and she had been sitting, bending over her work, her back to the stairway.

Frantically the two women searched the house, from attic to cellar. In the midst of their search, Ruth rang the front doorbell. Both Mrs. Townsend and Elvira rushed to the door to open it. Face to face with Ruth, Elvira's hatred broke loose in a torrent of abuse and accusation.

"Where's my sister?" Elvira shrieked. "You've taken her away. You've killed her!"

Ruth, aware that something unusual had happened, turned to Mrs. Townsend.

"What's going on?" Ruth asked, ignoring Elvira.

"She's gone," Mrs. Townsend said. Ruth parted the two

distracted women with a sort of breast stroke and rushed between them into the hallway and up the stairs. Elvira screamed after her, wildly and incoherently. In Alice's bedroom, Ruth found just what Mrs. Townsend had found, and one thing more. Alice's dainty lace nightgown had been wadded into a ball and stuffed into an old shoe box up on the clothes-closet shelf. This was unlike Alice, who folded everything neatly and carefully.

Ruth tried to calm Mrs. Townsend. "Tend to Elvira. Keep her quiet if you can. And leave the rest to me," she said. "If Alice got dressed and went out on the street, someone must have seen her. And where could she go? Maybe to Mrs. Preston's?"

"You've taken her somewhere," Elvira interrupted. "Ma. Call the police!"

"Keep your shirt on," Ruth said, severely. "If there's a big fuss about this, Alice'll never get over it."

She turned to Mrs. Townsend. "You stay here in **case** she comes back. I'll go down Lynn Street and look around. She can't have gone far, and the weather's mild."

It was just getting dark, and here and there in Linden lemon lights, and orange, flickered faintly on the window shades. The sidewalks and gutters were strewn with fallen leaves and over the low meadows and marshes the ghostly haze was suspended. The depths of the woods were already pitch-dark. Beyond the Broadway carbarns the low ridge of evergreens was brought into gentle relief by lingering streaks of turquoise green and deep rose. Distant memories of Linden are tinted always with sunsets and dawns, one after another, like faded silks on attic shelves.

Ruth was striding purposefully down Lynn Street. The Walkers' shabby little shack was first on her left. She mounted the short flight of steps and knocked.

"Come in," Irv said. He was lounging in a makeshift camp chair, his feet on the wood box. Big Gertie, his wife, was stirring something on the stove.

"You haven't seen Alice?" Ruth asked, trying to appear unconcerned. "She went out for a walk," Ruth added. "I thought she might have passed this way."

Gertie grinned. "So she took it into her head at last to get up," Gertie said, not unkindly. "What's the matter? Had she worn out the bedclothes?"

"She's feeling lots better," Ruth said, thinking fast.

"Glad to hear it, Miss Coffee. Right glad, I am," said the good-natured Irv.

At Mrs. Preston's across the street, Ruth also got a negative report, and concluded that Alice must have taken Lynn Street in the other direction, up towards Broadway. She lengthened her stride, starting westward, and saw ahead of her Mrs. Townsend, her head wrapped in a shawl, talking distractedly with the lanky stoop-shouldered "jeweller," "Ich" Drown. As Ruth joined them, disturbed because Mrs. Townsend was spreading the alarm, Mrs. Townsend was babbling.

"My little girl has disappeared," she wailed.

"Disappeared, my eye," Ruth said, sharply. "I told you I'd find her."

"She didn't come down to Lynn Street. Mr. Drown would have seen her if she had," Mrs. Townsend said.

"I was sittin' on my front steps, lookin' down this way all the time," said Drown. "I saw Miss Coffee go in, then I saw her come out again, and walk down Lynn Street. I knew something was wrong, from the way she walked. If Alice went out, she must have gone out the back way, up into the woods."

"What for?" demanded Ruth, but the thought that Alice had strayed into the woods was already uppermost in her mind. That puzzled Ruth, because Alice had never mentioned the woods, and as far as Ruth knew, had never gone walking there. It would have been completely outside her timid character.

Ruth knew the woods up by the quarry, near her own cottage, and along the Newburyport Turnpike, but the stretch behind the Townsends' was strange to her. There the slopes were steep, cut with dry rocky rivulets, and the humped granite summit that was called "Elephant's Back." Paths were few, and seldom used. There was a thick undergrowth of alders, sumach, briers, berry bushes, and the three-leaved clinging vine called "poison ivy."

Mrs. Townsend, made bolder by the presence of Mr. Drown, glared at Ruth and defied her. "You can say what you like," Mrs. Townsend said. "I'm going to call the police."

Ruth sighed, trying to control herself. "The police!" she repeated scornfully. "You mean Spike? He couldn't pour slops out of a boot, with directions written all over the sole. Why not call Doc Moody and see what he says?"

"I've had enough of him, too," said Mrs. Townsend. She turned to Mr. Drown. "What would *you* do, Mr. Drown?"

"I could ask a few men to lend a hand, and help look for her," he suggested.

"And in ten minutes the news'll be all over town," protested Ruth. "Poor Alice'll never hear the last of it. What if she *did* decide to take a walk?"

"You probably know more about that than I do," said Mrs. Townsend, bitterly.

Drown was already ten paces down the street. He had the vague idea that a search party should be organized, but it was very hard for him to figure out how to go about it. He was a slow thinker and very careful worker, with his old clocks and watches. Action in a broader field was not in his line. He decided that he should turn over the responsibility and the ini-

129

tiative to somebody else. He thought first of Spike, the Linden cop, but finding Spike at dusk on a pleasant evening was most difficult. The lanky jeweller would not have known how to begin. Irv Walker, whose door he passed first, was out of the question as an organizer. He would pass as a follower, if someone else would tell him just what to do. Mr. Preston, with all the will in the world, was not the man, because he was so nearsighted that he often mistook the hydrant in front of his house for one of his own kids, and called it repeatedly. The next house on the left was Daisy Hoyt's, and she had no man, unless Packard was around, in which case it would be most untactful to call. Then came Jim Puffer. Mr. Drown dismissed Jim without debate. Poor Jim would most likely set the woods afire and burn out the whole town, if he was sent up there to hunt for the girl.

Mr. Ford, kite-flying husband of the Congregational organist, had consumption, and could not stand the night air.

Deacon Clapp was a fine upstanding man, and sensible as they made them, but twenty years too old.

Then Mr. Drown had an inspiration. Dawson Freeman was just the man. Dawson, when the situation was put up to him, accepted with alacrity. He was a born organizer, in any emergency. Dawson had a loud, pleasant voice, black hair and black moustaches, snapping black eyes, smoked black cigars, and spoke with much assurance.

"Ring the church bell," Dawson ordered. "That'll bring men there, to find out what's wrong."

Dawson made up his mind, right away, to make his headquarters on the steps of the Congregational Church, and there instruct his helpers, organize his groups, assign the territory to be searched to each, and wait for reports.

"There's no question of foul play," Dawson said. "The

schoolmarm is a little cracked, got tired of lyin' in bed, put on her clothes, and strolled away. I don't blame her if she wanted to dodge that sister of hers.

"If the girl's in anybody's house, it'll soon be reported. If she's in the woods, maybe she fell down and hurt herself."

Dawson's new phone did not help him much. He could only call Norman Partridge, who could hear him without a phone, from the Congregational porch, or J. J. Markham, who probably knew all about it by that time. Horses were of no use in the woods. What he needed were lanterns. Dawson called to Charley Clapp, his brother-in-law, and sent him on the hotfoot to Black Ann's Corner to stop all trolley cars and warn the motormen to go slowly through Linden and keep their eyes on the track. Mario Bacigalupo and Frigger appeared, the news having already travelled across the railroad tracks. Dawson sent them in opposite directions to scour the neighborhood for lanterns and ask for volunteers. But ringing the church bell was not so easy. Deacon Parker, who lived way up on Revere Street, had one set of keys to the church. The Reverend K. Gregory Powys had the other. Neither of them were at home. Jim Puffer was handy, so Dawson sent him to the carpenter shop to borrow a ladder, in order that someone might get into the church steeple and get hold of the bell rope.

Ralph Milliken, a boy a few years older than I was, knocked at our back door on his way through the yard, to ask for a lantern. It was from him that Mother and I first learned what had happened. I rushed down-cellar to get our lantern, and tried to follow Ralph out, but Mother put on such a scene that I had to stay home. She was always nervous, but pathetically so when anything distressing was happening in town and I was not within her sight.

I was saved from missing the rest of the evening out-of-doors by Miss Stoddard, across the street. Ralph went to her house on the run, as soon as he got our lantern, and pulled the front doorbell.

"Alice Townsend's lost in the woods," Ralph said. "Dawson Freeman sent me for your lantern."

"What does Dawson Freeman think he's going to do with a lantern in those woods? He won't be able to see anything but his own legs and the shadows of them. With a lantern he might as well be blind," Miss Stoddard said.

Ralph did not stop to argue. He dashed away, muttering, "Old Maid Know-it-all," and decided to try Norman Partridge's house.

Miss Stoddard had been a good friend of Alice Townsend's, before and after the girl's collapse, and she also liked Ruth and knew the latter would be frantic. She got on her walking boots, put on an old skirt and coat that already had been torn by briers, got one of her old mother's stout canes, and came across to our house. When Mother saw her at the door, Mother felt a little faint and flustered, for it seemed to her that whenever Miss Stoddard got mixed up in anything, it turned out to be disconcerting.

"How are you, Lutie?" Miss Stoddard said. "I want to borrow Elliot."

"He hasn't had his supper yet," Mother said.

"No matter. He'll be hungrier later," said Miss Stoddard, who never would take "No" for an answer. I had heard what she said, and already was putting on my sweater and coat, and an old pair of gloves.

"This youngster knows more about the woods than all the men in town, with or without their lanterns," Miss Stoddard said. Mother was pale with fright at the thought of my going to the woods in pitch-darkness, but since Miss Stoddard was going, too, she could not refuse. She would merely lose her appetite for supper, and sleep more fitfully than usual that night, if she could quiet herself down enough to sleep at all.

Soon Miss Stoddard and I were hiking across Weeks' field, near enough to Hen Richards' rickety shack to start his crazy little dog to barking.

"By the time those men get up into the woods, Miss Townsend could get all the way to Sugar Pond," Miss Stoddard said.

We were both thinking along the same lines. The path that led into the woods from Townsends' back yard (which was tilted up at an angle of forty-five degrees) was nothing more than the loose, rocky bed of a tiny watercourse that was a torrent only in spring and after a cloudburst for an hour or two. It branched, one fork leading up Elephant's Back, the other leading to a grove of sugar maples that stood in stagnant water called "Sugar Pond." There were two danger points. On the west fork of the path, which was almost invisible in the daytime, there was a stretch where it was within a few feet of a steep cut bank, with a fifty-foot drop, the edge concealed with low bushes and briers on which it was easy to trip. The other grim possibility was the pond itself. If Alice tried, she might drown herself there, among the wet moss and roots and water snakes between the sugar maples. In certain pools the depth might reach six feet.

As we hurried along, Miss Stoddard discussed these possibilities with me. She always, from my earliest years, addressed me thoughtfully and talked with me as if I were adult, and in return I dropped the reserve and lack of confidence I habitually held as a screen between me and most grown people.

As usual, I had a theory about what might have happened, based upon a guess as to what would go on in another person's mind. Miss Stoddard listened to it respectfully, as I led the way along the path that skirted the border of the woods near Salem Street, and she followed, step by step. Without lanterns, in spite of the Indian summer mist, our eyes had adjusted themselves and we could see quite well. What brought most people into the woods, those who did not particularly care for them, was the sight of the Bulfinch State House dome in Boston from the summit of Elephant's Back. Now certainly Miss Townsend would not, in her right mind, start out to climb Elephant's Back at twilight, but if she had done so before she took sick, it seemed to me that she might repeat the process. Certainly if she were in the woods at all, she would have followed the one pathway with which her feet had been slightly familiar. The briers and underbrush would have prevented her going more than a few feet from the precarious path.

We had passed behind Grovers' sprawling New England farmhouse (which for years had been without farm), and farther along had started the hens clucking in Irv Walker's hillside hen house, and were nearing the junction of our lateral path with the uphill path from Townsends' yard when the church bell began to clang.

"That isn't Deacon Parker," I said.

"No," said Miss Stoddard. The frenzied clanging, which got tangled up in itself every few strokes of the bell, was the work of an amateur. Miss Stoddard had told me that my reasoning was good, concerning what Miss Townsend might do, and she grunted appreciatively when I remarked that the ringing of the bell was not in Deacon Parker's style.

We paused and looked down over Linden, between the parted branches of an oak. Little dark figures were scurrying here and there, most of them converging toward the Congregational Church. Lanterns were swaying and twinkling. There must have been three dozen of them. A few were clustered already around the church porch.

How far that panorama of mists and dark slopes and dimly lighted window shades and moving shapes and lanterns seems from today, which has its police cars and motorcycles with sirens, two-way radio telephones, to say nothing of modern psychology, psychiatry, psychoanalysis, neurologists, alienists, and all the Gospels and Apostles of St. Sigmund Freud. The community of Linden was responding to the call, as best it could, each man willing, and no one thinking of leaving a public emergency to be dealt with by paid officials who resented aid and interference.

Jim Puffer had appealed to Swede Carlson for a ladder long enough to reach the belfry of the Congregational Church. The carpenter responded readily, but the ladder was too long and heavy for one to manage, so Jim took the front end and the carpenter the rear. They trotted down Beach Street and when they came to our yard, they tried to cut through, on a beeline for the church, forgetting that Don Partridge, who lived behind us on Lawrence Street, had just put up a newfangled wire fence, without barbs, that was guaranteed not to rust. Jim, in the lead, ran his end of the ladder smack into the wire, the ladder bounced back, breaking his nose, knocking him flat, and also throwing Swede Carlson at the rear end, who fell and sprained a wrist and bruised an ankle. My mother and Leslie, at the supper table, heard the twang of the wires, the thump and groans, and got to the back door just in time to see Jim and the carpenter sprawled on the ground, both trying to get up. From the back porch Mother could see that Jim's face was streaming with blood, so she ran back in for some hot water.

Jim helped the Swede up, getting blood all over him; they both limped up the steps and into our kitchen where Mother stuffed Jim's nose with cotton batting, treated the carpenter's bruised ankle with Arabian Balsam, a patent medicine in which she believed as firmly as in Christ's miracles, and followed the Swede's directions about strapping up his sprained wrist. Of course it had to be the right one.

Meanwhile, Dick Lanier showed up at the church with his

climbers. As he was spiking his way up to the belfry, digging his spurs deep into the Congregational paint and clapboards, there was some discussion as to the propriety of his act, but Dawson Freeman settled that.

"The church needs painting, anyway," he said.

Norman Partridge had telephoned Markham's store to notify Dr. Moody that his patient was on the loose, and the doctor, driving Hip and his buggy through the ranks of the gathering posse, locked wheels with Packard, bound in the opposite direction, and a dozen men had to lift both rigs off the ground to get them untangled.

Suppertime had now arrived in all the houses, with women waiting and complaining, food spoiling in the oven and on the back of the stove, children either restless or missing, and the more active men about to search the woods with lanterns, while the staider ones had been assigned streets for a house-to-house canvass. Dawson, in assigning men to the various streets, had taken them as they came, so that most of the Protestant streets north of the tracks were canvassed by Irishmen who had never darkened the doorways before, and the Irish and Italian wives, on the south side of Linden, were interviewed self-consciously by the Protestant deacons, who did not fail to note the smell of cabbage in the entryways, the loose boards on the steps, and the empty bottles in the ash barrels, or thrown carelessly in piles.

Miss Stoddard and I reached the steep path down to Townsends' back yard long before the searchers under Freeman got started. I was still in the lead, and had not got halfway to the back of Townsends' house when I brought up short, causing Miss Stoddard to collide with me. She saw what I had seen, and kneeled swiftly. The body of Ruth Coffee, clad in her mannish blue serge, was lying prone, across the pathway.

"She's alive," Miss Stoddard grunted, before I could ask.

Then she added: "She's been cut." In the half-darkness I could see Miss Stoddard turning Ruth face-upward, and exploring a wound below her left shoulder, in front. At least, the coat and blouse were cut and soaked with blood. Ruth had a bruise on her forehead, where she had hit a stone in falling. That is what had knocked her out.

I thought I heard Dr. Moody's voice, and footsteps on the Townsend stairway.

"Go down and get Dr. Moody," Miss Stoddard said, and I slid recklessly down the rocky path, swerved before I crashed into Townsends' back door, and managed to reach the doctor before he reached the front porch. The house was lighted inside, but no one was in sight.

"Come quick, doctor," I said.

"What's up?" he asked, but already I had started back up the hill, and he scrambled after me, holding his medicine case in his hand.

When we got there, Ruth was conscious, sitting up, and talking in her hearty way with Miss Stoddard, who was nodding, and clucking, and agreeing. Ruth was holding her cut shoulder with a handkerchief to staunch the blood, but they were not talking about her injury, as if she were in danger. Seeing first me, then the doctor, Ruth glanced at Miss Stoddard, then at me again, and said, in a tone I knew was intended for me, and need not necessarily convey the facts: "I thought maybe Alice had wandered up this way, so I came up in the dark, stumbled and fell. There must be glass around here, because I cut myself."

She patted with the handkerchief the place below her shoulder.

"What time is it?" she asked suddenly, this time touching her bruised forehead.

137

"Almost six o'clock," the doctor said. "Let's have a look at you."

"Shucks. I'm all right," Ruth said, and started to get up. To her surprise, her legs gave way and she sat down again, hard.

The doctor turned to Miss Stoddard. "We'd better lug her into the house."

"Elliot," Miss Stoddard said. "I'll be busy at the house here for a while. Why don't you run down to the sand pit, below the cut bank, on Salem Street, and see if anyone has fallen down in there. Then take this path to Elephant's Back, as we said. If you don't find Miss Townsend at the summit, or around Sugar Pond, come back here, ring the front doorbell and ask for me, and I'll go home with you, and explain to your mother what kept us."

Reluctantly I agreed, somewhat hurt because suddenly the others thought I would be in the way, or find out about something they wanted to keep from me. Already I had a strong suspicion of what really had happened, and I was disappointed that Miss Stoddard, with whom I thought I had an understanding, would think that I would tell about anything she asked me not to, or would admit its validity even if the whole town were insisting on it.

Although I was depressed and resentful, I tried to conceal my feelings, and carried out Miss Stoddard's instructions. I raced down to the foot of the cut bank, which had its base fifty feet from the upper sidewalk of Salem Street. No one had fallen down there. When I retraced my steps, I tiptoed up the long flight of steps to the Townsend house, trying not to make any noise. I still had to make the long climb to Elephant's Back and the subsequent journey over to Sugar Pond. Through a back kitchen window I could see a strained group in the sitting room, Ruth, her shoulder bandaged, her manner cool and relentless; Miss Stoddard nodding judicially; Dr. Moody embarrassed, but obviously taking some kind of a stand; Mrs. Townsend at bay; Elvira sulking in an easy chair, refusing to take any part in the discussion, whatever it was.

I found no trace of Miss Townsend on the way to Elephant's Back, and the night mist made it impossible to see the Broadway carbarns or the gravestones in Holy Cross Cemetery, let alone the Bulfinch State House dome or the Bunker Hill Monument. By the time I had trotted down from Elephant's Back and taken the other fork of the path toward Sugar Pond, Dawson Freeman's men were in the woods, with lanterns, calling back and forth to one another, tearing their skin and their clothes on the briers, and getting thoroughly fed up with the search before they were well started. I rescued two of them. Spike Dodge, the cop, had been found and pressed into service at last. He had been playing Casino with the blacksmith and the blacksmith's daughter, who worked summers in the women's side of the bathhouse at Revere Beach, renting and receiving bathing suits. Leona, the plump young woman in question, was paired with Spike, in the search. Both were lost, and were headed for the Newburyport Turnpike, believing they were working their way back to Linden.

I went with them as far as Salem Street, then hurried back to the Townsend house, where I looked through all the back windows to see what was going on before I rang the bell. The doctor had gone. Mrs. Townsend was vehemently remonstrating, Elvira was still sulking, and Miss Stoddard was firm. More than anyone else in Linden, Miss Stoddard tried to mind her own business, or rather, to avoid getting mixed up in anyone else's affairs. Ruth was alone in the kitchen, heating some water in order to change her own bandages.

News of the woman-hunt had spread to the neighboring communities, Broadway and Maplewood on the west, and Cliftondale northeast, so in addition to the Linden men roaming the streets, inquiring at doorways, getting free rides to and fro on the trolley cars presumably in line of duty, and crowding the Massasoit bar, quite a number of non-Linden men, and their women, were sharing the excitement.

I saw Ruth, having bathed and rebandaged her sturdy shoulder to her satisfaction, leave the kitchen to rejoin Miss Stoddard and the Townsend women. When she reached the sitting-room doorway, I saw her look startled, then come alive quickly and stride over to the opposite side of the sitting room, where there was an old carved sea chest. Ruth raised the cover, gasped with relief, and Mrs. Townsend started screaming, until Miss Stoddard shook her exasperatedly to quiet her.

Alice, dishevelled and pale, wearing a shirtwaist that had not been tucked into her skirt, sat up, and reached toward Ruth, who clasped her in her arms.

"They tried to make me send you away," Alice said, and Ruth turned indignantly to Mrs. Townsend.

"The doctor warned you about that," Ruth said. "I hope you're satisfied."

"Every day they tried to make me send you away," repeated Alice, clinging, while Ruth, forgetting Mrs. Townsend and Miss Stoddard, held her tightly and patted her head as it rested on her shoulder.

That was the moment I chose to ring the front doorbell, and all of them jumped. Miss Stoddard came to the door.

"I think you'd better go home by yourself, Elliot," Miss Stoddard said. "Before you go in, tell Dawson Freeman that Miss Townsend has been found."

"Where?" I asked.

"In the woods, back of the house. . . . She lost her way, and fell asleep," Miss Stoddard said.

"Who found her?"

"Ruth," said Miss Stoddard.

"There wasn't any glass on that path, or anywhere near it
. . . I hunted all around," I said, looking her resentfully in
the eye.

Miss Stoddard relaxed and smiled ruefully.

"What folks don't know, won't hurt them," she said. "I'll
explain it all to you . . . when we go walking Sunday . . . if
I can. Now run along. Remember what I told you."

I found Dawson Freeman at the church, gave him the in-
accurate message, and hurried home to ease my mother's mind.
Just as I was getting into bed, before I fell asleep, the bell of the
Congregational Church began to ring again, but this time with
the soothing, steady strokes of Deacon Parker.

CHAPTER NINE

Black Ann's Corner and the Finns

❖

THE approach to Linden from the North Shore and the east was through Black Ann's Corner, where Salem Street took a ninety-degree bend, around the quarry, and Lynn Street branched off of it, to skirt the marshland toward the Square. Beyond the ledge, where the streetcars struggled up the hill and disappeared, were Cliftondale, Saugus, Lynn, Salem, Beverly, Marblehead, Gloucester, Annisquam and Rockport.

I have mentioned several times how vast and inexhaustible the granite quarry seemed, standing like an eternal bastion to deflect the force of northeast storms and channel them onto little Linden. That does not mean there was furious or antlike activity around the ledge or the old-fashioned stone crusher. Nothing or no one was too busy in our town. There may have been half a dozen men, all Irish, who worked for the quarry company and lived south of the tracks, about a mile away. A mile in Linden was a considerable distance then. It took twenty minutes to walk it, if the footing was good and one did not meet a few friends on the way. The going underfoot was seldom ideal, and friends were everywhere.

It may readily be understood that six easygoing Irishmen, with a neighbor for a foreman and an anonymous Boston contracting concern that furnished the pay, working against a huge gray background of ageless hard rock, did not create enough of a stir to be noticeable, except at blasting time.

Once or twice a day, two or three stone carts would drive into Linden, from Revere, and take Lynn Street at the Square, bound for the quarry. They would be loaded at the crusher, with a little unhurried bustle and much conversation, the horses would be changed or watered, odd bits of news from the city would be discussed, and a few hours later the loaded carts would head back to Boston. More often than not, they would get stuck somewhere between Black Ann's Corner and the Massasoit House, for Lynn Street dipped from the higher ground of Salem Street to the level of the marsh, and the mudholes lasted days and days after the other streets were dry. When Lynn Street got dry, it was very dry, and the passing carts set up a screen of dust that cut off the view to the east and slowly drifted toward the residential section.

Not far along Salem Street, from the quarry, in a clearing that faced the town, stood Weeks' barn, the only large one left in Linden. Mr. Weeks, the Linden milkman, was a Yankee, and his hired hands were Yankees. They were not the hayseeds of the vaudeville stage, but were definitely farmers and dairymen, who milked the cows, drove them back and forth between the barn and the various fields Weeks used for pasture, knew how to swing a scythe, to stack and dry the timothy hay, pile up colossal loads that dwarfed the hayracks and horses that pulled them, store the hay in the lofts, and pitch it down for the cows in the winter. Weeks had four men, besides his son Harry. They supplied milk for most of the stores and families in Linden, and quite a few in the neighboring communities of Cliftondale and Broadway. Also they shipped a dozen or more huge tin cans, not quite the Ali Baba size, both ways on the Saugus Branch, to Lynn and to Boston.

A field of Linden cows was not like any other herd on earth, but how they graced the meadows, sometimes one, sometimes another. Weeks, when things were going well for him, used

143

three or four fields at a time, one of the largest stretching all the way from Beach Street across the creek and up to Salem Street, directly opposite our house; from our porch we could watch the cows moving indolently about their business, hear them munching and sloshing in the mud, smell their fragrance, and as years went by, get acquainted with them, individually, and learn that they were no more alike than people were. The slow-moving, almost wordless Mr. Weeks did not go in for breeds and strains. In colors and markings, the thirty cows or more in any given pasture represented just about everything that could be done with shapes and hues and arrangements. Some were plain red, fawn color, yellow, white or black. Some were piebald, dappled, spotted, ringed or belted. Quite a few looked at us with large reproachful eyes, and represented tragic figures, animals who protested their status in a dignified way. Others, with rakish angles to their twisted horns, were obviously clowns. Now and then a cow would have horns that matched. Weeks had a bull, who was not of any special kind, either, and never two days alike. His name was Dave, and he looked as if he had never been able to decide whether he would be predominantly white or black. On days when Dave was feeling chipper, scenes were enacted in Weeks' barnyard, with spectators along all sides of the rickety rail fence, that were worthy of the jousts of old. Merely to hear one of these bovine debauches was an experience. I think it was there I got my obsession for sound effects, but the assorted colors of the victims enlivened the action as well.

When Dave was performing, all work stopped at the quarry and the blacksmith shop, and the Irish laborers and Yankee farmers met on common ground. More than once, the spectacle was so moving that the Irishmen knocked off for the rest of the day and headed, some for home, and others for the Revere cat houses three miles distant.

I remember Mr. Weeks, when he called at our back door to tell Mother that he would have to charge six cents a quart, instead of five. All the other milkmen around the region had previously made the change, and he was sorry, but wages were higher, whatever he bought cost him more than it used to. When his boy, Harry, had figured up the year's receipts, he had found that they both had worked hard twelve months for nothing.

"Some dratted new kind of double-entry figurin'," Mr. Weeks said.

Mother nodded, sadly and sympathetically. She knew that everything cost more, and worried about it, too.

Mr. Weeks never seemed to have a recent haircut, or work clothes that fitted him. He was lean and lanky, awkward and perpetually embarrassed, when it was necessary for him to talk at all. His men did not wear themselves out, nor did they loaf. They produced milk, which was rich and highly unsanitary, without seeming to exhaust the source, as the Irish at the quarry produced crushed stone. The milkmen voted Republican and read the *Herald,* the Irish voted Democratic and read the *Post.* Some got drunk whenever they had a chance, others stayed sober. I think they liked working and living in Linden. I believe they felt a mantle of security, with no suspicion that their employers were out to exploit them. Somehow they would always earn a living.

How much of their contentment was well founded, or sound economic or social doctrine, I leave to the reader to decide. I must insist, however, that in feeling the way they did, they derived a lot of pleasure from living, and a minimum of care. Their children went to the same schools, played on the same ball teams, and bought their clothes at the same stores as the rest of us did. The animosities that existed were almost purely individual, and not too many of those.

145

I wish all children could live a few years in a place where nearly everybody liked everybody else. There is nothing quite comparable to this. I will go farther. I wish all children could have lived a while in Linden. I should like to feel that they had seen Weeks' cows, in all the colors and patterns cows' promiscuity can achieve, against the background of daisies and buttercups, when the tide was high and they could stand in the cool water. And when it came to guidance about the facts of life, Weeks' barnyard had it all over the little bees and bluebells.

Another feature of Black Ann's Corner was the Linden blacksmith's shop, which stood with its back to the town, facing the Finns' stone yard across Lynn Street, with the Saugus Branch embankment and miles of marshland in the background. What first attracted me to the spot was its utter denial of Longfellow, whose verses I heartily detested. There was no "spreading chestnut tree," or any tree whatsoever. The foreground consisted of a muddy or dusty street, with unchiseled slabs that later would be gravestones. And the smithy, Bart Dickey by name, was less than the average in height, had dyspepsia of which he continually complained, and when he had any heavy lifting to be done, he called on a few of the unemployed men (unemployed by instinct, choice and temperament), who were always hanging around and were willing to help him.

Probably Bart, who was an indolent man, figured that the free entertainment he provided, mending wagon rims, shoeing refractory horses, making railroad spikes for the section gang, and pitching horseshoes against all comers, entitled him to the services of his audience.

The rusty scrap iron, broken-down parts of vehicles, mudholes and semistagnant pools, relieved by the smoky old ruin of a shop and the slabs and gravestones in the Finns' yard across the way, did not provide the most attractive setting for "loafing and inviting the soul." However, that was the rendezvous for idle and unattached Linden men, not of the tradesman class, like those who hung around the Square, but laborers, roustabouts, and tramps. Seldom were there less than ten or twelve in the group.

When I remarked to Miss Stoddard that the meeting place of the bums was unsightly, she pointed out that while they were in that desolate area, they did not see it, unless they were looking down at their feet. What they saw was the rugged granite ledge and the wooded hills to the north, the fog banks creeping in from the marshes to the east, a side view of residential Linden to the south, and fertile rolling meadows bordering the creek as it flowed westward, when the tide was coming in.

Not all the men who spent their time around Dickey's shop were from Linden. Many who liked to be idle, from Broadway or Cliftondale, and did not find it convenient to be seen doing nothing by their wives, families or creditors, shuffled over the Linden borders and converged on the blacksmith shop.

When the tide was right, in smelting season, there were always four or five men fishing from the granite rim of the conduit, smoking, dangling their legs, allowing the kids to take the smelts off their hooks and drop them in the pails. They all used spreaders, with at least four hooks and leaders, and when the fish were running, seldom caught less than three at a time. At other times they caught alewives, or speared eels, or seined for shrimps, but their fishing was never in the line of work. They took a few home, gave the rest away, and thought of fishing as another way of killing time.

A horseshoe game was always in progress, unless the weather was too cold or too warm. If it was too hot, the men would stretch themselves out on the higher ground and doze, and if it was too cold they would build a large bonfire, with scraps of driftwood and discarded railroad ties or wagon spokes that always were handy. Nothing around the blacksmith shop was ever picked up unless someone had an immediate use for it.

Pehr and Paavo, the Finns, worked steadily in their shop or out in the yard, not a hundred feet away, seemingly paying no attention to the fishing, or games, or bonfires, and the loafers never crossed the muddy street and sat on their stone slabs and pedestals. So the hardest work in Linden was performed within sight of the most complete and accomplished loafing in Middlesex County.

The blacksmith shop crowd was seldom drunk or disorderly. Now and then a bottle was passed around, but the loafers were more likely to finish their liquor, what little they had, before checking in at the loafing grounds. Most of them were men who handled very little money, although they would have resented being classified as "poor." They were able-bodied, but weak and unambitious in their minds. They were respectable, to the extent that they seldom got pinched, but their financial bracket was much lower than that of the men who watched the trains come in and the customers go in and out of the stores and shops in the Square. Their wives, if they had them, took in washing. Their jobs, if any, were seasonal or intermittent. They were house painters' helpers, ice cutters, teamsters without horses of their own, men with cricks in their backs or pains in their stomachs that no doctors could relieve, single-taxers, men who had been fired unjustly, or promised work that did not materialize. Their ranks were swelled by other men, a little more soundly placed in the social setup, who were temporarily out of work, or had sustained minor injuries, or were fed up with wherever they had been and were visiting indigent relatives south of the Saugus Branch tracks.

Actually their presence in the Lynn Street hollows incom-

moded no one. Ruth Coffee, my Great-Aunt Elizabeth, Mrs.
Weeks and young Mrs. Weeks, and the other women who lived
on the eastern reaches of Salem Street, would have chosen the
better footing afforded by Revere Street, in order to do their
errands in Linden, even if the gang of ne'er-do-wells had not
been gathered on Lynn Street. If transient or out-of-town customers drove to the blacksmith shop with women in their rigs,
Paavo, the stonecutter, would cross the street, doff his cap, and
offer the stranger the use of his front room and other facilities
he did not specify for the womenfolk. After a glance at the
Lynn Street bums, the women accepted the offer with relief
and alacrity, although probably they were in no danger at all.
I cannot remember a single incident in which a woman was
molested around the blacksmith shop. No Linden woman ever
risked going near enough for that.

Linden weather, forty or fifty years ago, was a formidable
consideration in any mode of life. It was amazing with what
ingenuity the blacksmith shop loafers adapted themselves to it.
Their rendezvous was without natural shade or shelter, but
they managed somehow, rain or shine, in the stifling heat of
summer and the bitter cold of winter. None of them had suitable clothing for either extreme. On the hottest days, when
the sun was strong, they would sometimes stray as far as the
edge of the woods beyond the quarry, but they detested
the ants and nettles, the snakes and poison ivy, while the flies
and mosquitoes that swarmed around the creek were companions they understood. It took a real scorcher, or the stickiest of
dog days, to drive them any farther than the stone wall, overrun
with brambles and berry bushes. In the morning, they would
lie on the western side of the wall, in the field. In the afternoon, when the shadows spread the other way, they would
stretch out on what was called, for lack of an accurate term,
the sidewalk. When it was raining hard, they would swarm

149

into the blacksmith shop. To slight showers they paid no attention, standing like bedraggled fowl and watching without purpose or interest, the spatter of the raindrops on the surface of the creek or on the mud.

On clear, cold days, there was no problem except wood for the fire, which they built on the ice that bound the still pools. In snowstorms, when the creek was frozen, they huddled in the conduit under the railroad embankment, heating the shelter with an old metal tank filled with coals.

They argued continuously, but seldom fought. Fighting required physical effort, and if they had been that kind of men they would not have been there. None of them bought newspapers, but there was always one or two around, and the headlines served as springboards for their talk. If a new building was going up, or an old one was being torn down, if the city was embarking on a public project, the pros and cons would be sifted, in a vehement but impersonal way. Clay pipes and cut plug were obtainable for one cent and five cents, respectively, and a few of them smoked Sweet Caporals or butts they picked up on the sidewalks.

Whenever there was a public ceremony or a ball game in Linden, the bums from Lynn Street were the most partisan rooters or spectators. They did not stick together, but mingled freely with the rest of the Linden population and showed as much animation as on other days they showed lassitude. Once, when after a dry spell the marsh grass caught fire and was fanned by a brisk east wind, they beat out the fire with their coats and green branches from the woods, and undoubtedly saved the town. But if Jim Puffer approached from the Partridge warehouse and wanted to hire a few extra men to unload leather, the variety of reasons they would give, as individuals, as to why they could not oblige that day, was a tribute to their ingenuity.

150

Black Ann's Corner and the Finns

Once, a hurdy-gurdy, pushed by an Italian and hauled by his strong young daughter, stopped in front of the blacksmith shop and the Italian started to grind out a tune. The bums looked at each other, annoyed and embarrassed, and slowly dispersed, before the young girl got around with her tambourine. They certainly would not put out the few coins they had for music, and wanted no favors free of charge. The Italian was bewildered, somewhat hurt, but he never made the same mistake again. He left Linden for Cliftondale by way of Revere Street and Salem, and kept away from Lynn Street and the blacksmith shop. The Lynn Street gang was made up of Irish, and what were loosely known as "Americans" or "white men." No Polacks or southern European or Scandinavians were among them. They had no interest in music. None of them ever sang songs, unless he was drunk, and then he was discouraged from continuing.

It always seemed to me that the loafers had a mild contempt for the respectable, hard-working people who had steady incomes, were looked up to by their families, and jumped when whistles blew. I never heard them express any quaint philosophy or profound socialistic ideas. They were not sorry for themselves, they did not seem to be ruminating on past frustrations or sorrows, like Hen Richards or Dick Trask, the hermits, for instance. None of them mentioned the fact, if they "had seen better days." The days they were seeing were good enough for them. They felt no obligation to be useful, or noble, or industrious. They liked the status quo and were irritated by innovations.

Bart Dickey, the blacksmith, made a few dollars now and then, in spite of himself, and I am sure he would have been lonesome without his shiftless companions. They did not mind his working, if somebody showed up with a horse to be shod or a wagon to mend.

151

"Doesn't it drive away half of your trade, having those bums around the shop, day after day?" J. J. Markham asked the blacksmith one day.

"I hope to God it does," Bart said, sincerely.

The Finns, Pehr and Paavo Wallenius, whose place was also a landmark at Black Ann's Corner, made a living by shaping up stone slabs and carving names and gems of hopeful statement on funeral monuments. Between-times, the Finns did the finest masonry work, for pavements, walls or porches, in New England.

The two brothers looked and dressed much alike. Pehr was slightly taller and had a tinge of orange in his sandy hair and moustaches. Paavo had shoulders not quite so narrow as his brother's. They worked equally hard, when there was stone cutting to be done, from about eight o'clock in the morning until the last blast sounded at the nearby quarry, just after six p.m. The remainder of the twenty-four hours, and all Saturday afternoons, Sundays and holidays, their pathways were separate.

Pehr, the older one, drank. Paavo, the younger and broader one in the shoulders, did not. Paavo read Swedenborg instead, and at an early age I had Mary Stoddard's word for it that the drinker had all the best of it, in so far as the effect on the brain was concerned.

From the moment the Finns had laid the stone walk in front of her neat cottage, and had fixed up her wall so the spring rains would not wash it out, had added a stone well, an outdoor fireplace, and a fountain with a sun dial in her flower garden, by far the most decorative and well planned in Linden, Ruth Coffee had been obsessed with the feeling that two such artists should not waste their talents. It was worth a lot to see the embarrassed, deprecatory smiles that passed over the boyish faces of the middle-aged masons when Ruth referred to them as artists. Good stone masons and cutters were respected in Finland, they admitted, but they were just plain working men.

"You're chumps not to cash in on what you can do," Ruth said. "Those summer people down to Marblehead will pay you more for a porch like mine than you get for a hundred lousy gravestones. Just say the word, and we'll skin 'em alive."

The Finns did not like to talk when they were working. A nod or a grunt or a gesture between them was sufficient for communication. They made no lost motions. Consequently Ruth was tactful enough not to harangue them in working hours. And except during working hours, the brothers were seldom together.

Pehr, the elder brother, was at the Massasoit every night. He went there straight from work, cutting across the fields when weather and footing permitted, instead of using the roundabout streets and sidewalks. At six o'clock, the whistle on the stone crusher blew, a hundred yards away. Pehr stopped whatever he was doing. If he was halfway up the "U" in carving a "Pause, Stranger," he did not hit the chisel another tap. He got up, dusted himself off, went to the yard between the shop and the blacksmith's to wash his hands, and now and then his face, and was cleaned up in time to see the blast.

Pehr got a childish pleasure out of seeing a section of the huge granite ledge crumple and slide down to the level of the quarry bottom, with its wicked puff of smoke, white and black, the lift, the fissure, the pull of gravitation, friction, dust, flying fragments that sometimes landed all the way down to the yard in which he stood, and the delayed sound of the explosion, followed by the rustle and clatter and roar of rock cascading downward against rock.

As soon as the workmen were safely away, two watchmen walked along the car tracks in opposite directions, with red flags, to warn pedestrians, vehicles and trolley cars not to approach. All day the drillers had been drilling, the powder monkey had been taking drills back and forth from blacksmith shop to quarry, the hard-rock men had been stowing away the black powder, for lift, and the dynamite for fission. The fuses had been measured, attached to the concussion caps, and laid. They were lighted with a match, and if one spluttered out and failed, there was dangerous work to be done.

Linden people got accustomed to hearing the blasts at the quarry, just after noon, and just after six. It was part of the day's punctuation.

The last blast meant more to Pehr than most of the people. It signalled his exit from a world of toil, to one of the imagination and retrospect, well oiled with Portsmouth Ale. His brother handled the money, fixed the charges, paid the bills, and after expenses were taken care of, divided the money, bill by bill and coin for coin, one for you and one for me. Before he took his own half, Paavo put whatever extra change or bills he had left over from the last division into a metal box concealed in his fireplace. The other half he gave to Pehr, who put it all in his pockets and headed for the Massasoit bar.

There was something satisfying and purposeful about the way Pehr walked from his shop to the bar. Anyone watching him would feel, instinctively, that there was a man who knew what he wanted, and was not likely to be frustrated or deterred. He took long strides, without undignified haste, leaning slightly forward without swinging his arms. Swinging his arms would have been physically uneconomical, and Pehr would have none of that. He would have use for his arms the next morning at eight o'clock, in the shop. Until then, no worry, no waste, no interruption.

The Admiral, the bartender, my Uncle Reuben, Hal Kingsland, Ruth Coffee, Ginger McSweeney, Mr. Wing, all the bottle companions assembled would nod and smile pleasantly as Pehr came through the swinging doors. He was never late, and never misbehaved. He acknowledged the greetings politely, with his warm, boyish smile. The glow of the lamps, the smell of beer and sawdust, the somber hue of the mahogany, the alluring high lights in the stout brass rail, sang a song of evening, a vesper hymn, a brotherhood in Christ and alcohol, a unity of mankind, what all bards and scalds and poets and drinking songs have, since the beginning of time, tried faithfully and inadequately to express. The sailor home from the sea, the beacons passed, the spiritual predicate. What mattered the hours of tapping with a mallet upon stone, the foolish phrases, the stupid patterns, the aching fingers, neck muscles, dust in the nostrils?

Ale and good brother Paavo, and the money to pay for what he had, by yumpin' Yesus. Pehr seldom spoke, unless the amenities made it necessary, but after a few good mugs of ale he smiled happily to himself, breathed deeply, flexed the muscles of his shoulders, and on one occasion, from pure inner glee, startled the other tipplers at the bar by exclaiming, to himself and apropos of nothing, in the middle of an evening, during a lull in the barroom chatter: "God damn it to hell!" With those words, he shook his head, with exuberance, and smacked the bar, gently but delightedly. Pehr loved existence, and the world.

What did Pehr experience, leaning so blissfully on his elbows, resting his foot on the brass? Snatches of song, of toil, of boyhood among the reindeer, or smoked reindeer, of northern lights, and northern minor music, with cleavages of major and minor, like faults in clear ice. Of a safe and ordered existence, with coins in his pocket, work always to be had, and always his little brother, supplying what in character Pehr lacked. He had never urged his brother to drink, or sung to him about drink's miraculous evocations. He had promised his

155

dying mother that he would take care of Paavo, and Paavo had sworn to take care of him. Both were fulfilling their vow, in their separate fashions.

Pehr never ate an evening meal, but depended on the free lunch at the Massasoit. Lucullus might have depended on less. Jeff Lee put out home-cured hams, steaming hot and redolent with spices; steamed Annisquam clams that had dreamed in the sand and seaweed fragrance and been turned up by understanding clam forks and given the blessing of hot vapors, not more than two minutes; four or five kinds of herring, one better than the other; roast beef or roast spring lamb, with homemade bread, white, rye or brown, for sandwiches; the pickled toes of swinekins, in a brine that would save sinners; baked beans and steamed brown bread. The beans deserve another chapter. If each bean were a bead of a rosary, and the cross made of fat salt pork, there would be no men of taste outside God's mercy.

Glimpses of fine, strong, blonde women in seaport dives. Song drunken, and song sober. Evergreens and salt air, and the patterns in the grain of granite, basalt, porphyry, and marble. Porches and pavings, poetical, and monuments stiff and trite. Days working and nights drinking, the roar of the breakers and the space between the stars.

A train steamed into Linden, stopped to let off a few latefaring passengers, then steamed along the edge of the marsh. This took place on weekday nights, just about midnight. Paavo, the younger Finn, heard this train, invariably, although he had been in a deep, placid sleep since nine o'clock. He got out of bed, hauled on his britches and boots, wrapped a scarf around his neck, took his corduroy cap with ear muffs (tucked up in summer), and started down Lynn Street toward the Massasoit. The Massasoit never closed, in the accepted meaning of the word, but Pehr softly and gradually folded as leaves are turned on calendars. Several of the steady drinkers would still be at the bar, and would wave and speak greetings as Paavo came in. The bartender would reach for the keg of root beer he kept on hand for customers on the wagon. Pehr would open one eye sleepily, nod to his brother, shake himself lazily like a dog, shove over his mug for one last and final ale. Paavo would gulp the root beer, smacking his lips approvingly. Stone dust gave a man a good thirst, whether he drank water or liquor. Pehr would drain his mug of ale, take out his purse and pay for his evening's drinks, which seldom amounted to more than two dollars and a half. If, toward the end of a week or a month, Pehr didn't have enough, Paavo would pay the difference and charge it to general expenses, or what has now become known as "overhead."

Together they would nod and say, "Gude-night, jentlemen," and would leave the barroom, side by side. It was a point of dignity with Pehr that he must go home under his own steam, and not stagger too much. His little brother, he explained, came to remind him, not because Pehr could not take care of himself. They would enter the shop, in the back of which they lived, do whatever undressing they thought necessary, say, "Gude-night, brother," and tumble into their bunks.

When the six o'clock train, Boston bound in the morning, whistled for the unguarded crossing on Lynn Street, Paavo would get up, wash in the yard, light a fire in the cook stove, put on coffee, warm over some beans or steak or whatever he had left over from his supper, fry about a dozen fresh eggs, break out some bread or sea biscuit, tidy up the sleeping room, and at seven he would wake Pehr. This was a project requiring restraint and patience, as well as ingenuity and adaptability. It seldom required more than a quarter of an hour. Once the advent of a new day had seeped into Pehr's consciousness, he would sit up, shake his head, say, "Gude-morning, brother," and go out to the pump. There he would not hold his head under the stream. That is for nondrinkers. Drinking men keep their heads up high, and raise the water in their cupped hands, until the worst is over. Jerry Dineen would have delivered the paper. The Finns read the *Globe,* passing the sections back and forth gravely as they ate a whopping breakfast. Paavo opened up the shop and made ready for business while Pehr washed the dishes. Then they settled down to work, with a maximum of accomplishment and a minimum of chatter.

Their joint income was about twenty-five hundred dollars a year, gross. Of his share, Paavo put aside between nine hundred and a thousand dollars. Pehr had never laid up a cent.

The only cross words that passed between the brothers were due to Paavo's thirst for the wisdom of Swedenborg. He would knit his brows, clench his hands, groan and suffer agonies of concentration as he read, in English, about the relation of the finite to the infinite, and the geometrical theory of the origin of things. He let his head ring with squared circles and the Swedish mystic's dreams, talks with the Lord and the angels. God, he learned, was like a man, only divine, and a sphere, glowing as the sun.

Once Pehr picked up the book he had seen his brother so strenuously devouring, frowned harder than Paavo, and pointed out a word with his calloused finger.

"Brother? What's this 'nexus'? I don't know what it means," Pehr said.

Paavo flushed and looked hard at his brother. "That's none of your business," he said.

"Maybe you don't know yourself, exactly?" said Pehr, surprised and nettled.

"The man who wrote that book had witnessed the Last Judgment and saw the Holy Ghost," Paavo said, taking the book and closing it firmly.

"And what did the Holy Ghost look like?" Pehr asked.

"That isn't for sinners," said Paavo.

"Maybe Mr. Swedenborg forgot to write it down," said Pehr.

"A great man is a threefold eternal incarnation, when he's seen the Last Judgment and the Second Coming, and couldn't forget, unless the Father, the Son and the Holy Ghost were so minded, and thus spake," Paavo said. "Now will you shut up and hold your tongue?"

"I didn't mean to get you mad, brother," Pehr said. "But if I did, you can kindly go to hell."

The Finns did not speak to each other again for ten days, and Pehr never asked his brother again about anything in Swedenborg's book. Pehr, nevertheless, brooded a bit about the meaning of the word "nexus" and sprung it on the gang at the Massasoit bar. Some thought it was an animal, like the sidehill gouger or the four-legged snipe, others believed it was a place, like Texas, only having people who spoke better English. Ruth Coffee did not know, but she saw Miss Stoddard passing, and invited her to come in. Miss Stoddard ordered tea, and sat at a table. She had heard volumes about the Massasoit, but had never been there.

The Admiral and Mr. Wing were very gallant and my Uncle Reuben poured a jigger of rum into the tea. Miss Stoddard sipped it and liked it.

"The Finn just stumped us with a word he saw somewhere in a book," Ruth said.

"I didn't realize you had spelling matches in here," Miss Stoddard said.

Hal Kingsland, who always found a way to insert an element of gambling into a situation, made up a book, offering odds of six to seven that Miss Stoddard would know what the word meant. My Uncle Reuben insisted on even money. Jeff Lee came out from the kitchen, his eyes glowing. He dearly loved a

159

sporting proposition, and had decided hunches on that one. He offered to back Miss Stoddard for any amount he had in his pocket, or could borrow.

When the money was all put up, and Pehr had been reduced to the depths of self-consciousness because he had made himself so conspicuous, Ruth asked Miss Stoddard the question.

"What is a nexus?" she said.

Miss Stoddard's humorous and tolerant smile lit up her homely face, warts and all.

"A nexus," she said, and already Jeff Lee was reaching for the money, "is a bond between members of a group. For instance, between you gentlemen, the nexus that holds you together is a thirst for strong drink."

She finished her tea, still smiling between sips, rose, said, "Good-evening," and departed.

The men looked after her, impressed, as she departed. For years, most of them had looked upon Mary Stoddard as a harmless eccentric. Now they were convinced that she knew a lot more than they did.

Miss Stoddard's speech at the mass meeting about the Balm of Gilead tree had provoked a lot of ridicule. She said that in her day the tree had been struck by lightning at least a dozen times, and that if it were removed, the houses in the vicinity would be in danger from electrical storms.

Linden was one of the prize locations in the world for thunderstorms. Something about the conformation of the northern hills, the currents of air that rose above the marshes, and the hot flat lands to the south, seemed ideal to attract the most vicious streaks of lightning and produce the most ultra-Wagnerian thunderclaps. Miss Stoddard had pointed this out, and the opponents of the tree, as well as many of its supporters had not taken her seriously until a few months after the last of the tree had been sawed down. Don Partridge, Norman's brother and junior partner, started building a house just back of ours, and when the rough work was finished, the new building was struck by lightning and nearly demolished.

The proprietor, as well as Mr. Carlson, the builder, were in it at the time, and both were stunned. It was then that folks in Linden began to believe that Miss Stoddard knew what she was talking about.

"What a shame," Uncle Reuben said, as she left the Massasoit bar. "A smart woman like that, with a face that would scare a dog off a gut wagon. Some of you young fellows ought to help her out."

"Not me," said Ginger. "There's nothing that throws a man off his stride like an educated woman. It makes him nervous at just the wrong time."

"Lots of girls feel bashful with an educated man," Big Julie said, "but they're kind of nice when you get used to them."

"Does it make any difference what a *man* looks like?" my uncle asked.

"You can always turn the page," Julie said.

CHAPTER TEN

Of Codfish Balls

IT WAS the codfish (*Gaddus calarius*) that brought to the New England coast a large number of its best inhabitants, not the misfits and the pious of whom far too much has been written, but mariners and fishermen with all the adventurous characteristics of men who pit themselves against the sea, where the ways are free for all and nobody owns anything except the fish he catches and the vessel he rides on. The Grand Banks off Newfoundland, and farther south, Grand Manan off what now is the state of Maine, and St. George's great submerged peninsula off Cape Ann, brought fishermen from England, France, all the Scandinavian countries, the Spaniards, the Basques and the Portuguese; many of them, finding it more convenient to winter on the coast of America than to sail back to Europe, spent a few seasons here, were challenged by the new continent's endless possibilities, and stayed.

Among those who chose Cape Ann, founding Rockport and Gloucester and other coastal cities and towns in what now is Massachusetts, a number left descendants who established themselves in Linden and the little communities just north of Boston. The first cargo ever to be shipped from Massachusetts was of sun-dried cod. And when the steam engine was invented, in the eighteenth century, and sails, one by one, disappeared from the seas, large numbers of fishermen stuck to the traditional schooners, and sailed out of Gloucester, Newburyport, Salem, and Boston, preferring one of the toughest known ways of making a living to swallowing cinders on steam freighters or going into New England factories to weave textiles or manufacture boots and shoes. The codfishermen did not work by the day or by the month. After the owner's and the skipper's cut had been taken from the receipts of the voyage, the crew shared alike.

Old Gimp Crich, who waited on the back room customers at the Massasoit House, had had his leg sheared off by a tow-rope, aboard a fishing schooner off Grand Manan. He had a cousin who had been one of his shipmates and who still sailed out of Bucksport, Maine, for the Newfoundland Banks, had got a master's ticket, and as captain and owner of a neat two-master, was prosperous. Captain Eldridge was his name, and he argued with Gimp by the hour to give up his job and act as watchman on the *Bessie B*. Gimp, over seventy and with a handicap that would have crippled a less agile man, was still independent.

Gimp explained to me once why so many New England sailing vessels had women's first names and only an initial afterward.

"Them's mostly hookers," he said. "Somebody liked 'em and couldn't remember their last name, if ever he knew."

Also, I think Gimp liked his Linden job because of the girls who came in each night.

"Gimp always was a hound," Captain Eldridge said, and, while Gimp looked embarrassed and snorted, his cousin told the back room crowd around Hal Kingsland's long table how, when "Gimp and him" were young punks together and had just got back from the Banks with a fine load of cod, Gimp started hell-bent up the street in Bangor, his share of the money still in his hand. Captain Eldridge hurried after him, caught up, and said:

"Gimp, hadn't you better give me some of that money? You'll be needing food and clothes this winter."

("This was the last trip of the season," Eldridge explained to the crowd.)

" 'To hell with food and clothes,' Gimp said," according to Eldridge. " 'I'm after whores and music.' "

Gimp shuffled off his bashfulness and was a little defiant.

"Well. What of it?" Gimp said. "I ain't starved to death yet, and I'm decently covered."

Gimp, in fact, was quite content. It will hardly be believable, in the light of present-day existence, how many contented men and women I report out of Linden. I do not suggest "going back" to those conditions. That is foolish and impossible, and not even desirable. Recapturing the contentment, striving for it, recognizing that it is most important is another matter. That we must do. No series of harassed and bitter generations will produce an improved mankind. What will happen, if contentment is sneered at and obliterated, is that the best qualities of humanity will be drained away, which is far from impossible. Scientifically it is even probable, unless enough of us persist in having a good time. Admitting that we still need Karl Marx, we need Omar Khayyam even more. They must be reconciled.

Linden, without codfish, would have lost one of its essentials, as would any seacoast town in New England. The matchless varieties of seafood, available and inexpensive, had their part in building Linden's people, balancing their precarious economy, strengthening their physiques and mellowing their character.

It was on Tuesdays and Fridays in Linden that Ezra Stowe, the fishman, called from house to house. The stores carried meat, which could be kept in the ice chest for days or weeks. But New England customers insisted that their fish be fresh—

right out of the water. They knew nothing about vitamins, but were right about what they liked.

Mr. Stowe was a small active man, incredibly swift and skillful with his hands, which, because of his occupation, were scarred, pitted, calloused and gnarled. He could clean a haddock with his thumbnail, in less time than most men could reach for a knife. He knew how to pack lobsters, alive, so they would not fight and maim one another, and without resorting to pegs driven into their claw joints.

"Don't never eat a lobster from a pound," he said. "He won't taste no better than you would, after you'd been in jail and practically starved."

I think there are few more beautiful sights, of shapes, patterns and colors, than were displayed at the back of Mr. Stowe's zinc-lined cart. The stupid and wasteful practice of chopping "filets" from fish and throwing the most useful and nourishing parts away before the customer saw the fish, had not then been conceived. Mr. Stowe, who had shrewd grey-blue eyes as merry as his cousin Mathilda's, liked best to deal with customers who knew fish when they saw them, and of those there were plenty in Linden. Folks who did not know what they were getting were instructed by Mr. Stowe, and he would sell them nothing that he thought they should not have.

"Mrs. Ford," he would say to the organist, who came from out west in Ohio and knew little about salt water fish, "you don't want me to skin them flounders. Where do you think the flavor is, if it isn't in the skin? Skin 'em after you've fried 'em, if the taste is too strong, but my advice is to eat it and get used to it, and if after three tries you don't like it, I'll give you the choice of my two horses. Is that a bargain?"

The fishman's two horses were named Moody and Sankey, and he used them on alternate days. He could drive them without any reins, which he frequently did, twisting the lines around the whip in its socket, and simply directing them around corners, back and forth across the streets, and wherever he wanted them to go. The Linden cats all followed Mr. Stowe and his cart, sometimes halfway around town, purring happily, with tails held high, and always were rewarded with scraps. He knew them by name, scolded the greedy, encouraged the weak and the timid. He had trained Moody and Sankey to look around, both sides, before they started, to be sure no cat had settled down to eating between the cart wheels, where it might get run over. It was Mr. Stowe who told the Italian hurdy-gurdy man how to keep his monkey alive, after two had died because of the rigorous climate.

"Get a cat to sleep with him," Mr. Stowe said, and the old Italian built a little house with an upstairs compartment for the monkey and a lower for the cat. In the fall, when nights turned cold, and through the winter, the monkey would reach down and haul up the cat, and they would cuddle together. In spring and summer, they rested on their separate levels. Where Mr. Stowe picked up these odd bits of practical knowledge, no one knew, but he solved a host of minor problems.

One of the Freeman boys had an awful case of hiccoughs, which started on Monday and lasted all night. When Mr. Stowe came around, he put a paper bag over the boy's face and told him to breathe ten times. The hiccoughs stopped and big Mattie Freeman stopped crying. Dawson, as generous as he was original, spent days and evenings trying to figure out what a fish dealer would like best as a present, and discussed the matter with all the regulars at the Massasoit.

"Thunderation. He don't smoke cigars, and he gets his liquor for next to nothing," Dawson said. The incoming sailors the fish dealers met around T-wharf in Boston every morning had no great reverence for the customs laws, and made a few extra dollars bringing in imported liquors and the best English cloth, as well as genuine meerschaum pipes, Toledo swords, snakeskins from South America, and other articles highly prized and easily disposed of. Dawson wound up by commissioning a Boston painter to paint a still life of wild ducks and fresh mackerel for Mr. Stowe's dining room. It cost Fred two hundred dollars, and everyone thought he was crazy, but Dawson Freeman never did anything in a picayune way.

I do not know what Mr. Stowe really thought about that oil painting, but he put up a good show, and never called at the Freemans' without admiring Dawson's collection of paintings and remarking how he prized his own.

Mr. Stowe bought his fish at T-wharf about five o'clock in the morning, within sight of the spot where the famous Boston Tea Party had taken place. His haddock were caught in the channels between the offshore islands; scrod and cod came from the hidden ledges off Nahant, Marblehead, Gloucester and all the way along Cape Ann; flounders were sweetest and best from the East Boston flats; smelts swarmed the tidal rivers and the creeks of Linden marsh; salmon came down on the daily Maine boat, alive, from the Penobscot; mackerel and bluefish abounded, in schools of hundreds of thousands that matched to the fraction of a centimeter in all their details; deep-sea halibut and swordfish were found in cold currents, over shell bottoms; lobsters prowled the floor of the ocean all along the North Shore and were taken from traps on the turn of each tide; the finest oysters were raked at Cotuit and Narragansett; the best of all clams were from Ipswich and Annisquam.

"Lutie," Mr. Stowe would say to my mother, whom he had known in Rockport for years, and my father, too, before he died, "Lutie. I've saved these cheeks and tongues for you."

Pollack's cheeks and tongues were a delicacy, comparatively rare. Each trip there were cod's cheeks and tongues, but the cod is a vulgar cousin to the less numerous and more elusive pollack, and the tidbits from the heads of the latter are esteemed by connoisseurs. If my mother had ever heard the words "gourmet" or "connoisseurs'" she would have thought of them as too highfalutin or affected to use. But Brillat-Savarin could have learned enormously from her about the choice and preparation of fresh fish.

So every Tuesday and Friday evening in Linden, when the trains began puffing and clanging to the Linden depot, and hungry men who had worked all day in Boston got off and started fanning out in various directions along the familiar tree-lined streets, the fragrance that would greet them and enliven their progress toward home would be a symphony of the steam from chowder; clams or lobster in seaweed; haddock baking, garnished with home-cured bacon and shallots from the yard; the mysterious and poetic exhalations from deep-sea snails who had strayed into lobster pots; bluefish pan-broiling on one side, to be grilled gently on the other; perfect mackerel, hake, and halibut. From some of the kitchens, where a local housewife was known for her careful cooking, the inviting smells would arrest the commuters, homeward bound, and I regret to say that on one occasion, a couple of good fellows, friends and neighbors for years, before and after, got into a fist fight over the question as to whether birch or willow twigs made the best live coals for grilling salmon.

Those were days. I am not writing about jaded gentlemen with stuffed pocketbooks, in city hotels, but of Linden men and women who thought of supper as a high point in a worthy working day, of dishes worthy of any king's table that cost eighty cents apiece, for a family of four or five, of recipes not from Parmentier, or Savarin, or Escoffier, but coming to Linden from Cape Ann settlers named Tarr, Griffin, Pool, Wetherell, Noble, Bly, Favor, Norcross and Paul. What is a meal? What was ever a meal? Should it be revolting and toxic, convenient and insipid, or evoked from nature's best with reverence, loving kindness and address? What have we, outside of our days and hours? Companions. And what is better for companionship than regard for the table. The kind of health good food engenders cannot be shot into arms or swallowed in pills, amid Philistines and bores. Except frequently at the Massasoit, and in some of the houses, the Linden mealtime conversations were neither witty or inspired. Hearty eaters said little or nothing, and that is as it should be. Civilization has never devised a more stupid convention than requiring a poor devil, faced with course after course of a banquet, to turn first to his right and then to his left and think of something brilliant to say. Talk as much as you like between drinks, but hold your peace while fornicating or eating. Simple abstract grunts, sighs, or ejaculations are sufficient, less distracting, more directly understood.

My Great-Uncle Elijah was one who came to Linden from Cape Ann in 1870, when his trade, that of ship's carpenter, began to show signs of its final decline. He was offered the job of foreman in a small shipyard near the mouth of the Mystic River, and about the same time a relative left his wife, Elizabeth, a snug white house on Salem Street, on the high ground near the top of the Salem Street hill, west of Black Ann's Corner. The house was not nearly as beautiful as many of the cottages Lije had built Down East for other men, but he shingled the roof, replaced the clapboards, and made the building sightly and weatherproof, in spite of its banal proportions.

The little section of Linden, sloping downward to the creek bed from the Salem Street hill, was neat and lovely because of the well-kept houses, yards and flower gardens along the sidewalk, and the fields, with hen yards and corn rows between the back of the houses and the main part of town. There was the rambling white house belonging to Great-Uncle Lije, and across the street, Ruth Coffee's little red cottage with white trimmings, a fountain and dial, and rock garden. Ruth's house was the only one in Linden ever reproduced on the cover of a magazine, but that was years later.

My Great-Uncle Lije was the strongest man in Linden. He could roll boulders with a crowbar that three or four men could not move, or bend horseshoes and pokers, tear decks of cards, and put any man's hand on the counter, at the elbow game. These tricks he did reluctantly and only after extreme provocation, because he was naturally shy and unassuming; and he was uneasy in his mind because, in his best years (between fifty and eighty) his work petered out and he could only be kept busy for wages or on contract, maybe half of the time. The other half of the time, Lije kept busy, and the results were picturesque, if not directly profitable. The land his wife had inherited had been part of a farm, like all the other land in Linden and vicinity; Lije thought he ought not to waste it, so he kept hens, turkeys and ducks, a milk cow that often had a calf, likewise a large and noble Newfoundland dog named Rover who took care of all the neighborhood children, preventing them forcibly from wading or falling into the creek when the tide was high and the water was deep. Lije also had a horse, with buggy, harness, a carryall, a dump cart and a spring wagon. The horse was named Zaccheus, because the first thing he had done as a colt, when Mr. Weeks had tried to hitch him, was to climb an overloaded apple tree and break it down.

Our Linden school copybooks in those days contained the verse:

> *Zaccheus, he*
> *Did climb a tree,*
> *Our Lord to see.*

Great-Uncle Lije was a deacon and a pious man, who could not swear in public and seldom did so in private, and his interminable contest of wills and forces with Zaccheus was epic and amazing. Being a seafaring man, of seafaring ancestors, Lije misunderstood horses in every conceivable way. He thought they were stubborn, like squarehead sailors, and could understand and do what was wanted if they felt like it. I do not know the source of the old English tale about the sea captain who had come ashore for good and was getting married, being late for the ceremony because, riding a saddle horse for the first time in his life, he tacked him back and forth across the field, not knowing he could drive the creature straight into the wind. But it looked as if Great-Uncle Lije was trying to maneuver a catboat, sometimes, when he hitched Zaccheus to a plough and tried to turn furrows, up and down the slope and side by side. The blade would hit a rock, the handles jump, Zach would kick his straw hat off, and the harness, nine times out of ten hooked up the wrong way, would rip or break. My Great-Aunt Elizabeth would watch from a back window, concealed behind a lace curtain, and protest and pray.

"Every ear of corn we raise costs us five dollars," she would say, to my mother and my Aunt Carrie, but never to Lije. A Cape Ann husband was the head of the house, if he was any good at all.

My great-uncle was not hard up for money. He had saved his pay and his profits, when young, and the banks where he deposited his savings were not the ones that failed. He had never had a sick day in his life, and neither had Great-Aunt Elizabeth. Their only son was doing well, with a hardware store in Bangor.

"If Lije would take it easy, when he's off from the shipyards, we could have a fine time and save quite a bit of money," my Great-Aunt Elizabeth said.

"It's no use talking. Men can't do what isn't in their nature," Aunt Carrie, my Uncle Reuben's lovely and long-suffering helpmeet said.

"I'm not asking him to do what's contrary to nature. I only wish the Lord would put in his head not to do what's contrary to his nature."

"The Lord has His work cut out for Him, puttin' things in some men's heads," Aunt Carrie said.

"It's harder taking things out than puttin' 'em in," said my mother reminiscently.

When Tommy Craven's girl, Abbie, our church soprano, married Barney Ewig, an undertaker's assistant from out of town (six miles, in Lynn), the stalwart little English grocer wanted to do things up brown, and held the wedding breakfast in Associate Hall, down behind the depot. Tommy owned the Hall and Abbie was popular, so everyone in Linden wanted to give her a good send-off. My Great-Uncle Lije shined up the buggy, with the wrong kind of polish that smelled like shoe blacking, oiled the harness with whale oil that smelled, according to Uncle Reuben, like sour owl turd, and insisted on driving Great-Aunt Elizabeth to the ceremony behind the outlaw, Zaccheus. My great-aunt began to tremble whenever she saw that horse. She was practically hysterical by the time she got near enough his hindquarters, holding up her long skirts away from the muddy buggy wheel while Lije awkwardly helped her in. It was a beautiful morning for the wedding and the breakfast, and Zach behaved like a thoroughbred all the way to the church. He stayed hitched during the wedding, did not kick or bite the other horses in the shed, refrained from gnawing away the soft boards of the manger, and practically bowed and smiled when Great-Aunt Elizabeth came from the church with Lije. They started toward the Square and the Hall.

"He's up to something," Great-Aunt Elizabeth said. "That miscreant can't fool me."

She was likely to use words out of Laura Jean Libbey, Louisa May Alcott or Harriet Beecher Stowe when other folks would use curse words or phonetic substitutes for profanity.

Zach allowed himself to be hitched behind the depot, then quietly reverted to type. As soon as he was left to his own devices, he unhitched himself, with or without the Devil to help him, crossed Lynn Street to the back entrance of the Hall, walked up a short flight of wooden stairs, let himself into a back pantry, and ate up all the bridesmaids' bouquets, which had come all the way from a florist's in Faneuil Hall, being tastefully arranged with small white rosebuds, forget-me-nots, and other rare flowers not plentiful in Linden. Having finished the flowers, Zach rubbed his head against a sliding panel and found himself looking into the kitchen, where Jeff Lee, his back turned, was doing his stuff. When Jeff turned around, Zach was on his third blueberry pie. The guests were called from the table to see the roguish horse, quite pleased with himself, in the pantry, his muzzle and head stained with blueberry juice almost back to his ears.

Great-Uncle Lije, who was painfully embarrassed when anything called public attention his way, was "mortified," but he would not sell, exchange or give away Zach. I think Lije felt that the Lord had sent Zach to him to see which one would give up first.

According to Linden tradition, my great-uncle was the only man in those parts to have a backhouse blown right out of his hand, without letting go of the door. Lije was one of the last men of adequate means who clung to the outdoor privy, in preference to the effete modern type that he heartily distrusted. To relieve himself, right in the middle of his own dwelling, always made him feel like the bird that sullies its own nest.

173

On a night like the historic one on which the *Portland* went down, Lije felt the urge when the storm was at its peak. Lesser men would have thought of some makeshift, but not Lije. He pulled on some woolen socks and lumberman's rubbers, slipped his heavy mackinaw over his long nightshirt, and tried to find the path through the drifts in the back yard. By the aid of a high rail fence around the barn, he guided himself to the backhouse, with the fury of the blizzard cutting diagonally across his course. Just as he pulled open the door, against the wind, a howling gust tipped over the backhouse, and left him with the door in his powerful hand. The hinges had been torn from their moorings.

So many generations of Lije's ancestors had lived within sight and hearing of the "stern and rockbound coast" that Great-Uncle Lije could not resign himself entirely to being miles up a creek, and he was one of the very few Linden men who kept a boat, in a boathouse just east of the railroad tracks, and navigated it through the labyrinth of the great Linden marshes, to a branch of the Saugus River and thence to the open sea. Both Lije and my father's father, Edwin Paul, had helped build and design the yacht *Petrel,* that, captained by my father, won second place in the toughest boat race then to be found, off Cape Ann; later, after Father sold it to an Australian, it won first money at Sydney, against a field of four hundred English and American craft.

So Great-Uncle Lije's little yawl, with sails and a four horse-power motor he despised, but had to use on the marsh, was called *Petrel II*. I can never remember being in a baby carriage, but have distinct recollections of rowing a dory and helping man the *Petrel II* while still in the first grades of school. Lije never ran her aground in the tricky, shifting shoals of Linden Creek, where the nine-foot tide raced like mad, in and out, for two hours at a stretch each way, and when high, overflowed the banks and hid the channel from all but the most discerning eyes.

My great-uncle and aunt seldom argued. She deferred to his opinions out-of-doors, and he to hers inside. That was the unwritten rule of Cape Ann. But they disagreed, wordlessly, on practically everything, in detail. As a whole, they got along through a marriage that lasted sixty years, and only ceased when Elizabeth died, aged eighty-one. Being cautious folks by nature, they had not married young, but had waited till she was twenty-one. That was because Lije was away, building ships in Maine, while she taught school in Pigeon Cove.

One thing they agreed upon thoroughly. Each year, Lije found time to make a trip in late summer or early fall to catch a winter's supply of cod, to be dried and used for making fish balls. And for that purpose, Lije did not try to raise his own potatoes. None would do, except the ones they bought in sacks from Aroostook County, Maine.

Just lately, some fine singers of American folk songs have sung all over the air a perverted version of one of the saddest songs in the world. The original title was "One Fish Ball," and it brought tears to my eyes whenever Charles would sing it, as he often did while he was attending M. I. T. and after.

There was a man of small renown,
Came to a tavern in the town.

Thus the words started, and went on to tell how this man, who had only a nickel in his pockets, looked fearfully over the menu. "Fish balls, 10 cents," was one of the items. The waiter was at his shoulder. Embarrassed, he ordered "One fish ball."

The waiter, who had few of the finer feelings workingmen should have, brought the single fish ball. The man said, "Some

175

bread and butter if you please." And then the waiter's voice "boomed through the hall."

We don't serve bread with one fish ball.

Modern Americans, from the middle of the country, now sing this song as "One Meat Ball," following the practice of Burl Ives and Josh White and Paul Robeson. Meat or fish, flesh or fowl, it is just as sad and discouraging. I have shed as many tears over those lyrics, and their forceful tune, as any song I know. I should be happy to see inserted in our Constitution a provision that with one fish or meat ball, at least a man is entitled to half a slice of buttered bread and a clean glass of water.

So one evening my Great-Uncle Lije was sitting on his front porch, relaxed and puffing on his powerful corncob pipe, and in the stillness of the twilight air a column of "twisted smokes" arose like incense to the God of his fathers. His mind worked deliberately, never hastily. He knew it was about time for him to go out for cod. While he was about it, he always got enough for us, Aunt Carrie, and a widow named Dunbar, who, old and infirm herself, was taking care of three older, badly crippled and bedridden relatives, in a house just back of the Congregational Church.

Lije glanced at the western sky, and found there what he wanted.

> *Evening red and morning gray,*
> *Sure sign of a fair day.*
> *Evening gray and morning red,*
> *Will bring down rain on the traveller's head.*

That was the proverb New England folks found reliable to heed.

The evening was red, several of the reds, with streaks of robin's-egg blue in between, and higher up, a mackerel sky in dove colors. Lije had seen Hen Richards, the hermit, go clamming that afternoon, and knew that, likely as not, if he met Hen on his way back, before he passed the Massasoit, he could buy a couple of baskets of clams for bait. Lije rose, therefore, left the porch and dumped the ashes from his pipe, being careful to tread them into the turf, and started for the Massasoit House. He said nothing to his wife about his project, because if he didn't get the clams he would have to wait until another day, and there was no use working up the womenfolks for nothing.

My great-uncle was a deacon in the church, and did not often go into the barroom, but he was not a teetotaler, and enjoyed a mug of ale if his wife were not present to feel badly about it. Nick Spratt kept his imported ale, Bass or Burton, at an even temperature, on its side in the keg, not too cold, not too warm, for six weeks before serving it in pewter mugs, so that it would be as still, when poured, as the surface of a pond. Through the windows facing the marsh, Lije saw Hen Richards plodding slowly westward, across the hidden paths through the reeds and sweet grass, and went out to meet him at the stone wall along lower Beach Street. Hen had a gait and carriage all his own. He wore an old derby, high crowned and out-of-date, and held his shoulders erect in an almost military way.

The tide was then low, and starting to come in, so the flats and creek beds gleamed, in mother-of-pearl and rose reflected from the sky. The salt air was fragrant. Late wild roses, sweet fern and bayberry grew along the roadside, and offered their mingled perfumes to the passengers of the open cars to Revere. The two men met, and exchanged a minimum of words, then together they walked back to the Massasoit, where Lije borrowed a couple of lard pails from Jeff Lee. They sat side by side on the worn stone steps, and started shucking. The empty shells dropped steadily on a newspaper spread between them, the clams went into the lard pails. When the pails were filled, Lije asked old Hen to join him in a mug of ale, and left the clams in Jeff's icebox, to be picked up in the morning. Around them sat the Admiral, his own best customer, and a number of the regulars, including Uncle Reuben.

"Going fishing in the morning?" my Uncle Reuben asked.

I arrived at the kitchen door, with a message from Aunt Carrie, just in time to hear the question and see Great-Uncle Lije nod. That was enough for me. Sometimes when he went out in his boat, Lije would send word down to me so I could go with him, but school had just started and I knew that unless I took independent action I would lose out on the voyage for cod that year. So I delivered the message to Reuben, after hearing him say he would go along to lend a hand, hurried home and went early to bed.

For that there also was a proverb:

Early to bed, and early to rise,
Makes a man healthy, wealthy and wise.

CHAPTER ELEVEN

Of Codfish Balls, Continued

I TOOK to bed with me, unobserved, a copy of the Old Farmer's Almanac, and puzzled over the pages that told about the tides. That was the only way I could be sure that I would not be too late. At Boston the next morning the tide would be high at four a.m. and a little later at Nahant. That meant, according to what Great-Uncle Lije had taught me, that at the boathouse in Linden, the high-water slack would start about five a.m.; the *Petrel II*, with its small motor, should shove off about four, buck a slight adverse current for an hour or so in order to reach the branch of the Saugus River, after twisting and turning like a snake for ten miles, when the tide would be going out at a moderate rate, faster and faster as the ocean was nearer.

A gull could fly, if he was so minded, from Linden to the cove inside Bass Point, without travelling more than four miles in a straight line. The *Petrel II*, following the tortuous creek bed, had to cover at least twelve, nine by creek and three on the river. Great-Uncle Lije would start, then, not earlier than four o'clock. I woke up at three, dressed myself silently, and stole downstairs in the dark, without awakening Mother. In the icebox on the back porch I found some slices of meat and some butter. From the breadbox in the pantry I sliced off six slices of bread. In the lettuce patch outside the Massasoit I picked a few fresh leaves, then went over and sat on the stone wall to fix

179

my sandwiches, eat them and wait for Great-Uncle Lije. I heard the clop-clop of Harry Weeks' milk wagon, intercepted him and bought a quart of milk, which I drank.

There was a light in the barroom, and I saw through the windows Uncle Reuben and a few other men who apparently had been up all night. When, just before four o'clock, I saw my great-uncle approaching down Beach Street, to get the clams for bait, I went over to the boathouse and sat on the landing. The tide was still coming in, but slowly. The moon was in the sky, reflected in the bends of the swollen creek. The marsh birds were still asleep. The sun, according to the invaluable almanac, would not rise before half-past five.

Great-Uncle Lije and Uncle Reuben, with lunch box, milk can, clams, and a case of cold beer, arrived at the boathouse ten minutes later and found me there. Only Lije pretended to be surprised.

"You here, my boy?" he asked.

I nodded, and started making myself useful.

They unlocked the boathouse, opened the door, and kicked out the blocks, steadying the *Petrel II* on rollers as it slid down the incline and into the water. While I hopped in and held the boat steady, with the painter half-hitched around a post, they brought out the masts and sails, put the former in their place, with sails furled, and started up the motor. Uncle Reuben stepped in, went to the bow, stretched out, and promptly fell asleep. Great-Uncle Lije took the tiller, and I went amidships, being careful to keep the boat in balance.

The moon grew dimmer as the eastern sky was streaked with white. The great marsh, in the dim light before the dawn, was boundless and mysterious, in dim neutral colors, on which were scrolled the winding creek. Soon, as we moved along, the put-put of the motor woke the water birds, who clucked and drifted. Some tucked their heads under their wings again, and went back to sleep, a few others started feeding. As the tide reached its height and was suspended, gulls, young and old, stirred themselves. Flocks of sandpipers wheeled in formation. A heron stood on one foot, on the bank. Some herring gulls went aloft, then plummeted down to catch minnows.

Patches of seaweed and driftwood bobbed on the surface. Stranded among the reeds were shells of horseshoe crabs. There was no vegetation higher than the coarse marsh grasses. In places the channel was narrow and deep, again it flared and shallowed on the bends. Between the boathouse and the river, Lije steered skillfully, not saying a word. I was busy watching everything, letting each detail of the dawn and the solitary landscape impress itself on my mind. The woods I felt that I understood, after a fashion. The marsh was haunting and vague. It held the quality of a dream that is disturbing but not terrifying, and can neither be forgotten nor remembered. There was restless, soundless life beneath the mud and sand and flowing water, so crazily etched and patterned, remote and primitive, inaccessible and cool.

I liked the feelings the marsh gave me, the chill of the early morning, the racier odors of the mud and clay, the wordless company of my Great-Uncle Lije, and the awareness that, when the time came, Uncle Reuben would awaken and be just as agreeable afloat as he was on shore. He was enormously sensitive about anything human, but moods of nature passed him by. That was not true of Lije, the devout and dutiful Christian. Lije relished all natural manifestations, as proof of the versatility of God. Still, neither Lije nor Uncle Reuben nor any of the men seemed to have much curiosity about the littoral, or the bottom of the sea, or particularly about the cod, which had always meant so much to Massachusetts.

When we were safely headed eastward on the surface of the river, where the currents were not tricky and the shoals were

easy to see and avoid, Lije turned the tiller over to me. He knew
I liked to steer. When we got near the ocean, he took it back
again. He knew where to find the best fishing grounds, where
the cod would be waiting, at a depth of twenty fathoms, over
a submerged ledge three miles off Nahant. The sky was still
cloudy and the water was unruffled when Lije baited his hook,
tested the sinker, and let his line over the side. I did the same.
When the first cod, about eighteen inches long, was hauled in,
hand over hand, by Lije, Uncle Reuben awoke, shook himself,
and glanced toward us.

"Mornin', Lije," he said for the second time.

"It's tolerable," Lije replied.

Uncle Reuben unslung another hand line, baited it skillfully, and started fishing. Lije pulled in another twelve-
pounder, I got a slightly smaller one. Uncle Reuben caught a
haddock.

"I'll save this one for chowder," he said.

"That won't square you with Carrie, for not going home last
night," Lije said. "You'll catch the Old Ned, and who can
blame her?"

"Not I," Reuben said.

"Don't you ever feel ashamed?" Lije asked.

"Shame?" repeated Reuben, with mock indignation. "Do
you know a better, more saintly woman in Linden than Carrie is?"

"Can't say as I do," admitted Lije.

Reuben looked at him gravely. "And who keeps her that
way?" he demanded.

"She does, and Our Heavenly Father," said Lije, drily.

"They don't do any such thing," Reuben said. "I do."

"Getting full every night, and chasing other women?" Lije
said, skeptically.

"I furnish her the trials and tribulations," Reuben said. "A fine woman like Carrie don't get the best in her brought out except by a sinful man like me. Just an ordinary husband couldn't do the trick. Her qualities wouldn't get a fitting workout. Some day, when she's sitting pretty, in the sky, she'll thank me for all this."

"You won't be there," Lije said.

"She'll find some way of sending me word, wherever I am," Reuben said.

They fished away in silence and, as usual when I found adult conversation interesting or illuminating, I pretended not to pay attention to a word. I was catching fish steadily, until my arms were aching: cod, with a few pollack, a hake and a haddock.

Lije was inclined to pursue the argument. "You mean to say," he said to Uncle Reuben, "that if I got plastered and was profane and idle, and couldn't pass up a skirt, that Elizabeth would be better off?"

"Sin don't come natural to you, Lije," Reuben said tolerantly. "Still, you aren't as bad off as some I could name. Now and then you have a good time."

"That isn't what we're put here for," Lije said.

"Any idea just what we were put here for?" Reuben asked.

"That's the Lord's affair, not ours," said Lije.

They stopped talking, and I began thinking about the cod, not only the ones that lay glistening and suffocating in the bottom of the boat, but the myriads below, feeding over the hidden ledge, and the quadrillions in the rest of the Atlantic. Miss Stoddard had made me feel profoundly about codfish, more numerous than all the peoples of the earth, dead or alive, from the beginning of time; pursuing their relentless existence in water far below the freezing point; devouring anything and everything that came their way. Hundreds of millions were caught each year, and those left behind did not even miss them. Looking out over the ocean, I thought how much more water there was than land, that formerly the earth had been covered with water, that there were fishes, and probably cod, before there had been trees, or birds, or animals or men. Miss Stoddard had told me about Darwin, and evolution. Our Linden marshes, or others like them, had been spread over vast areas of continents, slowly drying, she had said.

Every time I went with Lije, in a boat, from the boathouse across the marsh by the twisted little creek, to the flowing river, and thence to the sea, I felt that I was taking an excursion into history and prehistory, something far back of the Indians who had roamed in the woods, the Balm of Gilead tree, the *Mayflower*, the first Linden settlers. None of this feeling I communicated to Lije or Uncle Reuben. They were, like most New England people, a little hostile to anyone who thought he knew too much.

Just a year or two before, I had made myself unpopular by asking first my brother Charles, then Fred Tarr, Gimp Crich, Uncle Reuben, and Great-Uncle Lije, in turn, whether fishes slept. They had all spent their lives among fishermen, and not only were unable to answer the question, but showed by their manner that it surprised them and that they had not thought about the matter before.

I must not leave the impression that my Uncle Reuben was a weak or ineffectual character. In the Linden of his time, it took more stamina to be a sinner than to live by the Book. Uncle Reuben's personality, in spite of the efforts of his parents and relatives, and later his wife and her church associates, to reform him, went through life unchanged. What bothered those who wanted most to restrain him, or disapproved most strongly of his mode of life, was the awareness that his free-and-easy ways were not bringing him the remorse, anguish and disgrace that should follow a dissolute youth, as season followed season.

To me he represented good sense and freedom. From whatever angle I considered his life, I found myself warm with admiration. For one thing, he had no steady occupation which required that he rush his breakfast and catch an early morning train, or get into a duster and straw hat and work long hours in a store, or hold down a job as station agent in order to study law. He took his own time about everything, got up when he felt able, went to bed when he was too tired to drink any more, liked men and women, practically all of them, and even his sternest critics had a tolerant gleam in their eyes, and smiled when they did not mean to, in commenting on his activities. What made Uncle Reuben perfect, from my point of view, was the fact that he made considerable money, while having a riotous good time. How he managed it, no one ever knew, exactly. He bought and sold real estate, or boats, or horses, carriages, wagons, crops, and now and then, after consultation with Mr. Wing, took a flyer in what was mysteriously known as "the market," and which was considered by most of the conservative middle-class Linden folks as one of the more dangerous of the Devil's domains.

On our way back from the fishing grounds, after sun-up, we saw in the distance a three-masted schooner, with some kind of a foreign rig not in vogue with Down-Easters. It was motionless and listed at an angle that indicated it had gone aground, in the shallows off Nahant.

"Shall we take a look?" Uncle Reuben asked.

Lije was reluctant to digress or delay. He liked to finish trips the way he planned them. The question was solved by the appearance of a Portuguese fisherman in a big gray motor boat that smelled to heaven and, from Lije's point of view, had never been properly cleaned since it first had left the yards.

Uncle Reuben hailed the Portuguese, who was as easygoing as himself and was headed for the wreck just to pass the time. I wanted very much to go with Uncle Reuben, and he would have invited me, had he been sure that he would get home that night. Whenever I got home, I was in for a bad time because of school that day. In my eagerness to go fishing—or rather, to take that mysterious voyage across the marshes—I had ignored the fact that we would not get back until two hours or more after school had started. So I had to stick with Great-Uncle Lije, helping clean the boatload of fish as he steered the *Petrel II* into the Saugus River. The tide now was coming in, and had started to run rather fast. The Linden Creek that twisted and turned from the river to the Saugus Branch tracks and the boathouse, and all the way through Linden, would be a mere trickle of water between the still pools in the meadows, but by the time we got to it, the water would be high enough. As soon as we were safely on the river, Lije wordlessly relinquished the tiller to me and took over the fish-cleaning job. Whatever those old-school New England men did, they did skillfully. They raced each other, shucking clams, cleaning fish, or picking berries. If two of them were picking up potatoes, or nailing up boxes of sardines, or sawing in the lumber woods, or playing Casino on the morning train, there was stiff competition. One tried to keep ahead of the other. They wore themselves out, proving they were better men than others were. When once I asked my music mentor, Mr. Wing, a New Yorker, why it was the men who sang loud in church were always ahead of the organ and each other, he explained this New England characteristic.

"It wouldn't do for one of them to let the others beat him," Mr. Wing said.

I had felt the instinct to race with everyone, and all my life have alternately yielded to it or fought it on principle. I cannot say which is harder. But I always envied, and still envy, men like my late Uncle Reuben who felt no urge to surpass their fellows in unimportant ways.

The Portuguese who picked up Uncle Reuben and took him to see the wreck off Nahant had been a sailor, years before he sailed to America and stayed here. He had a small supply of red wine in a leather flask. Uncle Reuben shared it. They learned that the wreck had a cargo of dried herring and cheese, then headed for Bass Point, hove to, and went to a fisherman's saloon for more refreshment. The place was lively that morning, because most of the crew from the stranded schooner, all Portuguese, were drinking there, and had brought up a bunch of women from Lynn.

With a few good drinks under his belt, my Uncle Reuben seemed to be able to communicate with men or women in practically any language, although he did not know more than six words of each. Having spent two hours with Jorge, the Portugee, whom he called Horky, they were already firm friends. The only music available for the foreign sailors and their women from Lynn to dance by was a small accordion in bad repair, played by a local blind man who could see much better in saloons than in the streets, during the busy summer season. However, the Italian proprietor of the saloon brought out a fiddle and a bow, and Uncle Reuben took over. Not only could he play the old square dance tunes, with gusto, but could turn in a creditable "Over The Waves," "My Bonnie Lies Over The Ocean," and another waltz tune the words of which concerned a brave sea captain who went down with his ship.

Soon the Bass Point saloon was very gay. The solid old flooring of pumpkin pine, strewn with sawdust, rumbled and clicked beneath the tread of seamen's boots and women's high-heeled slippers. The Italian proprietor drafted two male cousins into service to take advantage of the boom in business.

Seated on a stout barroom Windsor atop an equally stout table, was my Uncle Reuben, bearing down on the strings and singing, in his hearty baritone:

> *I'll stay by the ship, boys,*
> *You save your lives.*
> *I have no one to miss me,*
> *You have each other's wives.*

From somewhere, a strapping Swede girl showed up, and danced and drank with Uncle Reuben while the sailors sang foreign songs to the tune of the accordion. When the lobstermen got in, the Italian sent his fat wife down to buy enough to fill two wash boilers.

Reuben, smelling the fragrant steam of the lobsters cooking, dragged his Swede girl out back, to the kitchen, and insisted on making Johnnycake. The fat Italian wife looked on, beaming, and the proprietor, ordinarily fiendishly jealous, did not mind when Uncle Reuben flattered her outrageously and patted her playfully under the chin. He, and all the others, had taken a great fancy to Uncle Reuben, and felt as if they had known him all their lives. When they tasted his Johnnycake, along with the steamed lobsters and butter, not to mention the strong black coffee, Italian style, that cleared their heads for the afternoon and evening drinking, all hands liked Uncle Reuben even more.

There were a couple of bedrooms upstairs, not intended for transients. They were occupied, ordinarily, by the two young daughters of the Italian, but, having seen the way things were starting out that morning, the proprietor had exercised his customary forethought and sent the two young girls, under protection of a very strict aunt, all the way to Chelsea, where they were to stay, carefully nurtured and chaperoned, until further notice.

Uncle Reuben was having the time of his life. That is what he seemed to do at least every other day. Alma was strong and receptive, jolly and handsome, and seemed to be wholesomely unattached. She and Uncle Reuben withdrew, from time to time, to have a look at the rest of the house. So did various couples of Portuguese, and an Irish girl or two who came over after the shoe factories in Lynn closed for the night. In the kitchen, at evening, the fat Italian wife had prepared two or three huge roasts of beef, a couple of hams, Italian squash, and took down from a rafter a large Provolone cheese.

"What kind of cheese was in the schooner?" Uncle Reuben asked Horky, as they ate fresh Italian bread and Provolone, at the end of their second huge meal.

"It wasn't like this," Horky said. "This comes from a—a— what is it, Mr. Paul, you call in English a horse with two ass holes?"

"You mean a mare," my Uncle Reuben said.

"That's it!"

"Was it Portugee cheese?" Reuben persisted.

"I think it was Dutch," Horky said, after consultation with the Portuguese sailors.

I do not know all the details of the gamble that, along with the harmless revelry, was forming itself in my Uncle Reuben's mind. I picked up several of them, one way or another, after he had got home to Linden, about four days later. He did not return, bleary eyed and tired, with wrinkled clothes and soiled linen. Instead, he got off the Boston train, the 6:10, one evening, debonairly. He had on a new dark gray suit, of the finest imported woolen, new boots with elastic sides, a diamond ring and stickpin, a light-colored vest, a new derby, with a fine wide

189

brim, a plum-colored four-in-hand tie, leather gloves, and a topcoat "too light for winter and too heavy for fall."

He had remarked the angle at which the stranded schooner was listed, had made a good guess as to where the cargo was stowed, and how it lay, with respect to the water that had leaked into the hold. He knew that tubbed salted herring would not be damaged much by a little sea water, and that there was a lively demand for Holland cheese in the Faneuil Hall market just then. In the course of his pleasant adventure, he had met the captain, found out the name and address of the commission agent who handled the cargo, had drawn from the Boston banks all the money he had, and Aunt Carrie's money that had been left her by her father and Reuben had promised her he would never touch, and had taken a chance that most of the cargo could be retrieved and sold before the schooner went to pieces. Uncle Reuben knew the sand bar and the ledge where she was hung up, the way the tides and currents ran. He had used his best judgment about weather prospects, and he won his flyer.

When he showed up in Linden, four days after our fishing trip, the merchandise had been salvaged and resold, at a good profit. Aunt Carrie's money was back in the bank. My uncle had two or three outfits of new clothes and some diamonds. Aunt Carrie had a fur coat and yards and yards of Chinese silk. The Swede girl had a nice room in Boston, which she had badly wanted, some good clothes, and a job with the commission agent. Our fishing trip had netted him at least five thousand dollars, and fifty of the excellent cod which were drying on the racks in Lije's back yard.

Some Widows and Old Maids

NO MATTER how reticent a Linden resident might be, or how he shunned contact with his neighbors, no one's life was entirely his own. What he said and did, or what he failed to say or do, was noticed, discussed, embellished, interpreted and disseminated throughout the town, as public property. If a man seemed too anxious or insistent upon having folks believe this or that about his past, his current situation, or his prospects, the instinct of the Linden people was to scrutinize his claims extra carefully. Their minds would not be closed, but open just a crack. On the other hand, if anyone in Linden seemed to have anything to conceal, his neighbors would dedicate themselves to acquiring information without asking it directly from him. And if a man brought the focus of the community's attention upon himself as an equation with unknown quantities, a woman in Linden who had elements of the mysterious was yeast to everyone's curiosity.

In Linden today, few people would recognize many of the men and women who lived two streets away. There are other things to think about, other problems, other entertainments. Who is to decide which is the more interesting and worthwhile: the daily fate of Stella Dallas, or the movements of Hen Richards, Linden's hermit, whose past was never disclosed; the deductions of Hercule Poirot, or the detective work concerning Daisy Hoyt and Packard, in the Ladies' Social Circle; the astronomical proportions of Lend Lease, or the microscopic depletion of the bills and coins in Mrs. Townsend's vase.

The majority of dwellers in old Linden had never exchanged a word with the Dexter sisters, for instance, and even fewer had been inside their house, where in the front rooms on the street level they conducted their pitiful "Bazaar." Still, how many of our neighbors and townspeople felt sorry for them, perhaps made fun of them, wondered how they paid their rent, what they ate and how they cooked it, how much it cost them for their slightly grotesque clothes. Linden people whom the Dexter women had never bowed to, and whose names they did not know, discussed the weird sisters, tried to find out if they had relatives somewhere, and, if so, why the relatives never put in an appearance. Where had the sisters been born? Their way of speech and formal manners, prim, but not subservient, mild, but with a certain inner assurance, indicated an aristocratic origin, in a family that had seen better days.

Laura and Ottilie Dexter had lived side by side so many years, in the kind of seclusion that was defensive, against the world outside, and suffered mildly from what the French call *folie à deux*. That means the merging of two personalities, isolated from all others, into one that is eccentric or mad. When Laura spoke, Ottilie was likely to finish the sentence or supplement it with a similar one that confirmed it. Whatever they said to tradesmen or customers was likely to end with: "Isn't it, Laura?" or "I'm right, am I not, Ottilie?" They stood side by side at the range or the kitchen table as they prepared their frugal meals, functioning like a piano duet in a sister act. They dressed almost alike, but never exactly alike. It seemed as if they were trying to present an identical appearance, but, like whatever else they attempted, their skill was not equal to their conception. Somewhere their hands and eyes were sure to go astray. It was the same in the tiny articles of embroidery

192

and needlework they offered for sale. The patterns looked like children's drawings. The embroidered flowers, forget-me-nots or pansies, seemed to hide idiot cherubs' faces in their lines and curves and spots. Their borders were never quite even. Their embroidered puppies and kittens were insidiously monstrous and sent a chill down one's spine.

Aware that they were unable to costume themselves with distinction, they did not dare to attempt dressmaking, which, if they had been able to do it, would have been more profitable, or less unprofitable. On one occasion, they presented themselves, trembling with dread and sure in advance of the failure of their mission, to the manager of a Malden dry goods store, asking employment as salesladies. They offered to do the work of two for the wages of one, to counterbalance their lack of experience. Naturally, the man was obliged to refuse them. Their vibrant anxiety defeated them. He was unnerved himself. They were fifty years old, and forty-eight, respectively, unworldly in appearance, and both had voices that were high and hollow, large eyes that rolled like those of owls, beak-like noses and very small mouths. They were tall, for women, and painfully thin. What their excursion to Malden cost them, in days and weeks of tremulous conferences and long pressure of necessity, no one knows. I only know that Dawson Freeman, admirer of Tom Lawson and his revolutionary "Frenzied Finance," and the terror of every hired girl his wife brought into the house, heard about the application from some of the thoughtless neighborhood boys who thought it was a joke. Dawson showered the boys with a torrent of reproach, until he actually had tears in his eyes; then, quietly, he slipped around the back way, via Clapp Street, Oliver Street and Elm Street, getting mud on his spats, entered the Dexter sisters' "bazaar," hoping to God that none of the Massasoit regulars would see him, flattered and jollied the tall despairing sisters until they were giddy, and bought practically everything they had on display: absurd pin cushions, pathetic tea cosies, doilies, handkerchiefs, sachet bags.

Long into the night, after Dawson had left them, the Dexter sisters sat silently, in their front room lighted only by the nearby street lamp on the sidewalk (which saved them buying kerosene), on a ridiculous undersized sofa of stuffed plush, sighing happily, saying, "Think of it, Laura," or "Ottilie, we should have had more faith," and holding each other's long and bloodless hands.

What Dawson Freeman did with his collection of embroidery no one knows. He said nothing about it to his wife, or anyone in Linden. The next morning, he had some large packages when he took the train for Boston. As usual, he waited for the other three businessmen who occupied the two seats facing each other in the smoking car to finish their newspapers. That occurred by the time the train got to Malden Center. From there on, through Edgeworth, Bell Rock, East Somerville and into the North Station, Dawson, fine Havana cigar in hand, talked to them with resonant voice and gleaming eyes, about the evils of State Street and Wall Street, and Teddy Roosevelt's latest crusade.

Dawson was a collector by instinct. First, when he was furnishing his new house, diagonally opposite the Clapp mansion where his wife was born, and exactly opposite Don Partridge's house, where his wife's sister presided, he took a fancy to a Boston landscape painter who exhibited in one of the art galleries near the Boston Public Library in Copley Square. This painter, Claude Barnett, had lived most of his artistic life on Huntington Avenue and no doubt was tired of the city streets and buildings, blended into a dirty gray by the cinders from the New York, New Haven and Hartford locomotives. So Barnett painted mostly sheep and cattle in lush green meadows, à la

Constable, on the banks of streams that were a tribute to Corot. He belonged to the school that laid the paint on thick and roughened their textures with a palette knife. The skies were in the prevailing American style, dim near the horizon, breaking up into cirrus clouds like puffballs a little higher up, with a clear band of blue.

Through Barnett and his canvases, all framed in heavy gilt mouldings, Dawson brought contemporary art to Linden. As far as I know, he was the only one in Linden who ever paid out good money for oil paintings. If a man of means had two or more daughters, and one of them was learning to play the piano, it was not uncommon then for another daughter to study drawing and painting. Anne Partridge, née Clapp, took lessons from Barnett and in the course of time turned out creditable examples of his style and subject matter. Because I was obsessed in my grammar school years with the desire to paint, and had covered yards of canvas, beaverboard and Japanese drawing paper with sketches in pencil, pen and ink, water colors and oil colors, Mrs. Partridge kindly relayed to me the lessons Barnett gave her.

Painting, as then taught by the successful painters and teachers around Boston, involved a copious use of one of the muddiest colors and stickiest substances known to man, called "Bitumen." Barnett advised his pupils to cover the entire canvas first with a layer of bitumen and wait for it to dry. In that way, one started with a groundwork of what my Uncle Reuben called "deep fart color," instead of the dim white or light gray of the canvas. The sky was left until last, but as the painting progressed, one was encouraged to wipe one's brushes not on rags, but where the clouds would be, to build up an appropriate sky, as well as to effect an interesting minor economy.

The walls of Dawson Freeman's new house were covered with gold-framed landscapes by Barnett, and when all the wall space was filled, Dawson leaned a few against some of the tables and chairs in the parlor, the sitting room, and the spare bedrooms, and stood a few on the floor of the "finished" attic, to the slight inconvenience of the men who played pool or billiards there. More than once, a player put his heel or the butt of his cue through a Barnett masterpiece, and afterward Dawson would display the painting, skillfully mended by the master so that the break was invisible, with greater pride than the unrepaired scenes.

The first man in Linden to throw himself, heart and soul, into the collection of phonograph records was Dawson. He had every cylinder record that Edison put out, and I daresay that if his collection is intact today, it will be worth as much money as the Freeman house, the Barnett paintings, and the rest of the personal property he left his children when he died. Dawson deluged the countryside with Liberty Bonds during World War I, and escaped disillusion by dying before World War II broke out.

Oriental rugs were the target of Dawson's next burst of zeal. He tangled with an Armenian named Hagop Bogigian, who had a flourishing rug business on Boylston Street and a large experimental farm in Brighton. They met in the halls of the Massachusetts State House, where both of them were seen yearly, in support of their pet legislative projects, neither of which seemed to have any other adherents.

Dawson's bill, which was defeated year after year, was designed to separate policies of life and endowment insurance. That, in Dawson's eyes, seemed essential to the future of the race. Bogigian, the huge Armenian, jousted as gallantly for the protection of game birds. Bogigian loved exotic fowl. He kept peacocks, pheasants, quail and ptarmigan on his Brighton estate. When the Boston Elevated Railroad terminated one of its first suburban surface car lines in his vicinity, hunters from

dier than most. By the new schoolhouse she would cross the tracks to Eastern Avenue, take a back lane to avoid Linden Square and the sight of the depot where Charley had worked so faithfully and long, and at the moment the five o'clock fire alarm sounded, first the Maplewood bell, then the Malden whistle, she would open the front door of her little yellow house, where she lived alone, and disappear. A schoolgirl in her neighborhood was paid twenty-five cents a week for doing her errands. Aside from the daily walks, by the progress of which one could set his clocks, Miss Carberry showed herself only in church. A deep hush was felt when she entered and started down the aisle. She looked neither to right nor left. Her pew she shared with no one. She was never referred to as an old maid, but was grouped with the widows, at the head of the class.

Rena dropped out of the Ladies' Social Circle when Charley died, as she had dropped out of everything else. Her small yard, with its willow tree and chokecherry tree, and blackberry bushes, the tiny lawn and flower beds, which previously had fairly exploded with huge peonies, was left untended. The picket fence rotted, and fell away in small sections, leaving a few pickets and posts in disarray.

On lovely days, the sight of this dark wraith, as she moved around the edge of the town, speaking to no one, seeing nothing clearly through the mazes of her veil, thinking thoughts with ill-matched wings that floundered in circles—was a harbinger of misfortune. Women who watched her would wonder why, if she wanted so badly to die and join her fiancé, she stuck so grimly to her program of daily exercise. On stormy days, folks said she was trying to catch pneumonia, in order to die as Charley had died.

After church each Sunday, the minister stationed himself at the head of the right-hand aisle, facing the pulpit, to shake hands with his departing parishioners. Miss Carberry, to avoid having to shake hands or speak to anyone, went hurriedly out on the left-hand side. The members of the Social Circle tried calling on her, without success. She received them, and sat with them in her parlor, the windows of which were obscured with underbrush growing wild outside. They tried to sustain a conversation. She could not. The minister was helpless in the matter. She had not renounced her faith in God. She was not able to decide about it, and wanted no help or interference.

Her face, seen dimly through the veil, seemed to get smaller, as years went by, and as yellow as old parchment. Her neck became leathery and scrawny, as thin as a turkey's. Her hands looked like claws.

At first, everyone in Linden was shaken with sympathy on account of her loss. It was Linden's loss, too. Charley Moore, always so genial and accommodating, always stooped over his books when the trains were not due or the telegraph ceased clicking. He had been so honest that he was chosen as stakeholder, no matter who was betting. He arranged purchases and deliveries in Boston for the Linden housewives, through a practicing Christian brakeman on the Saugus Branch line. He umpired football and baseball games, and no one questioned his decisions. He spoke when flagpoles were dedicated on the Fourth of July, and in Republican rallies when the politicians needed someone whose integrity was beyond cavil. In another five years, added to the ten he had studied out of school, he would have been a self-taught lawyer. That his relations with Rena, during the twelve years of their engagement, had been strictly decorous, was never in doubt.

There are not many communities today in which the widows and old maids form such an important section of the social structure. Deep mourning, among Protestants at least, is almost a thing of the past. And unmarried women today have so many fields of endeavor open to them, and care so little about sexual technicalities, that in some respects they are looked upon as luckier than women with husbands, and who have to open cans, run vacuum cleaners, make formula for babies, ask their husbands for money, and at the same time keep their looks and figures, and dress like motion-picture stars.

Along the entire length of Beach Street, from Salem Street hill down to the Square, the houses containing women without men were numerous, indeed. The Dexter sisters at the top of the hill were spinsters. A few doors down on the left, the widow Plummer mourned Deacon Plummer, all alone, their only son having gone west (to Cleveland) because the only factory work for which he had been trained had shifted westward, too. Mrs. Channing, who lived opposite, facing Spring Street, was a widow, too, but she was occupied morning and night, with her son, Edgar, and it is hard to see how she could have been happier if her husband had still been alive. Candidly, it was well known that Mrs. Channing had not got on very well with the late Mr. Channing after Edgar had been born. The uncharitable ones said she had neglected her husband shamefully. Others, with only children, believed the late Mr. Channing was unreasonable in his demands for attention and that her treatment of him served him right.

The untimely death of Edgar, on account of a brain tumor no doctors then were able to diagnose in time, in his early high-school years, transformed Mrs. Channing into one of the most irreconcilable widows, who would have nothing whatever, from that moment onward, to do with a God who could treat folks that way.

Mrs. Ford, the patient, sweet-faced organist and Sunday School teacher, was a semiwidow, that is, her husband was unable to work or to be an active husband because of tuberculosis, in Linden called "consumption." She encouraged her husband's hobbies, the making and flying of magnificent box

kites and the collecting and classification of sea plants. He had
an entire room filled with albums (loose-leaf records had not
then come into vogue), and I spent many an afternoon, bewildered, stimulated and enchanted, enjoying the variety of
colors, patterns and forms and trying to picture to myself the
meadows, plains, ledges and forests, and the silent life that
flourished in submarine areas, far greater than those of the
continents. Mr. Ford, tall, mild-mannered, with a wistful kind
of humor, spent as much time and effort with his kites and
seaweed as almost any man in Linden did with profitable ven-
tures. Mr. Ford was never known to make or collect anything
salable, and his consumption never seemed to get the better
of him. In fact, he outlived his healthy wife by several years.
Mrs. Ford did plain and fancy sewing, gave piano lessons,
played for weddings and funerals, and in sundry quiet ways
earned their living. They must have been deeply in love, at
one time, and the charm of it lasted, dim and plastic, like the
tints and designs of the pressed sea plants, reminiscent and
unchangeable. I liked to be in their flat, above Puffer's store,
looking over Clapp's truck garden from the front windows,
and the creek and Weeks' field on the eastern side. It was one of
the calmest places indoors in Linden. Technically I learned
exactly nothing. I seemed to be allergic to formal learning.
The scientific or common names of the sea plants I ignored,
unless the sound of them struck my fancy. I cared little for the
groups and species and families. The physics and mechanics
involved in making kites that would soar while others dived
and crashed ignominiously meant nothing to me, but I reveled
in their proportions and lines. If Mr. Ford had four kites in his
little upstairs workshop, and I selected one because it struck me
as being beautiful, he would be pleased, because more often
than not it would also be the one that flew the best. In fact, he
often asked me about the "looks" of a kite and if I thought it

looked lopsided or topheavy he would adjust it, and both of us were happy if I had been right.

Next on Beach Street came number 63, our house. My mother was another of the widows and while the main compartment of her life was closed and never entered thereafter, when my father died in 1895, she did not wear mourning long, except on the thirtieth of each May, when she took the train to Rockport and put flowers on his grave. She did not ask any of her children to accompany her until twenty years later, or so, when my brother Leslie used to drive her down in the Ford. Mother's occupation was in fitting the small bills and coins into the family necessities, and this she did, by dint of constant application and ingenuity that was tinged with fear. Mother's nerves had been shaken, by Father's illness and death, to such a point that she worried all the time she was awake, and suffered from frightful nightmares much of the time she was asleep. My own nerves responded, like the strings of an instrument that vibrate sympathetically when another instrument is played, and I felt easier on the days and nights when Mother was worrying about small things than when she was harassed by more menacing problems. I slept as lightly and fitfully as she did, and many times each night awakened her, to stop her screaming, while Leslie, in an alcove nearby, slept like a top. The result was that Leslie, with his steady nerves and even disposition, was the best company for Mother, and soothed her, while I increased her anxiety and uneasiness. She got up early and built the kitchen fire, or revived it, planned and cooked the meals so that we ate like princes without spending as much for the family as most people spent who lived alone. Mother not only cleaned the house daily, and did the washing and ironing (except the stiff collars and boiled shirts), but twice a year gave the premises such a going-over that nothing seemed the same for weeks afterward. Rugs and carpets were taken up and beaten, odds and ends in the attic and the cellar were shifted and rearranged. Sometimes the piano was in the sitting room, again it was rolled into the parlor. The writing desk, the chairs, the sewing machine, the dining-room table and highboy and lowboy, the beds and commodes and dressers upstairs in the bedrooms, all seemed to be moving and swaying, forward and back, swinging their partners, sashaying, *dos à dos*. Finding one's way in our house, after dark, following the spring and fall housecleaning, was hazardous in the extreme.

Mother did the morning "chamber work" at a furious, almost desperate speed, and her footsteps, usually so soft and uninsistent, would thump back and forth, until it seemed, downstairs, that a number of recruits were practicing squads-right and left.

Monday was the day for washing, and if the weather permitted (grudgingly, if at all), the Linden clotheslines would be strung from corner to post and on them the washes would be spread, white and colored, striped, spotted and checkered, until the little community looked like a giant battleship in full array of flags and pennants. The day when Linden housewives first sent their "white wash" to steam laundries was the occasion for many quarrels, and broke up quite a few families, as did the shift from homemade bread to the baker's product. Those were crises, on the path to progress, the catch being that no steam laundry ever did the white wash as well as my mother and her neighbors did, and no bread made in commercial quantities could compare with the delicious, fragrant "staff of life" my mother and the others brought forth from their bread pans and ovens. Today I can recall the smell of yeast, as Mother mixed the dough and left it overnight, to rise. I stood watching it, sometimes, trying to see it rising, and forming a conception of changes infinitely slow, to match the speeds that all around us were increasing.

204

Mother did remarkable things with the leftovers from the Sunday dinner, to feed us on Monday, dishes that did not take too much time to prepare, so that she could finish the washing and hang the clothes out on the line. Tuesday was ironing day, with a fragrance of its own, and either a chowder would be creating itself slowly on the back of the stove, or the fresh fish brought by Mr. Stowe would be fried, creamed, baked or broiled for supper.

Saturday was the heavy baking day. No pies or cakes or puddings in our house were brought in, ready-made. Mother started baking early in the morning, and finished in the middle of the afternoon. All week she planned breakfast, dinner and supper, for whoever was at home, and when she was alone she ate the things the rest of us did not like and she liked particularly. Each individual taste at the table was considered. Leslie did not like raisins and I did, so the mincemeat was made, some with raisins, some without, and the pie was composed in sectors, with marks on the upper crust to delineate the raisin and non-raisin areas. Mother knew which part of a roast each of us preferred, which cuts of fowl, which kinds of fish. If one of us got the worst of it in the entrée course, he was favored for the dessert. Mother had a dainty appetite. She took small helpings and ate them slowly, her principal interest being focussed on the rest of us. Her only worry about my eating was that I ate like a longshoreman, and stayed thin as a rail. She was afraid I ran too much, or had a tapeworm.

In Mrs. Stoddard's house across the street, there was Lydia Stoddard, a widow of forty years' standing, and her daughter, Mary, the town's most dynamic old maid.

Lydia Stoddard lived in her attic, in her high four-posted bed, her rocking chair, and at the clover-leaf table. In her day she had been a steady and discriminating reader, and must have had a dozen correspondents, contemporary men and women in society and diplomacy, with whom she exchanged letters during decades. Mary Stoddard was criticized for many, many acts, of commission and omission. Every Sunday a number of the Linden women would call her to account, behind her back, for letting her eighty-year-old mother get on a street car alone and ride to Malden Center to attend the First Baptist Church in Malden Square. The fact was that Mary tried, every Sunday, to go with her mother, not caring particularly whether she went to the Baptist Church, to her own Episcopalian, or to none at all. Lydia, the old lady, was more headstrong even than her willful daughter, and insisted that she had not reached the point where she needed a nurse or a keeper.

I think no one in Linden understood her times, recorded history and science, and her neighbors better than Mary Stoddard did, but she was helpless to influence them. She was too ugly for anyone to marry, and if she had been handsome, any suitor of hers would have had to leave his will and opinions outside on the coat and hat rack.

When she was about forty-five, Mary succumbed to a lifelong desire to have a pet cat. One Saturday she brought him home, quite a while after her old mother had died, and she had sold her house and rented a room at the Dexters'. Miss Stoddard placed the handsome yellow half-Persian tomcat on a garnet plush chair and stood back to contemplate the spectacle. Schley, named for the Spanish War admiral, was aloof and very photogenic. Daintily he lapped his milk, waved his plumy tail, and almost as daintily rode big dogs down Beach Street hill, clawing steadily the while, if they annoyed him.

Mary Stoddard turned to me, as near to a companion as she had, and said, shaking her head judicially and ruefully:

"Elliot. I shall end by being too fond of cats. You will see."

That is just what she did. More and more she confided in Schley, talked to him aloud, sang to him, and then, one unlucky day, when she left the offices of Photo Era on a Saturday noon, she saw a starving, draggled cat in an alley nearby, and, trying to approach it, frightened the animal, which was frantic, and spent the afternoon unsuccessfully trying to find it.

On the first streetcar to Boston the next morning, Sunday, Miss Stoddard rode forth, with milk and liver, flea powder and a comb. She haunted the alley and because that district was quiet on Sunday, she found the stray cat, won its confidence and intended to carry it to the Animal Rescue League. The cat, when Miss Stoddard tried to take it up, scratched and went into a panic, getting clean away.

From then on, for many days, Miss Stoddard did not get home to supper until eight or nine o'clock. Her supper, eaten in her room above the Dexters', consisted of cocoa, cheese and animal crackers. As soon as her office work was done, Miss Stoddard took from her desk drawer the milk, meat, powder and comb and fed and groomed the alley cat, which now was tamer and seemed contented with life. Thinking of the cats in cages, waiting for homes in the Rescue League haven, Miss Stoddard decided that the alley cat was happier as things were. The cat, a female Miss Stoddard named "Minerva," improved in health until she became attractive to the Boston stray toms and what resulted posed another problem to Miss Stoddard.

"Elliot," she said. "There is no end to this. I know this is folly. Intelligent people, like you and me, should not be softhearted. We start by doing what we can, and finish by being overwhelmed."

Nevertheless, she spent a night in the alley, helping the cat with her kittens, tramped all the way to the Charles River and drowned all but one, a semitortoise-shell color. The re-

207

bellious agony she suffered, because she had to do this, I sensed very well, but she did not ask me to accompany her.

"This is their reward for being females," she said, grimly. "I am being kind."

When she lost her job, on account of her age, Miss Stoddard devoted all her time and her savings to hunting stray cats, between dawn and business hours, in the alleys of Boston, among the ash cans and milk bottles and other modern manifestations of the rosy-fingered goddess, Aurora. My first few books were published before Miss Stoddard died, and although trite remarks had always been discouraged between us, I can say now, truthfully, that without her influence they never would have been written. I have an almost pathologically strong sense of my own individuality, and seldom feel as if I were another person, or as if another person were I. Temperamentally, I feel closer to the late Mary Stoddard than anyone else, except possibly my late Uncle Reuben, Ulysses to my Telemachus. That the combination has not split my personality wide open and left me the prey of psychiatrists, psychoanalysts and other roving swamis, is a tribute to the Paul physique, inherited from my father's side, and which has stood all of us in good stead, as compensation for Mother's supersensitive nerves.

CHAPTER THIRTEEN

About the Relatively Worthy Poor

HEN RICHARDS was the Linden hermit, and nothing his neighbors could not directly observe was ever known about him. Webster's dictionary defines a hermit as "one who abandons society and lives alone," a line which seems to me to be worthy of the ultimate poet. Hen did not abandon society, exactly, but he certainly lived alone. Over in Concord, Henry Thoreau, when he decided to withdraw from it all, went a little farther from the town than an expert can drive a golf ball, and settled on the shore of Walden Pond. Hen Richards found his supreme isolation in Weeks' field, fifty yards from our house, in the spot that was not far from the geographical center of Linden.

He was not a beaten man, or inferior in any way, and no one thought so. There were plenty of people in Linden who their neighbors thought were mildly crazy. No one thought that of Hen. He walked slowly but steadily, in a most correct and dignified way, not like a soldier, not like an actor, not like a statesman. Like a gentleman who was thoughtful and preoccupied. His voice was neither loud nor soft, but was well modulated, and although he used it infrequently, when he spoke, his words were to the point and well chosen.

Old Lydia Stoddard, whose house was nearest Hen's small shack, was the first one Hen spoke to, when he came into town. Several times, in my hearing, she told about his entrance. It was on a pleasant morning, while the Civil War was still in progress. Hen was a young man then, but he looked and acted about the same as he did forty years later. His clothes were shabby, but decent, quite formal, but worn. He had a plug hat, which he wore at a slight angle, a long coat Jeff Lee described as a "Jim-swinger," and cowhide boots without buttons or laces. His trousers had been black, but had gathered a faint *patin* of green.

"Good morning, ma'am," Hen had said to Mrs. Stoddard. He had raised his plug hat.

"Good morning, sir," she replied.

Hen looked over toward Weeks' field, where the pathway passed over the creek on a small wooden bridge without a rail.

"May I inquire, ma'am, who owns that field?" he asked.

"It belongs to Mr. Weeks," Mrs. Stoddard said, and indicated Weeks' barn, up on Salem Street. "He's probably up there in the cow barn," she continued.

"I thank you, ma'am," Hen said, bowing as he raised his hat again.

"You're welcome, sir," she said.

Hen had started along the path toward the creek, neither slower nor faster than he had walked up Beach Street. Just before he crossed, he had gathered up a few pebbles. There was a little patch of meadow, flat and fifty feet square, that was five or six feet higher than the ground around it, and from its appearance it was higher than the level of an ordinary tide. At flood tide it was usually an island, for an hour or two. Hen looked it over carefully and by snapping the pebbles with his thumb, he indicated the dimensions of the one-room house he later built from scraps, driftwood, tar paper and tin placards advertising Bon Ami, Mayo's Cut Plug, and Mrs. Pinkham's Vegetable Compound. The placards he turned inward, so the shack would not be too unsightly.

That day, the shack was only in Hen's mind. He walked into Weeks' barnyard and saw that three or four men were gathered around a pigpen, higher on the hill. There was plenty of space in Linden, then, and no one objected to pigs on the outskirts of town.

Mr. Weeks was young, then, and just married. He had only a few animals, and each one meant a great deal to him. He was doing all his own work, establishing a small milk route, and curing hams and bacon. The men who stood with him were neighbors. They saw Hen approaching, and something in his attitude prompted them to make way, at the rail of the pen.

Hen, taller than the others, and looking more so because of his plug hat, looked down, and saw four pigs wallowing in the muck. They evidently were ill, and about ready to give up.

"Good morning, gentlemen," Hen said.

Mr. Weeks and his fellow mourners responded or nodded.

"A bucket and a pitcher," Hen said.

Mr. Weeks scratched his straw-colored hair, and started toward his house. Hen followed. The others watched them. There was nothing much to say.

When Mr. Weeks and the stranger emerged from the kitchen, both were carrying pails of soapy water and Hen had an enamelware pitcher in his hand. Careful not to soil his trouser legs, Hen opened the gate, went into the pen, took hold of one of the sick hogs, held open its mouth, and poured in dishwater from the pitcher. This process he repeated, with the other three hogs. Mr. Weeks and the men watched, spat tobacco juice, looked at one another, noncommittally, and waited. Hen came out of the pen.

"They ought to be all right by tomorrow forenoon," he said.

"Are you a vet?" asked Mr. Weeks.

"No, sir," Hen said, and helped him take the buckets back to the house. Then he said, "Good day, sir," and before the somewhat awkward and diffident milkman could recover, was on his way again. The men watched him take the steep and rocky road, just wide enough for wheel tracks, and go over toward the Pike.

The next morning Mr. Weeks got up before dawn, as always, and the hogs were eating corn and swill. Meanwhile, the advent and exit of the mysterious stranger had been relayed from one end of Linden to the other. Whoever was up early went up to Weeks' barn, then told the folks in the Square and the stores that dishwater cured hogs when they had colic.

About seven o'clock, when the sun was well up and Linden was completely under way, Hen Richards came down the rocky road and turned up Salem Street to Weeks' barn. Mr. Weeks met him, with bashful cordiality.

"You did the trick, all right," the milkman said.

Mr. Weeks looked troubled, as he always did when money matters had to be discussed.

"How much?" he asked. "Them hogs were as good as dead."

"Oh, that's all right," Hen said, then he extended his arm toward the field, a quarter of a mile away. "I should like, if you don't mind, to build a small house just over the creek, near the wall."

"Why certainly," said Mr. Weeks. "Glad to have you. Go right ahead."

"I'm obliged, sir," Hen said.

"My name is Charley Weeks," said Mr. Weeks, extending his hand.

"Mine is Henry Richards," said the hermit. He did not mention that he had abandoned society, and if he had, it certainly would have thrown Mr. Weeks, whose figures of speech were of the plainer order.

Bit by bit, Hen's simple shack went up. At first he used a mallet he had made with his jackknife, and wooden pegs for nails, until Mrs. Stoddard and Mary, who at the age of ten was as homely as she was forty years later, told him there were tools in their shed, and plenty of old nails, and he was welcome to use them. What had attracted Mary Stoddard, aged ten, to the hermit was the way he looked at the snakes, and refrained from molesting them. There were a few days each spring where, in the back part of the Stoddards' land, and nearby, in Weeks' field and on the other side, in the swampland owned by Norman Partridge, as if by prearrangement, hundreds and thousands of garter snakes came out of hibernation, with brand-new skins, a zest for life and spring sunshine, and the grace and poetry of motion that only creatures so simply designed can possess. Mary Stoddard had her first brush with the law and the thoughtless brutality of mankind when she had taken from the chest an old horse pistol and driven away the men and boys who liked killing snakes. Hen felt about them as Mary did. He would not kill a fly, unless it was biting a horse or a cow.

Hen's house had two windows, and an old stove, one missing leg of which was propped up with books. The furniture, consisting of a kitchen stool, a rocking chair with boards nailed over the missing cane bottom, a wooden bunk, with an old mattress but no springs, and a few makeshift shelves, pots and pans, tin plates and a few odd forks and spoons, had been acquired slowly, as the need arose. Mr. Weeks never thought of asking him to pay for use of the land. The price of four hogs covered that, for a lifetime.

Hen never bought anything except salt, salt pork or bacon, condensed milk, sugar, coffee, and infrequently a few pounds of flour or corn meal. To get the necessary cash for this, not more than twenty-five dollars a year, Hen trapped and sold eels to the Italians in Chelsea, and shrimps, clams, and worms for bait, to the sportsmen whose headquarters were the Massasoit House. He liked to read old almanacs and magazines, but did not care for books. He wore the same clothes, year after year, until some man he liked would offer him a derby, straw hat, or a coat, pair of pants, or a pair of old boots. This had to be done tactfully, and in strict privacy, or Hen would politely refuse. In my time, wherever Hen went, he was followed a few yards distant by a small shaggy dog with hair hanging over its eyes.

In the woods, Hen found nuts and berries, and plenty of perch, bass and pickerel in the ponds. Sometimes he shot partridge with a slingshot, not wishing to become involved in the purchase of ammunition for a gun. In wild duck season, when the hunters went to the great marsh for sport, in the frosty dawns, Don Partridge, or Admiral Quimby, or my Uncle Reuben would lend Hen a shotgun and shells, and he had a way of preserving the ducks in a light pickle, so that he had a supply the year round. His only reference to the past was a remark he let slip, and could not recall, that he had learned about marinating ducks in Bilbao.

When anyone passed him on the street, or on the pathways across the fields, Hen would say, "Good morning," or "Good afternoon," in an absent-minded way, and that is about all he ever said to anyone. He used as few words as possible and kept his human contacts down to an absolute minimum, although he showed no fear or distrust or any pathological symptoms when he found it necessary to seek out someone and communicate with him. He avoided all the women except the Stoddards, his nearest neighbors. Most Linden women were a little nervous about him. He set a bad example, from their point of view, getting on without work, or money, or a wife.

If Hen had a barrel of eels he wanted to take over to sell to an Italian saloonkeeper in Chelsea Square, who bought his supply for Christmas each year from Hen, Hen would go over to Clapp's field, a hundred yards from his shack, to see Mario Bacigalupo, Deacon Clapp's hired man.

Mario might have been rated by statisticians as a poor man, but he felt like a rich one, only better. He had immigrated from Sicily, with his wife, Giovanna, and had lived in the slums in the North End of Boston, while digging ditches for a contractor at the rate of one dollar a day, of which he saved fifty cents. Life in America was not what he had expected, but Deacon Clapp had watched him work with pick and shovel from the window of an organ factory the Deacon had on Hanover Street. Something about Mario had set him apart from the others in the gang, and the Deacon had asked him if he knew about farming.

The words with which Mario had replied meant nothing to Deacon Clapp, but the way Mario's eyes had lighted, and the rapt look on his face, had decided the matter. So Mario had come to Linden, with Giovanna, had rented a house south of the tracks, and had raised two boys: Julio, known as "Frigger," the newsboy, who was very smart, and Romeo, two years younger, who was very good, and dreamed of playing the violin when he was not actually practicing.

Giovanna was a fine cook, red wine was cheap in Chelsea, and the fertile acres Mario cultivated for Deacon Clapp were so luxuriant that they seemed as proud of Mario as he was of them. As the first Italian to settle in Linden, Mario was accepted as an example of his nationality. He knew everyone in Linden, and exulted or sorrowed when fate dealt his townsmen this or that. The Linden folks made fun of his dialect, praised his work, and when, a few years after his arrival, the Raggios, the Sorrocos, and the Marincolas came, they were introduced and guided by Mario, as dean of the Linden Italians.

If Hen Richards, the hermit, was the most aloof man in

215

town, Mario was sociability personified. Mario felt a proprietary interest in Linden, and all it contained. Once, when Luke Harrigan, the most beloved of the Irishmen, was soliciting small contributions so that the Linden baseball team could wear uniforms, Luke got five dollars from Deacon Clapp, ten from Dawson Freeman, and five from Don Partridge, all within sight of the field where Mario was spreading manure.

That afternoon, at milking time, Mario hung his head, and a tear dropped into the pail. He went home, through a back gate and the deserted school yard, would not eat, and went to bed with his clothes on, his face to the wall. In the middle of the night, he told Giovanna, in Italian, what was wrong. He was hurt. He was desolate. He had his first papers, and knew the answers which would win him his second papers. People spoke, said, "Hello, Mario." His children went to school, got promoted. Still, he did not belong. Other men gave money for the ball team. He, Mario, was not asked. His son Frigger, the newsboy, heard what was said, and stopped in at Luke Harrigan's that morning, when he delivered the papers. Luke, as a cosmopolitan, took both the *Herald* and the *Post*. If Mario missed his supper, Luke Harrigan could not swallow his breakfast. He had a fine position, at Houghton and Dutton's and was needed there, but Luke stayed home from work. At ten o'clock, having put on his best clothes, and stuck a flower in his buttonhole, he made a list of all the Italians in Linden, ruling it with red ink, and writing it ornamentally, with elaborate Spencerian scrolls and curlicues. Mario Bacigalupo's name was at the head, and there were neat columns.

Luke called on Mario, who was plowing doggedly, along the creek, not hearing the birds, or smelling the fresh earth, or noticing the passersby.

"Mario," said Luke. "You're just the man I want to see. I've canvassed a few individuals, but the boys had asked especially to appoint you head solicitor of the Italian-American colony. Pep Marincola, as you know, will play center fielder on the Linden team. We want the Linden boys to have uniforms, so will you ask the men I've listed here to chip in?"

No one had a better sense of the dramatic, or could create an illusion like Luke Harrigan. Suddenly, in Mario's ears the songs of the orioles started ringing, and the day was so bright, the soil so fragrant, that he smiled and accepted the list. He saw the red ink, and the columns, and his name at the top. He understood, now, why, in canvassing mere individuals, and not the deans of racial groups, he had not been approached the day before.

"How much did my boss give?" Mario asked.

"In confidence, two dollars," Luke said. He knew what was coming, and knocked down the Deacon's five dollars by sixty per cent.

"For Mario Bacigalupo, his wife, Giovanna, and his sons, Julio and Romeo, three dollars," Mario said, and after Luke had left him, Mario talked to his horse about America, and the Constitution, and the people who were all alike, rich and poor. He told the horse that the Linden boys, with Pep, the son of his old friend, Marincola, would never be beaten, that when they got to bat, in the very first inning, the game would go on until dark, and the Lindens would never be put out. He said that Mario was a by-Jesus-Christa big damma fool, who suspected his friends, unjustly, for which he would burn a church full of candles, and not the cheap ones, but the best. And that some day Giuseppe Verdi would visit America, and hear that in Linden there were respected Italians—Bacigalupos, Raggios, Sorrocos, and Marincolas, including the then-famous athlete Pep—and that the Maestro would later compose an Italian-American opera with a chorus in Linden baseball suits.

In December, when Hen Richards sold his eels, no orioles sang in the elms, which were bare, and the rich black earth of Clapp's field was frozen to a depth of two or three feet and covered with snow. For the winter months, Mario saved odd jobs of shucking corn, grinding fodder, mending harness, and, in December, preparing for Christmas and New Year's Day. The family feast at the Clapps' included at table the Deacon, his wife, his two unmarried sons and one unmarried daughter; Mattie and Dawson Freeman with their children (a new one each year); and Anne with her husband, Don Partridge. In Mario's rented house across the tracks he entertained about the same number, but in a different way, with more varieties of food and seasonings, and instead of sweet cider and milk, red Chianti and grappa. In the big house, roast turkey with dressing flavored with sage, mashed potatoes, turnips, squash, and cranberry sauce. In Mario's place, pizza, piquant pickled peppers, sliced sausages from Genoa and Barcelona, Giovanna's superb canelloni, a roast stuffed fish, entire, and brought in on a plank for the company to see and cheer, veal scallopini so tender they were cut with a fork, if at all, a partridge apiece, from the woods, garnished with home-cured bacon and a touch of garlic, four kinds of cheeses, three of which would have driven a Protestant family and their pets from home, special holiday pastries, fruit selected from the best that Marincola sold, music by Romeo on his soulful violin, Uncle Bartolomeo's accordion, two mandolins and a guitar. And colors of the Old World in the old folks' holiday costumes, and what young America wears displayed by the younger generation, with the racial jauntiness, the tints of shirts, the points of shoes, the belts, neckties, angles of hats and pads in shoulders, that still set them apart from the *Mayflower* descendants.

Lest the reader forget that this chapter is about poverty, I must remind him that after one of these holiday feasts, the cash reserve of Mario and Giovanna Bacigalupo would not exceed sixteen dollars, and that no one in Linden, except possibly Dawson Freeman, who might be several thousand in the hole at the time, felt richer or more thankful to be in Linden and alive.

Mario lived December in two worlds. He brought evergreen branches and holly for the Clapp mansion, and his own. He did errands with his pung for the combined force of hired girls under the direction of Mrs. Clapp. Between-times, he observed American customs, which never ceased to astonish him by their restraint, and tried, in his own little home, to combine the best elements of New England celebrations with those of Italian fiestas. How many times I have wished that the willingness to acquire treasures of tradition and goodfellowship had been mutual, between the immigrants and the earlier settlers. Because while Mario's Christmas and New Year's were amplified and enriched by quite a few New England customs, the Clapps' sedate dining room, with its heavy silver service, Duncan-Phyfe table and Sheraton chairs, remained as always, menu, service, deportment, cigars and all. I do not mean that Mrs. Clapp's mince, apple and pumpkin pies, and her plum pudding with hot and cold sauce, were in any way inferior to the Italian baker's pastries, from Chelsea. My point is that Mario profited by both traditions of dessert, while the Deacon's household learned nothing.

Early in December each year, Hen Richards would walk over from his little house to the Clapp estate, his ridiculous old dog at his heels, and as Hen entered the driveway, the dog would sit down a moment and look up at him. Hen would turn. If Hen moved his head to one side, the little dog would sit down and wait, knowing there might be a larger dog ahead.

If Hen nodded in the affirmative, the dog would jog along, secure.

Year after year, Hen had said less and less, and at first he said very little. His initial request of Mr. Weeks was the only one on record. He would go to where Mario was working, say, "Good morning," or merely nod, and wait. Mario, knowing what he wanted, felt that it was friendly to tease him a while. Mario would look up at the sky and hold his finger to the breeze.

"It's gonna be a fine day," he would say.

Hen would nod, expectantly. Then both would wait. But in waiting, the Latin was no match for the recluse.

"You wanna something I can do?" Mario would finally ask.

Hen would nod again, but shyly.

"You wanna go somewhere, maybe?" Mario continued.

This time Hen would nod and ever so faintly smile.

"Maybe Lynn?" Of course Mario knew exactly where Hen wished to go, but he tried a few other places first.

Hen shook his head "No."

"Ah. Everett! That'sa fine place."

Like a bashful boy, almost, Hen shook his head again, from side to side. The little dog was looking up at Mario, his dark eyes appealing under their thatch of shaggy hair. The dog felt the tension of expectancy in his master. Mario, noticing the dog, would feel ashamed of himself.

"Well. Perhaps Chelsea," Mario would say.

This time Hen would wordlessly agree.

So eventually Hen and Mario would hitch up Clapp's horse to the pung, drive over into Weeks' field, take down the tailboard, use a plank for an incline, and roll into the pung the barrel of eels.

For men of frugal habits and fixed itineraries, eels are among the most accommodating food fish in nature. They may be caught at almost any time of year, if one knows where to look for them, and will stay in traps, feeding royally from the minutiae that flow through, so that before Christmas-time they may be gathered into barrels and grace the feasts commemorating the birth in Nazareth of Him who must have found a few fine *morenas* in His miraculous draught of fishes. Hen bored one-inch holes, with brace and bit, in the sides of his eel traps so that little eels could come in, find company and shelter, and feed until they were too big to swim out.

The five dollars that Hen got for this barrel of eels from the Chelsea saloonkeeper was the largest lump amount he handled in a calendar year.

I knew as a child as well as I know now that Hen Richards, because of some shock, infirmity or disappointment, had sought to disassociate himself and escape from what formerly he had thought of as "life." I know all the modern routines about the dangers of trying to "escape," how reality (what a word) must be faced, and all that, and all that. It has been my observation that many men and women who have tried to secede from the race have come to grief. So have many others who tried to be captain of a leaky and unseaworthy soul, and master of a botched-up fate. Whatever haunted Hen Richards, he kept to himself, and his eyes, when he gazed at the horizon, were not too wistful. He liked to spend the pleasant days walking around the countryside, picking up what was useful or edible and belonged to no one, watching things grow, the buds, the birds, the flowers, and in autumn wither or grow a protection from the cold. There were plenty of ways in which he would have made more money, or found steady employment. He did not want more money, or more employment. He liked to walk, and he had to breathe and think. In the simplest way imaginable, Hen made the best of it. My guess is that he placed too much confidence in some young woman, and, having been brutally double-crossed, did not care to risk it again. Surely he had never cheated at cards, because he played solitaire frequently and showed no aversion to the pasteboards.

I got to know Hen very well, because we both liked mushrooms, and they grew in the pasture he shared with Weeks' cows. Each morning in season, a fresh crop would appear, where the evening before had been none.

"That isn't a miracle, Elliot," Miss Stoddard would say. "Some things grow faster than others, that's all, and taste better, too. Whatever isn't growing, wears out."

Hen Richards never stole anything. No one was afraid of him. He spent his life not making money and not needing it, which in Linden, gem of our land of opportunity, was just as easy as becoming President. Perhaps some predatory woman had snared him, had nagged and demanded too much, and Hen had walked out as silently as Longfellow's Arabs, only minus the tent. No one in Linden ever knew. In my time, after Hen had lived in Weeks' field thirty-odd years, most of his neighbors did not criticize his mode of life severely, because it involved only himself, as far as they could find out.

With Irv Walker, the poorest man in Linden with a family, the verdict of his townspeople was more reproachful. Irv liked to be carefree and idle as well as Hen did, or even better, because when Irv had nothing in particular to do, he did not waste his energy walking or work up a headache thinking. He lay down somewhere and dozed, until further notice. Irv was tall, quite good-looking, and only betrayed his role as the poorest family man in town by greeting his fellow townsmen a little more politely and respectfully than they treated one another. No one disliked Irv, or any member of his family.

When Irv had come to Linden as a young man, and had patched up a shanty on the edge of Grovers' abandoned hillside farm, he had been accompanied by his young wife, Gertie, who was firm and well-rounded, with dark roguish eyes, and a manner with men that indicated that she was neither prudish nor helpless. Probably at least a third of the men then in Linden made advances to Gertie, more or less discreetly, according to their natures, the first few months she was in town. There was something about her that made this inevitable, some subtle witchcraft or musk. Gertie understood this, at times was pleased and at others regretted her attractions. But according to the Linden grapevine, Gertie was one hundred percent faithful to her shiftless young husband long enough to become pregnant. From that time on, she was either great with child—and Gertie could get greater than almost any other young woman her size—or nursing an infant, without the excessive modesty that characterized her neighbors under similar circumstances.

Irv never went after steady jobs, and often left temporary ones before they were completed. One drop of rain in the morning was enough to make him smile and stretch out for a quiet day at ease. Gertie went about her modicum of housework, the babies cried and cooed. Irv, on his side of their crude wooden bunk, dozed through it all. In winter their shack was kept red-hot, and was less drafty than more complicated houses. The stove Irv had found on the Linden dump, just west of town, and the wood he picked up for nothing, in the woods behind the house. Heating cost him nothing but a little effort which, as soon as his children were old enough, was contributed by them. For a long while, Irv and Gertie had only daughters, five of them, all of whom were too pretty and well-formed to be ideal offspring of a poor man. Even "Big Gertie," as Irv's wife came to be called after their third daughter "Little Gertie" was born, remained handsome and tempting, in spite of her shabby clothes.

The house Irv Walker and his family lived in had originally been a large hen house on the corner of the old Grover estate. He had built a sort of godown on the end farthest from the door, after his fourth daughter was born. When all eight of the Walkers were there together, four of the girls had slept in two-tier double bunks in the godown, with hooks and homemade chests for their clothes and belongings. Irv and Big Gertie had their double bunk curtained off with plush hangings (bought for two dollars in an auction sale), the youngest daughter and Young Irv had folding cots set up in the combination living room and kitchen. By the time he was twelve, the boy could have strolled through a dressing room of a girl's gymnasium without batting an eye. The kitchen window behind the stove was not battened down in the winter, so Big Gertie and her helpers could throw the tin cans they opened out on a pile in the back yard. As soon as they were old enough, and had fulfilled the minimum requirements in school, the girls got summer jobs at Revere Beach, and slept out from June until fall. Irv went his way, hauling ashes, mowing and trimming lawns, shovelling snow, and helping the gardener and stable man around the Norman Partridge place. What the Walkers lost in privacy, they gained in lack of mental strain and social obligations. Irv voted the Republican ticket each year, suspecting naïvely that if he went against the wishes of his various employers, the deception would show on his face when he came out of the voting booth. No doubt it would have. He was a candid man.

In the house, Big Gertie was no more adept at work than Irv was outside. The whole family lived from cans, which in those days were not common or inexpensive. Corned beef, sardines, salmon, beans, corn, and apricots were about all that could be found in cans in Puffer's store. Puffer's store, where the stock was meagre, was nearest the Walker shack, so none of them would walk an extra quarter of a mile to trade with Markham or Sampson. Also, Irv worked intermittently for Norman Partridge, who was Mrs. Puffer's brother, and therefore Puffer gave Irv a certain amount of credit which could be safely exhausted before Irv felt the pressure of necessity and had to look around again for something to do.

The youngest of the Walker family, "Young Irv," was quite like his father. Of the five girls, Nancy, Gertie and Agnes had plenty of brains, got on easily in school, and knew as much of what they should as what they should not know. The other two, Maisy and Dot, were slow thinkers, reacted indolently, and, without malicious intent, drove their teachers half-crazy by their good-natured inability to associate ideas or remember facts and figures, and kept their schoolmates of the opposite sex in a ferment of reprehensible desire.

The Walkers never missed a meal, were warmer, as I have said, than other Linden folks, thrived without ventilation or sanitation, had as many friends as anyone, and lived, on the average, just as many years. What was wrong with being poor, with a family, in Linden, had to do with women's clothes. Old Irv and Young Irv never cared a hoot how they were dressed, if their duds were fairly comfortable. As soon as the children were old enough, Big Gertie began to take renewed interest in her appearance, and instead of prodding and aggravating her husband, as less considerate women would do, she used to ride into Boston on the streetcar, and go to Raymond's, on Washington Street, a secondhand store that was unique and famous all over New England. Not a lumberjack from Maine, who came periodically to Boston to get drunk, did not know about Raymond's where, in spite of cut prices, the goods were as represented and nobody was cheated. Raymond's welcomed and solicited especially the hard-working men.

The New England lumberjack's idea of Boston was confined to a limited area, beginning at the North Station and extending no farther than Raymond's, two blocks beyond the Old State House. One of these stalwart woodsmen would work six weeks in the Maine forest, ride a pung to Bangor, in time for a Boston train. In Bangor he would provide himself with a jug of whiskey, called redeye, and a tin cup, and install himself in the smoking car. The cup was not bought for ten cents because he could not drink out of a jug, but if he made friends on the way to Boston and wanted to share his booze, he wanted to know how much the other guy was getting.

That requires a little side-explanation. In Boston, saloons where lumberjacks, sailors and other roving proletarians were welcome, there were "whiskey machines" where a man, almost broke, could get for a nickel all he could drink before coming up for air, that is, at a single swallow. The quality of the nickel whiskey was not strained, and probably some of it had dropped from heaven, but the bums, by long practice, learned to open their throats and let it run down, without moving their Adam's apple, until they were full or the tank was empty. A bum with this background could deplete a jug in no time. A lumberjack coming into Boston would cross the street from the North Station, spend his six weeks' pay on drink, women and food (mostly steaks) at the Hotel Haymarket, fill himself up in a nickel whiskey machine with his last jitney, then go to a neighboring pawn shop on Canal Street, and hock his lumberman's rubbers (worth three or four dollars) and his mackinaw, worth three dollars more. For these the Jew would lend him five dollars. Back he would go to the Haymarket, and drink until the five was gone. The bartender would give him a nickel, he would find another machine, drain it, then go sit on the curb in front of the North

Station, without shoes or mackinaw, until a runner from the lumber company or an acquaintance came along and staked him to a ticket back to Bangor, from whence he would return to the woods for another six weeks' Herculean labor.

Lumberjacks did their shopping before they got drunk, so they were to be found at Raymond's in a relatively sober state. The single gallon-jug of redeye, for the long trip from Bangor, was not enough to addle them. Big Gertie would linger in Raymond's, near a counter where heavy flannel shirts for men were on sale on one side of the aisle, and ribbons by the yard on the other. Few lumberjacks fresh from six weeks in the woods would fail to notice such a woman. One of the bolder would ask what she was looking at, and would buy it for her, and she would go with him to the Haymarket, to keep him company until it was time for her to catch the last Linden train. Big Gertie was strictly scrupulous. She never struck up an acquaintance with a man in or from Linden, and she never stayed out all night. If she returned to Boston the next day, and bought herself a decent outfit, Irv did not ask questions, as a less agreeable fond husband might do. He was glad that, somehow, in spite of the fact that he was a notoriously poor provider, his wife "held her age" so well, and looked better than most of the other women who had money to burn.

Big Gertie was careful not to teach her growing daughters anything wrong, but Little Gertie was smart, and followed her mother one day, taking an earlier streetcar and waiting for Big Gertie to get off the Chelsea car in Boston, at Adam's Square. First Little Gertie, then her sisters, began to dress much better, and the only shadow on their contentment which had been cast by their poverty was dispelled.

When the oldest and slowest-thinking Walker girl found herself in a family way, without a husband, Irv and Gertie did not throw her out into the snow, although the snow was deep that year. They took care of Maisy in their tender and casual way, also the little grandchild, and a few months later Maisy married an iceman in Lynn, and when Dot got into trouble, Dot went to stay with Maisy and her husband, had *her* first baby, and all of them lived happily ever afterward, as the story books say. They never seemed to need another man around the place, to clutter it up.

After I left Linden, I heard that Ginger eventually married Little Gertie, and that Young Irv was decorated for services beyond the scope of duty at Belleau Wood in World War I.

CHAPTER FOURTEEN

Being Seen and Not Heard

IT WAS on a Thursday evening that Alice Townsend hid herself in a sea chest, and had the whole town looking for her. I awoke the next morning filled with a sense of uneasiness. Because of what I had seen and heard, I knew more about what really had happened than others did who were not directly concerned, but my mind was troubled because I could not understand the situation well enough to stop wondering about it. That Miss Stoddard did not want me to talk about the matter was clear to me, and I believed that she had a good reason for wanting me to be silent. There was a question of friendship involved, several questions, in fact.

Anyway, before breakfast I slipped into the woods and in the daylight, damp and dim, I examined the rocky path where Ruth had fallen and we had found her. Not far from the spot, perhaps four or five feet, partly concealed by the leaves and tendrils of a vine, I found a paring knife, such as Mother used in the kitchen, and it was stained. This did not surprise me, much, but it excited me, and I tried to decide what I should do. I had not had a chance to talk with Miss Stoddard again, and normally I would not see her until Sunday afternoon, when we usually went for a walk in the woods, or along the streets into neighboring towns. So I took the knife with me to the summit of Elephant's Back, and as the sun picked up the various landmarks of Boston, Charlestown, Everett and

Broadway, I hid the weapon where no one else would be likely to find it and I could recover it whenever I wished. I sat down to think, not so much about what had happened, as why. Ruth had been helping the Townsends. Alice was fond of her. The others hated her. Why?

From another angle, I approached the riddle. Miss Stoddard liked Ruth and believed Ruth was right. Why did they not accuse Elvira? Of course, I knew that Mrs. Townsend had not tried to kill Ruth. The mother was not at all attractive, to me. But she was careful what she said and did, and acted sanely enough. Mrs. Townsend was worried, in a way I felt deeply, because since I could remember, the question of money had been the menace, the problem, the thing that made life unstable and tinged the future with amorphous dread. Why did Mrs. Townsend want Alice to send Ruth away? Why was she not glad that her daughter, who saw so few people, had made a new friend, and a warmhearted, generous friend, one who was known and trusted by some of the people I liked best?

Was Alice crazy? What did it mean to be crazy? How would it be different than being as we were?

Mother noticed that I was moody that day, and it disturbed her, so I pretended I was not. I disliked waiting, and tried to reconcile myself to waiting until Sunday, when I could have some kind of a showdown with Miss Stoddard.

I did not have as long to wait as I had expected. Friday afternoon a strange nurse, in uniform, got off the streetcar in the Square and was driven by Dr. Moody, a little later, through Beach Street to the Townsend place. My mother saw them pass, looked at me, then said nothing. I said nothing, too. But as soon as I could, without being too conspicuous, I slipped out the back door and walked up to Great-Uncle Lije's house, right across Salem Street from Ruth Coffee's cottage. I wanted to have a look at Ruth, see how she seemed to be feeling and what she was doing.

My great-uncle was not at home, and my Great-Aunt Elizabeth was busy. I did not disturb her. Rover came to meet me at the gate, and walked with me, or just behind me as he had been taught, to a small grape arbor near the fence and the sidewalk. From there, Ruth's windows were not sixty feet away. They were open and before I saw her, I heard Ruth singing "They Dragged Him 'Round the Room." She was not singing happily, but rather nervously, it seemed to me, as if she were anxious about something and was singing to make the time pass faster, and give her something to do while she was waiting. I heard her bustling around, cursing good-naturedly between words of the song as she bumped this or that. I knew that kind of sound, which only came from women cleaning house. A mild fury took possession of Linden women when they got their heads wrapped up in flannel and took dust pans, dust cloths, feather dusters and brooms in their hands, and started moving furniture out of place, then back again, or to some other place. Casters were always slipping from chair legs, tables caught on the edge of rugs, bric-à-brac got knocked from mantels, books were opened and shut, and the dust made the women cough.

I caught swift glimpses of Ruth as she was cleaning her living room. Ruth's cottage contained no parlor. The living room occupied the front, left of the entrance hallway, and had a stone hearth, with fire tools and andirons, old furniture that looked fragile and proved to be strong, rag rugs, a table with an inlaid chessboard on which she played with Millicent Partridge sometimes, or Swede Carlson, the carpenter, or Mr. Ford, who had consumption. Ruth's left arm was in a sling, so she blundered and cursed more often than usual, trying to work with one arm, or forgetting her left one was sore and giving herself an unexpected twinge. There were no venom and petulance in Ruth's expressions. They had a wholesome, spontaneous effect.

At the same instant, Ruth from her side window and Rover and I from the arbor heard hoofbeats approaching along Salem Street, those of Hip. Rover got up, looked at me, I signalled to take it easy, and he sat down again. Ruth took the cloth from her head, and put away the dustpan and broom, quite hastily, it seemed to me. She did not want the doctor to know she had been working. No doubt he had told her not to use her left arm. Still, I had seen her using it, and was sure that the nurse in uniform, taking Ruth's place at Alice's side, was not there because Ruth was incapacitated. Neither did Ruth seem crushed or disappointed, or too much worried. The more I observed of the Townsend affair, the farther I was at sea.

All I learned definitely was when the doctor came out again, and Ruth saw him to the cottage door. The bandage around her shoulder was a fresh one, and Ruth said, cheerfully:

"Well. See you tomorrow, Doc. I'm betting on you."

"I hope we're right," Doc said, got into the buggy, and drove away.

The next day was Saturday. It was easy to remember when anything happened in Linden on Saturday. There was no school, so the boys and girls were all over the place, some working at odd jobs to make a dime or two, others playing "Run Sheep, Run," "Hide and Seek," baseball or football in season. Those who had bicycles rode them up and down the streets, and, when they were sure the cop was not around, on the sidewalks as well. A lot of agitation against riding bicycles on sidewalks was in the air just then. Quite a few minor accidents had occurred, letters of protest appeared in the newspaper, and Spike Dodge, the Linden cop and the last person to get tough about trifles, had warned all the boys to be careful and not get him into trouble. Of all the men I knew, I think Spike was the most reluctant to get into trouble. For him, the absence of trouble was the ideal state, and work and trouble were synonymous.

There were two extra trains on the Saugus Branch on Saturday afternoons, and most of the men got home early from Boston, loaded with bundles from the Faneuil Hall markets and the Boston department stores. The Massasoit bar was crowded and once in a while the swinging doors would part and a couple of men in fisticuffs would hurtle out, or a drunk would be propelled by Nick Spratt, not toward the Linden line where he might be pinched, but toward the open spaces of Revere.

Doc Moody, that Saturday, drove across the street to the depot to meet the 1:15 train. A tall man about thirty-five years old, dressed quietly in gray, with pale blue eyes, slender but capable hands, and a reserved but confident manner got off and shook hands with Dr. Moody. The stranger was a doctor, without doubt, and through Dawson Freeman, who had talked with him on the train, the news spread that he was Dr. Alfred Worcester, of the staff of the Massachusetts General Hospital, a man well-known and respected by the entire profession, and a teacher at Harvard. That was where Dr. Moody had known him before.

Again I went to Great-Uncle Lije's house. This time, Great-Aunt Elizabeth saw me before I got to the arbor, so I went to the front porch and sat with her. She was watching Ruth's cottage, too, and Ruth apparently had finished cleaning the ground floor rooms the day before. She was working upstairs, humming and whistling.

"You've been in Miss Coffee's house?" my great-aunt asked.

"Once or twice," I said.

233

"Isn't that the spare bedroom, where she's cleaning?"

"It looks like it," I said.

"Now what's she doing that for?"

My great-aunt did not expect an answer. She sat on the porch, watching and listening and wondering, until it was time for her to take pies from the oven and water the bean pot. I waited and waited, two hours. And while I was waiting, something I had seen on Beach Street, and should have impressed me at once, came back to me. Dr. Moody was not using his buggy, to take the strange doctor to the Townsend house. He had hitched Hip to the carryall.

So it was the carryall I looked for, and I saw that Ruth had stopped work and was changing her clothes. She put on a fresh white shirtwaist, and a blue suit, freshly pressed, dark blue stockings and patent leather shoes to match. I saw her arrange her hair before the mirror, and put a red flower in her coat lapel. She smiled into the glass and squared her shoulders, and I noticed she had discarded the sling. Her cut must be better, I thought. Again I wondered why neither Ruth, nor the doctor, had said a word around town about how she got hurt. Was it to keep the knowledge from Alice, who might have another relapse if she were shocked? I did not think Ruth would take so much trouble to shield Elvira, or would stand that amount of nonsense from anyone, man or woman, without satisfaction.

When the carryall came into sight at last, I saw that Dr. Moody and the nurse were in the front seat, and that two persons, a man and a woman, were in the back seat. I assumed the man would be Dr. Worcester, so I concentrated on the woman and was astonished to see that it was Alice Townsend, fully dressed for the drive. By the time they were abreast of the porch, Great-Aunt Elizabeth was at the window, inside, watching from behind the lace curtains.

"Now don't that beat all?" she said, under her breath.

I was too absorbed in watching Ruth, who was standing, radiant in the afternoon sunshine, on the porch. She hurried to the sidewalk, as the carryall stopped, reached up and helped Alice descend. Ruth was not demonstrative, this time. She held both of Alice's hands and from a little distance looked at her, eyes shining.

"I'm here," I heard Alice say, hesitantly.

Dr. Moody interrupted. "Break, you two," he said. "Ruth. Meet Dr. Worcester."

"Glad to meet you, doctor," said Ruth, and with a sidelong glance at Alice, added questioningly, but confidently: "How about it?"

"I agree with Dr. Moody," Dr. Worcester said.

They all went inside, where Ruth served tea for Alice and the nurse and whiskey and soda to the men.

Great-Aunt Elizabeth was surprised enough when Alice appeared, but when the two doctors and the nurse left without her, and it was evident that Ruth was putting her to bed in the spare room, my great-aunt put on her summer shawl and started for our house, leaving me to watch the beans and put them on the back of the stove when the oven would be too hot.

"Tell Lije I'll be back in time for supper," she said.

I scarcely heard her, I was thinking so hard, and getting no results but circles. Eventually Great-Uncle Lije came in, and was a little surprised and put out because his wife had gone off and left the beans. He had already heard that Miss Townsend had ridden with the doctors to Ruth's house, but he did not know the sick girl had been installed in Ruth's spare bedchamber. He pretended not to care very much, one way or the other. Although my great-uncle never said so, it was easy to see that he did not approve of Ruth Coffee. Her robust use of the language bothered him, although Uncle Reuben talked

235

about the same and Lije never gave a thought to that. I had noticed before that when Great-Uncle Lije came home, expecting to find Great Aunt Elizabeth in the house, and she was out somewhere, he seemed to lose his grip. He was inattentive to what was said, and disapproving of what he heard, until he saw his wife coming over the Salem Street hill. She only came that way, because of the gang of loafers around Black Ann's corner.

There were other things about Ruth that rubbed Lije the wrong way. He was not sure it was decent for a woman to go out shooting or fishing with a gang of men, dressed in men's clothes. He never complained because she could make vegetables and flowers grow, and make things out of wood with her lathe. Of course, he was handier with tools than she was, but whatever he touched in the yard showed the kind of perverse resistance to his will that Zach displayed. A few years back he had decided, for instance, to plant some summer squash, some pumpkins, and some cucumbers, so he bought some seeds in the little narrow alley of Faneuil Hall, prepared the soil, and planted them in rows, side by side. Now when a man in Linden did anything like that, the innocent way in which his neighbors let him go ahead, was marvellous to see. They would come and lean on the fence, as the plants were coming up, and talk about how nice it would be to pick fresh squash and cukes and pumpkins from his own vines. Even Mr. Weeks, as shy and free from malice as he was, came over two or three times that season, and walked up and down, as Lije was weeding. When the vines grew luxuriantly and flowered, the bees came over from the nearby clover fields. It seemed as if they never could get enough, as they crawled and burrowed and rubbed their wings.

Ruth Coffee, sensing that Lije was not enthusiastic about her, and taking it in good part, did not join the other neighbors at the fence, but Lije had seen her looking at his garden in a mischievous way, and had heard her laughing afterwards, when he saw nothing to laugh at.

Zach got loose that year, several times, as he always did, and tramped and nibbled quite a few of the other vegetables, but he seemed to be scrupulously careful not to go near the cucumbers, the squash or the pumpkin vines.

Packard, when he stopped to deliver groceries when Lije was home, asked my great-uncle if, maybe, he would not have some cucumbers left over, that Markham could buy, and knock off the price from Lije's bill.

Nothing in *Alice in Wonderland* could compare with what appeared in Lije's garden that summer. A cucumber would start out at one end as a cucumber should, then develop an abnormal series of knobs and bumps like summer squash, and flare out into a pumpkin shape, with the colors all patched and mingled. The dark green of the cucumbers was splotched all over the pumpkins. The same men who had watched the vines grow and the bees wallow in the flowers made believe they were astonished and impressed at the riotous mixup that nature had achieved.

My great-uncle gritted his teeth, and bore it for a little while, then he hitched up Zach, ploughed up the whole mess, and glared at his wife all evening, just waiting for her to smile. She controlled herself until, about nine o'clock, she heard Ruth Coffee and three or four men who were over in Ruth's cottage playing seven-up, let out peals and bellows of laughter. She started laughing, choked and could not stop, and for three nights Lije slept in another bedroom and said nothing at the table or between meals in the daytime. He noticed, of course, too late, that Ruth and all the other good gardeners had planted their cucumbers, squash and pumpkins, and whatever else grew on similar vines, in separate patches at a safe distance from one another, but those vegetables did not appear on

Lije's table for three or four years, and my great-aunt, the first time she risked serving squash in a pie, was careful to invite the minister for dinner.

The Saturday evening Dr. Worcester was in Linden, he went with Doc Moody to the Massasoit for supper, and praised Jeff Lee's baked beans and brown bread. According to Uncle Reuben, who was not exactly talking to me, he made quite a hit with all the regulars, although neither of the doctors would say a word about what was uppermost in everyone's mind. They let it be understood that the schoolteacher was going to get well, and that was all. That took a heavy load from Ginger's mind.

As the evening wore on, Mr. Wing asked Dr. Worcester about Packard's powders, whether it was possible to mix up a medicine that stirred up the women, without doing any harm. Packard was present, but maintained his usual noncommittal air, neither admitting nor denying any knowledge of such a formula.

Dr. Worcester smiled in his quiet, unassuming way, and the Admiral, Mr. Stowe, the fishman, Walt Robbins, Ginger, and the others hovered around expectantly. All the talk in the back room quieted down, so those at a distance could hear.

"In Burton's *Anatomy of Melancholy*," Dr. Worcester began, "he quotes some old authorities of the time of Charlemagne. The great emperor, it seems, for years had been in love with a woman who was ugly and old, and none of the courtiers or ladies of the court could understand why a man who ruled the world, and could summon any beautiful young girl to his chamber, was content with an old hag whom even the stable hands and roustabouts would not have stayed with."

"You mean this old party would really stop a clock," said Ginger. By that time, even Pehr the Finn had overcome his diffidence and was standing by.

"Clocks were not invented until fifty years later," Mr. Wing interposed.

The doctor nodded. "That one would have stopped an hour glass," he said. "And even after she died, Charlemagne had her body embalmed and kept her in the palace, inconsolable. He would not leave her side, his appetite fell off, he paid no attention to the public welfare. It got to such a point that the bishop, trying to find out what could be done, prayed to the Lord, and it was revealed to the bishop, according to the testimony of contemporary writers, that the hideous old woman had some kind of a love charm on her person.

"The bishop waited until the emperor was asleep, then stole into the royal bedroom where the old witch was lying in state, and found the love charm, a stone or some powders tied up in a sack. The bishop took it from the folds of her gown and started away."

"Did that cure the king?" the Admiral asked.

"That made things worse," the doctor said. "Charlemagne awoke while the bishop was still in the room, tackled him from behind, and what happened to His Grace can better be imagined than described, in company."

"Let's hope it was a Protestant bishop," said Ginger, fervently.

"The bishop, as soon as he could get away, threw the love charm into a lake nearby, and from that moment on the great emperor loved the lake, and would not leave its shores. He built a palace there, and there he died."

The listeners chuckled, roared and applauded, and as soon as the commotion died down, Mr. Wing turned to Ginger.

"I ought to tell you, Ginger," he said, "that there were no Protestant bishops until six hundred years later."

Ginger crossed himself and groaned.

The Admiral urged Dr. Worcester to stay the night, but

239

the doctor said he had to take the last train back to Boston, because there were sure to be several cases of Saturday night paralysis brought into the hospital, and the interns did not know exactly how to handle them.

"Saturday night paralysis?" asked Uncle Reuben, suspecting a gag.

"We never have less than a dozen cases over the week-end. It's the same in all large cities," said the doctor. "A man, or, unfortunately, sometimes a woman, gets drunk, lies in a gutter to sleep it off, and rests an elbow on the granite curbstone. The sleep is so deep that the blood circulation in the arm is cut off for hours, and when the drunk wakes up he can't move his arm, sometimes for two or three days."

"I never get any cases as simple as that," Doc Moody said, ruefully.

Before Dr. Worcester started for the depot, he asked to use the telephone.

"I've surely got to put in one of those things," the Admiral said, apologetically.

"You know," Dr. Worcester said. "It's got so that around the hospital we use them, just to save ourselves running up and down stairs."

CHAPTER FIFTEEN

Pursuits of Happiness

◆

SUNDAY was bright and clear. A little earlier than usual, I finished dinner and went across the street to Miss Stoddard's yard, where I sat under the sassafras tree to wait for her to come out. There were two large trees in the Stoddard yard, the sassafras, with leaves shaped like mittens on a remnant counter at Raymond's, and a tall cherry tree from which I picked the fruit each year. The rest of the front yard had small pear trees, very old, and a long grape arbor which, each fall, was loaded with the finest Concord grapes.

From the back of the Stoddard house to the creek, the land sloped downward, and was a sanctuary for the frogs and garter snakes which elsewhere in Linden were not properly esteemed.

We took the path to Elephant's Back that day, Miss Stoddard and I, and sat to enjoy the broad panorama below, within a yard of where I had hidden the paring knife. Usually our conversation was brisk and touched a variety of subjects. On that afternoon not much had been said, because Miss Stoddard was reluctant and uncertain as to how far she should go, and I, being entitled to an explanation, was not willing to delay it by talking about something else.

"Elliot," she began, at last. "I'm not sure how much I ought to tell you. The truth is not free, like the air. Little chunks of it belong to other people, and those we can't pass around, without their consent. Suppose you tell me what you think happened the other night, and then, perhaps, I can explain."

That was a typical Miss Stoddard subtlety, which I understood. The more I had found out for myself, the more she could discuss, without violating a confidence.

"I think that Elvira doesn't like Ruth Coffee. Elvira's jealous because her sister likes Ruth, and will do what Ruth asks," I said. I saw from Miss Stoddard's expression that I was on the right track.

"Go on," she said.

"I think that when Ruth started out of Mrs. Townsend's house to look for Alice in the woods, when it was dark, Elvira followed her and stabbed her," I continued.

To emphasize my words, I leaned over, took the knife from its hiding place and handed it to Miss Stoddard. This really surprised her, and broke down what was left of her reluctance to speak.

"Where did you get that?" she asked.

"Not far from where we found Ruth, Friday night," I said.

In her anxiety, Miss Stoddard asked: "Does anyone know?" I looked at her reproachfully.

"Excuse me," she said. "You are doing our friends a very great favor."

I sighed. I was still in the fog.

"Last Fourth of July, when some Dago from Boston. . . ." I said.

She interrupted. "Some Italian," she corrected.

"When some Italian from Boston got drunk and cut Pep Marincola's father, the man was arrested and got sixty days," I said.

"Ruth does not want Elvira arrested," Miss Stoddard said.

"I know that. But why?" I asked.

Miss Stoddard took her turn, and shook her head, smiling

at me ruefully. "Why seems to be your favorite word," she said.

"Isn't it better to find out about things?" I asked.

"That," said Miss Stoddard, thoughtfully, "is a very hard question. But if you're built that way, you have to find out. You don't sleep as well nights as those who are not curious. Too bad. There's no alternative."

"Why doesn't Ruth want Elvira to be arrested?" I persisted.

"As long as Ruth has that hold over Elvira and Mrs. Townsend, she can make them agree to do what's best for Alice," Miss Stoddard said.

"You mean, for Alice to stay with Ruth?"

"Exactly," Miss Stoddard said.

"Forever?" I asked.

"Forever is only a word. Nothing goes on after it is finished and done with," she said. "Right now, while Alice is so nervous, it is bad for her to have two other nervous people around her all the time. As long as she stayed with her mother and sister, she would never get well."

As she spoke, Miss Stoddard looked with distaste at the stained knife in her hand. She rose, tucking it into her belt, handle upward, and we started walking toward Sugar Pond.

"The doctor from Boston," she began.

"Dr. Alfred Worcester," I said.

"That's right. Good man," she said. "You heard that old Dr. Goodenough from Malden said Alice was crazy and incurable."

"*Dementia praecox*," I said, nodding in agreement. "Dr. Moody didn't agree."

"You seem to know as much as I do," said Miss Stoddard.

"I don't yet," I said. "What did Dr. Moody and Dr. Worcester think was wrong, that made her act so queer, make such

243

a fuss over nothing, sleep for days, lose her job, and hide her-self in a chest?"

"Hysteria," Miss Stoddard said. "Strain and worry, day after day, year after year. They tested her brain, and found it was as good as anyone's . . . who didn't have a better one to start with."

"Don't brains get better, as a person gets older?" I asked.

"No," Miss Stoddard said.

I did not like that much, but it was not the moment to start Miss Stoddard on another track.

"What's hysteria?" I asked.

"Nerves," she said.

"Just nerves," I said.

"Dr. Worcester told Ruth that sometimes he thought the doctors knew as much about brains as about people's nerves. That would be next to nothing," she said.

We had reached the edge of Sugar Pond, where the sugar maples, spaced a few feet apart, just far enough to make room for boughs and branches, stood with their trunks in the water. Between were frog's eggs and lily pads, with tips of rushes sticking up, and water spiders skipping nimbly in zigzags. Some turtles who had been sunning themselves, slid casually into the water. A water snake, whose eyes and the flattened top of his head were just above the surface, ducked under, but not too hurriedly, and by virtue of effortless motion, more liquid and perfect than Annette Kellerman or Pavlowa could ever achieve, moved from where he had been to wherever he was going.

I watched him fade into the Rembrandt background of depth and brownness, and so did Mary Stoddard. Then I looked up at her, she looked at me and then at the knife, and slowly drew it from her belt and, as I nodded assent, tossed it into the water, where it sank, not ungracefully, and hid itself forever in the ooze.

I had one more question.

"What is Mrs. Townsend going to do. . . ." I stopped, always loath to talk about money.

"Without Alice's salary, you mean?" Miss Stoddard asked.

I nodded.

"We are coming to that, later," she said.

Before the afternoon was over, I knew what she meant. A maneuver of diplomacy was afoot, in a characteristically Linden way.

When it became apparent to Dr. Moody that Alice would have a better chance, away from her tremulous family, he had at first thought of an institution or a nursing home. Ruth had been horrified by that suggestion, and she and the doctor were sure it would throw the Townsend women into a panic. Mrs. Townsend would accept aid, services and occasional donations of food for the invalid, but never cash. And obviously the mother could not pay for Alice to be kept in a sanitarium. The public institutions and clinics were all for the feeble-minded or the insane, and Dr. Moody would as soon have thought of chloroforming Alice himself as sending her to an asylum.

Ruth had money enough, or could make enough, to take care of Alice, but that would still leave Mrs. Townsend and Elvira without funds, so Ruth used her excellent head and figured out a solution. Cobb, Bates and Yerxa, fancy grocers and importers in Boston, had started a department where fresh "homemade" cakes, pastry, rolls, crullers and doughnuts were on sale, or could be delivered on order in the metropolitan area. Like S. S. Pierce, "Cobb, Bates" had built a reputation for integrity that went back almost to Colonial times, and when they advertised goods as "homemade," it meant they had to be made in somebody's home. So they had made arrangements with housewives in the Boston suburbs to install large baking ovens and equipment, to be paid for as used, and furnished by the gross the delicacies Cobb, Bates sold. The store supplied the materials and the recipes, which had to be followed scrupulously, and thus many women, by working hard and long, in their own homes, were able to make a good living. "Cobb, Bates" tried to locate worthy women who had children they could not leave alone, and no men folks to support them.

So Ruth went first to Dawson Freeman, as who did not when favors were sadly needed, and Dawson made such an impression and stated the Townsend predicament so eloquently that all the partners of Cobb, Bates and Yerxa were making free use of their handkerchiefs and readily consented to make an exception to their rule of employing mothers with young children. Ruth insisted on paying for the ovens and baking equipment outright, and letting Mrs. Townsend believe it was furnished by the firm. The only hitch, then, was Mrs. Townsend's frenzied hatred of Ruth, who she believed had bewitched and stolen her daughter, and turned Elvira into a potential murderess.

Miss Stoddard had suggested to Ruth that she ask my mother to talk with Mrs. Townsend about the opportunities for baking for Cobb, Bates and Yerxa, so Mrs. Townsend would never know the idea had come from Ruth. Ruth, in turn, believed Miss Stoddard had more influence with Mother than Ruth did. So on that Sunday afternoon, before Miss Stoddard and I finished off the day, at twilight, with chocolate and animal crackers, and a story she read from Tolstoi or Chekhov, we stopped at our house to ask Mother if she would see Mrs. Townsend and put over the deal that would save them from starvation.

Mother understood readily that Mrs. Townsend might be resentful and suspicious of Ruth. Although Mother seldom took sides, if she could help it, she had listened to those women in the Social Circle who thought Dr. Moody and Ruth and the stranger from Boston had acted highhandedly in taking Alice from her mother's house. That those good women did not know about Elvira and the knife, had led them into hasty conclusions.

"They all think it's Alice who's crazy, when really it's Elvira," I said later to Miss Stoddard, when we were alone.

"Dr. Worcester said, and I have also noticed, that when one member of a family is cracked, some other member is the one who breaks down," Miss Stoddard said. I thought about that a long time, and have often thought about it since.

Of course, my mother warmed to Ruth, when she learned how much trouble Ruth had taken to provide for Mrs. Townsend. So on Monday, my mother put on her best hat and coat, her Sunday shoes, and sweetest, most persuasive expression, and not only did Mrs. Townsend consent to the proposition, but welcomed it, prayerfully, as coming, through my good mother, directly from God. That made my mother a little ashamed of herself, taking credit for a plan that was not hers.

Anyway, Mrs. Townsend and Elvira were soon busy from morning until night, and their mental and physical health seemed much improved. The deliverymen from Cobb, Bates and Yerxa, swore roundly because of the thirty outside steps down which tray after tray of hot homemade rolls and tarts had to be carried, but the partners, on account of Dawson Freeman's eloquence, had told the superintendent to tell the drivers to give the Townsends every consideration, and the drivers were helpless to protest.

The little red cottage, trimmed with white, and surrounded by sweet peas, sunflowers, phlox, asters and petunias, in which

Ruth and Alice lived, turned out to be one of the snuggest and happiest homes in Linden. Ruth in dungarees and simple blouses worked indoors and out, her cheerful voice resounding. Alice, as dainty and fragile as a rose, grew more lovely, more confident, and shyly radiant each day. I often found reasons for calling on them, or lingering in their antique shop or yard, because I felt the same harmony, the same unspoken understandings, the tenderness that was not objectionable because it was restrained, the mutual esteem and the relish of the passing hours that soothed me, and intrigued me, when I had visited Mr. and Mrs. Ford, or Lawyer Perkins and lovely Cousin Ella. I cannot tell you how deeply I believed, as a child, that people should have a good time, should do things they liked to do, and live with those who loved them. Again Telemachus.

"*Tuan?*" Alice would ask softly, of Ruth. She called her *Tuan*, or master of the house, to tease her. "*Tuan?*" she would say. "What shall we have for tea? Fresh raspberries, from the bushes beyond the fountain? With thick cream, from Mr. Weeks' pans in the well? From a pan without a mouse? And nut wafers?"

Ruth seldom agreed right away. She liked to make a counter-suggestion, and talk a while, watching Alice's expressions, her naïve gestures, her blooming health and timid joy.

"We might have cinnamon toast and bayberry preserves, and a little shot of Medford Rum in the tea," Ruth would say.

My Great-Uncle Lije, across the way, if he heard, sometimes got so upset that he squashed an egg in his hand, in picking it up from the yard, where some hen had strayed. Lije's hens laid eggs almost anywhere except in the nests. The more trouble he took to keep the hen house clean and dry, the more the hens ignored their conveniences. They often roosted in the willows down by the creek, where the muskrats could find them, while the ducks waddled up from the water and plucked young pansy plants from the front yard.

Lije's cucumbers and summer squash were famous, all over the county and the Cape. He topped them, later, with his rabbit house. Instead of building it up in the barnyard, where he would have to water the rabbits from the pump, he conceived the idea of putting it near enough the creek so the rabbits could drink when they felt like it, if the tide was going out and the water was fresh. Again, the neighbors watched, in all innocence, and offered no advice. But Mary Stoddard, when she heard about it, and the rabbit house was half-built, and the runway surrounded with chicken wire, laughed until the tears ran down her cheeks, between the warts and moles.

"Lutie," she said to my mother. "Tell Lije that rabbits don't drink."

"They don't drink?" my mother asked, astonished.

Then she could not help smiling. My gentle mother was not going to be the one to spring this information on Great-Uncle Lije, but she told Great-Aunt Elizabeth. My great-aunt did not care to tell her husband, either. So she resorted to what, for her, was a wily subterfuge. She wrote the *Boston Globe,* which Lije read every day, asking the editor if it were true that rabbits did not drink, and if so, how they got along without water. Day after day she watched the *Globe's* correspondence column and the morning it appeared, she was so nervous that she burned the muffins twice, before she got the breakfast table set. The *Globe* confirmed Miss Stoddard. Rabbits got the moisture they needed from the dew on fodder and lettuce and the juice the greens contained.

"What's got into you, Lizzie?" Lije asked, when he noticed that her hand was shaking so that the saucer was shimmering and the coffee slipping over when she passed him his moustache cup.

"I don't know why I feel so nervous this morning. Must be the change of moon," she said.

"That's all tommyrot," Lije said, then his eye hit the little Doric head over the letter signed "Housewife" about rabbits. He did not say a word. Grimly he finished the eggs, fried potatoes and country sausage on his plate, ate four buttered muffins and drank three cups of coffee. My great-aunt waited and watched. Lije was not going to the shipyard that day, and she saw him cross the street. Ruth and Alice were at breakfast. They had some pet rabbits, because they could not bear to throw away the lettuce they had left over. Each head had been tended so carefully, as was everything that grew around the cottage, that Alice said she felt she knew them personally and that their feelings would be hurt if she tossed them on the pile with grass-cuttings and raked-up leaves for mould.

"Mind if I look at your rabbits?" Lije asked.

"Why, no. Go ahead," said Ruth. "I haven't fed 'em yet. I'll be out in a jiffy."

When Ruth went out, with a dish of clover and lettuce in her hand, Lije was glaring into the rabbit hutch. No dish for water was provided. He made the rounds of several barnyards that morning, and his observation was the same. When he got back home, in a most difficult mood, he found that Tom Bagley's local express had delivered a wooden case addressed to him. Bewildered, he opened it, while my Great-Aunt Elizabeth looked curiously on. It was a case of what was called "tonic," that is, soft drinks flavored weakly with strawberry, lemon or sarsaparilla, in half-pint bottles with tin caps on top.

"Did you order any such hogwash as this?" Lije asked his wife.

"Why, no," she said.

Then Lije saw a card, picked it up, turned green and gray, and stuffed it quickly in his pocket. It read:

"To Elijah Prentiss Griffin, Esq., for his rabbits.

Compliments of his fellow-members of the

Linden Improvement Association."

Rover, who had been sitting behind the stove, got up quietly, made his way to the screen door, pushed it open, and crossed Salem Street into the woods, and was not seen again that day. When something got Lije mad, the sympathetic Newfoundland was likely to do that. He was not afraid of his master, he liked better not to witness the manifestations of his temper.

Lije started pell-mell for the south side of the tracks, to find Tom Bagley and find out who gave him that case of tonic to haul, but Tom was not home, and by the time the day was over, Lije had mastered his emotions and set out for a voyage to Rockport in his boat. While he was gone, my Great-Aunt Elizabeth hired Irv Walker to dismantle the unfinished rabbit house by the creek and carry all traces of it away.

She did not know until later that Lije, when his motor had kicked back and hurt his wrist, had jerked it out of the *Petrel II* and dumped it over the side, although it weighed four hundred pounds, avoirdupois, and had negotiated the difficult course over the marsh, and along the coast, threading in and out of some of the world's most treacherous reefs and hidden shoals, with nothing but sails and a stout pair of oars. Lije felt better after that, because nobody else in Linden could have done it, and not more than three men on Cape Ann.

That was the year the Italian women, not the ones who had settled in Linden, began searching the woods and fields for dandelion greens, slippery elm, spruce gum, and various roots, herbs and simples. They were as conspicuous and mysterious as Gypsies, with their gaily colored bandanas on their heads, shawls around their shoulders, earrings and loops in their ears, and six or more full petticoats.

When a Greater Boston meat packer, one of the pioneers of streetcar advertising, bought a vast truck farm in Revere, not two miles east of the Linden line, he hired a lot of Italians—men, women and children—who moved from Boston's crowded North End to the land on the border of the marsh. The Linden housewives, from below the Square, could see them moving, with push-carts and borrowed junk wagons, cloth bundles and innumerable babies. Every Saturday and Sunday the immigrants would swarm to the new settlement, where they had made first payments on small tracts of land, which they staked out, fenced, planted, and made ready for ramshackle little houses. They were under the protection of Senator Mangini, an Italian from Chelsea, and one of the first of his extraction to be elected to and attain wide influence in the Massachusetts legislature. The Senator was known and trusted by all Italians and Jews north of Boston, and preserved the reputation as long as he lived of never cheating a countryman or a member of a minority race, or permitting such men to be cheated with impunity. Immigrants in those days had small trust in banks, or understanding of their impersonal functions. They kept their savings in their socks, or hid them in buried lard pails, until they were ready to turn over a sum to Senator Mangini, for transportation of incoming kinfolk from Italy, to post as bonds for small subcontracts, to buy expensive musical instruments on the installment plan, or for the purchase of land. That was the dream closest to each immigrant's heart, to own his home and a plot of ground in free America.

Thus, weekly feasts and celebrations enlivened the former stretch of wasteland between the Massasoit's skating pond and the meat packer's farm, the last of its acreage and scope in northeastern Massachusetts. Accordion music was borne on the breeze, red wine flowed, and one by one, small tar-paper shacks went up, with detached little backhouses, all kinds of makeshift fences, and small trees transplanted from the woods or orchards. To the immigrants, the settlement was a heaven on earth, which could be tasted, smelled, and touched. To the middle-class Lindeners, it was an eyesore.

So when the Italian women used to come across the Linden line, with huge clothes baskets and flat kitchen knives or trowels, to pick bushels of greens and pecks of mushrooms, few citizens took pleasure in meeting or greeting them, partaking of their dreams and traditions, or sharing what went on in their hearts. This is sad, but it is true, and thus was lost much education.

Frigger Bacigalupo, one of Linden's smartest boys, tried to talk with these newcomers, but the dialect his parents had taught him, Siciliano, was not understood by Italians from provinces on the mainland, so when Frigger noticed that the old and wise Italian women were collecting certain plants, roots and bark, the uses of which he did not comprehend, he called on Palmira Di Brazzio as interpreter.

When Palmira relayed to Frigger what she had learned from her *paesani*, his delight knew no bounds. He made her promise, on pain of revealing to her father what went on at the Massasoit, not to say a word about the new discoveries to anybody, until he could get the proposition organized on a commercial scale. Some of the natural stimulants the Italian women gathered were believed to have all the virtues attributed to Packard's powders, and others would relieve the unlucky consequences of having loved, not wisely but too well.

This was the apex of an inverted pyramid of prosperity that Frigger Bacigalupo is enlarging to this day. It chanced that soon after Frigger had bought all he could of the medicines, prepared and wrapped by the immigrants at very low rates, Big Julie had been obliged to confide to the girls at the Massasoit, who passed on the information to their men friends, that she was in trouble. The big good-natured girl made little fuss about her condition, but she was worried, and when Frigger offered her, for only five dollars, a sure cure for her woes, and she had tried the stuff and it had worked, Frigger's stock went up promptly around town. Because of the success of his birth-control preparation, more men were willing to try out his aphrodisiacs. Through the grapevine the news spread among the women, as far as the ultrarespectable Social Circle, and a mild mass hysteria developed which began to step up Linden's birth rate, and decrease the percentage of lovers who had to leave town.

Poor Dud Shultz was bombarded with questions, not only by the Massasoit jokers, but by his most reputable customers, and was on the verge of a nervous breakdown again when Uncle Reuben, the Admiral, Mr. Wing and others among the patrons of the bar, framed up another prank, of which Dud was to be the butt.

As everybody knew, Dud continued his weekly excursions to Boston on the trolley car, without ever saying a word to anyone as to where he went or how he spent his time. It was Dud's night to roam, and Big Julie had told the men she was going to town that evening, so they suggested that, no matter how few people there were on the car, she sit right up close to Dud and try to lead him astray.

"He can't edge away no farther than the end of the car," Ginger said.

"Go on. You're twice his size," said Hal Kingsland. "Make him give in."

Big Julie looked a little sorry for the nervous little man, in advance, but she agreed to do what she could.

"Tell him you took some of the Italian herbs, and can't sit still," the Admiral suggested.

When the 8:15 car jolted past the Massasoit that evening,

many pairs of eyes were watching. It was one of those old-fashioned cars with plush seats along both sides and an aisle in the middle. The Massasoit regulars were convulsed with laughter when they saw that little Dud and Julie were the only passengers. And notwithstanding that, they had the entire car to themselves, Julie was sitting, knees wide apart, right up next to Dud, whose face showed consternation.

That was the last they saw of either of them for quite a while, and when they came back, they were married. Julie never would tell anyone what had happened, and with her to protect him, no one could take advantage of little Dud again. Julie watched over him like a mother hen. She kept house, cooked his meals, washed his ears, shampooed his hair, and even cut his toenails. When Dud was resting, upstairs, and Julie tended the drugstore, she gave back the ribald customers as good as they sent, with all her former gusto. The Linden folks began to respect the little druggist, who lost his sense of inferiority and became quite cocky.

I am proud to say that the Linden gallants were as capable of chivalry as of mischief, so Julie's past was allowed to drift back into oblivion.

"Upon my word, he calls her 'Twinkle,'" said Mr. Wing, a few days after the honeymooners had returned. I think Mr. Wing, always a restrained and courteous gentleman, took as much pleasure in the unexpected romantic development as anyone in town. Mr. Wing did not exaggerate. The tiny little druggist, five feet three, with a husky, squeaky voice, addressed his six-foot strapping wife as "Twinkle" and she called him "Bunny."

"Twinkle," Dud would say, rather pettishly, when things got too much for him, "come here."

"Yes, Bunny. Why sure," Big Julie would reply, and drop

255

whatever she was doing, instantly, to go to his side and resolve his minor difficulty.

Sometimes the efforts of the customers to rattle Julie—now they seldom got a chance at Dud—turned out constructively. For instance, Hal Kingsland, soon after he became a full-time fireman, said one day to Julie, while Dud was fussing and pottering at the prescription counter:

"What's the matter around here? Don't you know all first-class drugstores have soda fountains these days?"

"It's better to be a second-class druggist than a first-class jerk," Julie answered, right off the bat.

But two weeks later a soda fountain and all the necessary equipment were delivered at the Linden depot, addressed to Dudley R. Shultz, Esquire, and with "Twinkle" presiding as the first local soda-jerker, the innovation became a Linden institution.

There, where loneliness and anxiety had been, was another happy home.

"Darned if it isn't nice to have something turn out decent," Uncle Reuben said.

CHAPTER SIXTEEN

Of Racial Minorities

◆

THE problems of race antagonisms, in a world that was growing more complicated daily, were neatly simplified in Linden.
The middle-class Protestants who lived north of the Saugus
Branch tracks constituted the majority group, about two-thirds
of the population. The proletarian Catholics on the south side
of town numbered nearly one-third. There was one Negro,
Jeff Lee, the justly famous cook at the Massasoit; two Jews,
little Moe Selib, who ran the tailor shop and lived two miles
away, in Faulkner, and Ben Friedmann, the junkman from
Lynn; and one Chinese, Wong Lee, who toiled in steam and
Oriental fragrance from early until late, every weekday and
all the holidays except Christmas and the Fourth of July.

In the course of the years I was in Linden, there were three
Wongs Lee, one after the other, but the sign over the laundry
doorway was never changed. A few of the customers keenly
sensitive to personalities, like the Admiral, Uncle Reuben, or
Mr. Wing, noticed the switch, when a different Chinaman appeared behind the little counter. Lots of the Linden folks did
not.

Chinese coolies in those years had a fixed price in the Boston
area, and Chinese laundries flourished in every small community and nearly every city block. There was absolutely no
awareness among Linden people of the awakening in the
Orient, of Sun Yat Sen and his Republic, of clouds and dreams

and global unity. The Linden Chinaman had little or no connection with the civic life or the body politic, except to do a prodigious amount of work for a paltry sum of money, even according to the nineteenth-century standards. Starched shirts were laundered for five cents apiece, and stiff collars, two cents. Detached cuffs were two cents the pair.

The little one-story shack in the Square which was occupied by Wong Lee had a front room with shelves and a counter and a smaller kitchen behind it, which was screened from public view by a bead curtain which portrayed, in a very free style, Jesus among the little children. The only English words in sight were on a Chinese red pasteboard placard on the wall of matched boards. This read: "Suffer the little children to come unto Me, and forbid them not, for of such is the kingdom of Heaven." The first two Wongs Lee did not know what those words meant. They could neither read nor write English. But one of the boss Chinamen in Boston had given Number 1 the placard and had told him it was a good thing to have on his wall. Wong's not to reason why.

The standard price in Boston, for specific Chinese coolies smuggled in, was six hundred dollars. They were brought, for the most part, by Chinese theological students of the better class, who had been induced by missionaries in China to come to Boston in order to prepare themselves for the Christian ministry and to help convert the 600,000,000 of their heathen countrymen to the religion that bore the name of Jesus of Nazareth. Now the Chinese students cared relatively little for Jesus of Nazareth or any of His teachings, except that somehow the setup gave them a free trip to the Western world and the opportunity of learning English and American languages and ways. The educated Chinese preferred the Taoist philosophy and Confucian ethics to those of Christ, but they were careful not to let the missionaries or their teachers in the seminaries know that, since it might have made them feel badly, and be more careful with their funds.

So the Chinese theological students who were opulent bought one or more coolies in Boston for six hundred dollars apiece, put them to work in small laundries, and took enough of the profits to enable them to live a lifetime in luxury in China. When the rich students had completed their courses and felt the urge for their homeland, they resold the coolies to incoming Chinese freshmen, or to one of the Tong bosses who could always find use for a good industrious man who spoke and understood little English.

The chief smuggler of Chinese into Massachusetts lived at the Castle Square Hotel in Boston. But one of his leg men, a mild-mannered, studious-looking expressman, with a soft voice and wistful brogue from the old sod, the laugh with a tear in it, and all the equipment of the professional or stage Irishman, Tom Bagley by name, lived in Linden, and, when he worked at all, helped the "Chief" bring Chinese over the Canadian border. Tom had freckles, pale-blue eyes, mild red hair, and would talk with anyone by the hour about anything except what was really on his mind. Tom was the first man I ever met who, by instinct, or on principle, never told the truth. Periodically he would disappear from Linden for about a week. His wife, Nora, was a quiet, pious woman who kept their two red-headed children, a boy and a girl about my age, spic-and-span, accompanied them to and from school, much to the boy's embarrassment, walked regularly to Maplewood for Mass, and seemed to be beyond reproach.

Tom Bagley owned a horse and wagon and ran a "Private Express." In cases of emergency, he would consent to haul a trunk or a box to or from the Linden depot. Usually he found some reason why he could not accept the commission. He and his family lived well, but not extravagantly, and it was not until years later, when Tom and Frigger Bacigalupo were in the rum-running organization of the same chief smuggler, that the word got out, explaining Tom's mysterious absences from home, over a period of years.

Tom used to drive over the Canadian border, from Vermont, with an empty wagon and return with sacks of potatoes or onions. The Chinese, hunched into one or two of the bottom sacks, thus gained their entry into the land of the free. There was an "underground" route, carefully mapped out and kept in operation by the Chief, from a Canadian port of entry to St. Johns, then through the province of Quebec to the Vermont line at Philipsburg, and through northern New England to Boston and Providence. Most of the coolies went to Boston operators. The opium went to Providence.

It is not likely that those astute men who guided Sino-American affairs in the metropolitan area would have assigned a laundryman to a town in which lived the man who had brought the coolie over the border. So Wong Lee and Tom Bagley had no previous acquaintance.

Most Linden people were firmly of the opinion that all Chinamen looked alike, and it was not until some years later that I learned, from a charming normal school student, a Chinese girl who had been sent by the Republican government to Salem to learn to be a teacher, that to the Oriental eye Americans are hard to distinguish, one from another. She said that she spent several weeks in the normal school before she could tell her teachers apart.

Wong Lee fascinated me, from the beginning. There were a few men, like Jerry Dineen or Mr. Weeks or Charley Moore with his law books, who showed a fair amount of application, but the Chinaman never let up for a moment. When the first train left Linden for Boston each morning, Wong Lee was working in his tiny kitchen, prodding wash boilers full of shirts and soapy water with a forked wooden stick. Later he appeared at the counter where he did his ironing, squirting water from his mouth to aid him in achieving a flawless polish. Wong seemed to know that I had no unfriendly intentions toward him, and made no objections when I stood silently in the shop, after having received and paid for my brother Charles' laundry. I watched Wong with black ink and a brush write Chinese characters on red squares of paper, then tear them in two, one for the customer, one for the package on the shelf, when the work was finished. I tried to ask him, or to figure out for myself, what the strange marks meant, whether they were words, mottoes like those in our penmanship books, pictures, or numbers. Now and then I asked him to tell me the Chinese word for lichi nuts or joss sticks or firecrackers or shirts and collars, but he would smile briefly and evade the question, if he understood it. Nothing interrupted the tempo of his work. Whether he was at the washboard, or the ironing board, or making change, or preparing slips of paper, Wong moved swiftly, quietly and efficiently.

On Saturday evenings, Wong caught the last streetcar that moved across the marshes toward Boston, and returned on the last car into Linden on Sunday evening. He dressed in loose black trousers, a loose black jacket, and wore heelless slippers which made a soft shuffling sound when he walked. The first and second Wong Lee had queues, the third had a sort of convict's haircut. It was the common belief in Linden that Chinamen who cut off their queues could not return to China. Also, most Linden people were sure that Chinese women were curiously unlike white girls. In fact, one of the minor articles that Frigger Bacigalupo had for sale, before he broke into the big-time rackets, was a post-card picture of a Chinese woman exposed in such a way as to confirm the popular belief about the Chinese female anatomy. Already, when the century was so young and the art of photography still in its infancy, trick photography was commercially exploited.

I always wondered about Wong Lee, and the mysterious far side of the world he represented, what his childhood had been like, what he thought and felt, what made him work so hard and endlessly, whether the world as he saw it made sense, and, if so, what kind of sense. I wondered what I should do, if I were in China, with no one to talk to or listen to from Sunday midnight until Saturday midnight, week after week. I envied him his knowledge of the strange and beautiful writing, with paint brush and black ink; his having travelled such distances; the lure of Chinatown in Boston; his haunting singsong speech; the colored sketches on his boxes of tea. Without Wong, I should have doubted my geography books. My Great-Uncle Lije and several of my seafaring relatives had touched the ports of China, but they said as little about it as Wong Lee did. I wondered if I should ever go there, or go anywhere. When I learned how Chinamen were smuggled in, and had their existences mapped out for them, I felt sometimes a little regretful that there were no corresponding arrangements in Peking or Shanghai. Only I was sure that I would never be good at doing laundry or wrapping packages. I was fairly sure that I would never be very good at doing anything useful. I only hoped that I should be happy and lucky, like my Uncle Reuben, and urbane, like Mr. Wing.

No Jew ever lived in Linden. All of his customers liked Moe Selib, and found his workmanship satisfactory, but Moe did not stay in Linden overnight. For sleeping, and the rest of his home life, he walked to Faulkner where nearly everyone was Jewish, or rode to Chelsea, where the Irish, Jews and Italians ran the city, and made up seven-tenths of its population.

Quite early in the century, when surrounding communities were receiving a steady influx of Jews, the Linden Protestants, and the more prosperous Catholics who owned their homes, banded together into what was called the "Linden Improvement Association." No one, in my hearing, questioned its propriety or called it un-American. There was no personal anti-Semitism, because Ben Friedmann, the itinerant junkman, and Moe Selib were personally very popular, smart and amusing. Ben bought and sold the junk. Moe made and pressed the suits, honestly, gaily, and in a citizen-like manner. Moe had taken out his first papers. Ben had not, although he intended to some time, and never got around to it until his son came home from Dartmouth College in time for the First World War.

The purpose of the Linden Improvement Association was to protect real estate values in Linden, which meant a thoroughgoing understanding between all property owners that neither houses nor lots would ever be sold to Jews. It was purely a business proposition. Wherever the Jews crowded in, as they had already in Chelsea and Faulkner, property values went down, and the Jewish children swarmed into the schools, Jewish adults bought up all the small and large businesses, and Gentiles had either to become a minority without influence or pull up stakes and move. The men I liked most, the most liberal and jolly and tolerant and companionable, were charter members of the Improvement Association. These included my Uncle Reuben, Great-Uncle Lije, my brother Charles, practically all the Protestant deacons, small business men, and Protestants who worked in Boston.

Occasionally a Jewish travelling salesman would stop at the Massasoit. The Admiral would receive him with his unfailing geniality; Jeff Lee would cook for him with the talent that had given Jeff a state-wide reputation; Nick Spratt would serve him flawlessly at the bar. Big Julie, little Gertie Walker, Palmira Di Brazzio, the solemn-faced Irish girl, Maive Bagley, or any of the more accommodating and sociable of the young Linden women who were easier than most to get acquainted with, would sit at the Jewish drummer's table, drink with him, and later inspect the current equivalent of what are now referred to as "etchings" in his room. They would assure each other, men and women alike, after the Jew had departed, that there seemed to be nothing wrong with him. He was neat, clean, amusing, a good spender, a good business man, considerate in behavior, not too loud. He cheated nobody, offended nobody.

In cases where a visiting drummer was a Gentile, ninety percent of the time in those years, the same accommodations and companionship would be offered, but afterward no one would feel the obligation to defend him. That distinction, trivial or abysmal, obtains in Linden to this day.

It was from Moe Selib that I got my first direct insight into Jewish life in old Russia and Poland. Concerning America, Moe voiced no complaint. If Jews could not buy homes in Linden, there were places nearby where they could buy the city hall. Moe was not embarrassed in talking about Jewishness, and when I got used to that fact, I lost much of my self-consciousness in listening and asking questions. I was really on the defensive. Our friendship started out when I called at his shop one afternoon to get Charles' dress suit he intended to wear that evening in a minstrel show. I had a book under my arm about Dick Whittington, I think. At least, the hero was a poor English boy who became important later.

Moe smiled his rueful knowing smile, behind the thick-lensed glasses.

"I want you should read about a Jewish poor boy in the old country, one hundred percent as it was," he said. And the next time I went to his shop he handed me a paper-covered edition of *Herschel the Yid,* by B. Borovsky.

When I read the book, I was flattered because Moe had not considered me too young to read about things as they were, in whatever country. I saw at once that Moe understood much better what was going on in the outside world, at least in Russia and Europe, than almost anyone in town. Miss Stoddard had no political interests. Mr. Wing's reading was mostly of the English classics, with a bit of Hawthorne, Poe and Melville, not to mention Thoreau, Emerson, the Lowells, Longfellow and Whittier. *Herschel the Yid* was one of my first excursions into the realm of realistic literature and I found it so refreshing and satisfying, in comparison with the mutilated English stand-bys we had to read in school, that it marked an enlargement of my horizon. For contrast, I got hold of Victor Hugo's *By Order of the King* about that time, a vigorous dose of the romantic approach. Miss Stoddard had introduced me to Chekhov's short stories, and some of Tolstoi. My grandmother, without knowing it, got me started on Rabelais. I liked to read practically anything that was not handed me by a school teacher, or that was free of what is known as "whimsey." That quality sickened me then, and does today. When I read that in a New York theatre, Maude Adams, dressed as a boy, had asked the audience of grown people, "Do you believe in fairies?" and the customers had shouted, "Yes," I had felt the kind of profound discouragement that has come over me many times, in later years, when my fellow Americans have shown themselves in unfavorable lights.

Moe Selib told me that when he was about my age, his father got permission to take him to a theatre, in Kharkov. In the middle of the performance, the Cossacks rode in, and made everybody get out. They did not say why. Cossacks did as they pleased. As Moe and his father filed out, with the other members of the audience, a mounted Cossack at the door thought Moe's father was not stepping along quite fast enough, so he snapped his whip and caught Mr. Selib in the seat of his pants with a crack like a revolver shot. Moe pronounced the word:

"revolver" something like "rewolower," which threw me for a minute.

"My father was a very dignified man," Moe said. "Naturally he couldn't say anything to a Cossack, and get himself beaten to death with sticks or tramped under the horses' hoofs. But when he got home, and inside the house, he turned and looked at me. I knew his pride and dignity were very hurt. Maybe there was something in my eye not respectful enough, so he batted me one across the ears that knocked me flat."

Moe smiled understandingly, knowing just how his father had felt.

"Here, cops don't carry whips, and ride horses into theatres," Moe said.

"Why did the Cossacks close the show?" I asked.

"The Tsar didn't like to have too many people meet together," Moe said.

I never saw a man as sad as little Moe Selib when he got the first news of the unsuccessful revolution of 1905. He closed his shop, but he sat inside it, sorrowing—not wishing to go home where his wife would try to talk. He told me, later, how he had studied in a revolutionary school, in a cellar, and how, when the school was betrayed or discovered, when luckily he was not there, the Tsar's officers had shipped in three or four wagonloads of Polish peasants to burn down the Jewish houses, do what they liked with the women and massacre the men. Moe's father, that time, was not humiliated. He was murdered; "I hope quickly," Moe said. Moe's mother escaped with him through a vegetable garden that had deep trenches between rows, and they had walked about a week, he thought, to some other village where she had an uncle, and there she got a few things together and opened a little store, "not as big as a shoe-shine stand."

From this enterprise came the price of Moe's transportation

to America. He was smuggled into Austria, and from there to Hamburg, in Germany, and had landed, after a prolonged Gethsemane in the steerage, in Portland, Maine.

"So if they don't want me to buy a house in Linden, I buy one somewhere else," Moe repeated. "And if my young cousin can't belong to a fraternity in high school, he gets good marks and has friends who like him anyway. Myself, I can't belong to the Linden Improvement Association, so I don't have to pay dues. Everyone, to be happy in America, should live one week in Russia."

Moe sighed and took up his iron again. He did not work with steady desperation, like Wong Lee, or potter around like Dud Shultz. Moe worked hard when lots of customers were in a hurry, but normally he took his time, enjoying America and the brotherhood of man, in dreams and reality, and relative freedom, and good talk when he could get it. He never got rich, and never was poor, once he got started.

Jeff Lee got through a long and happy life in our town. In fact, after the big Balm of Gilead had been demolished and carted away, Jeff was the nearest claim to distinction Linden had. On one of the few occasions when the Lieutenant Governor and the Governor's Council visited Linden, on a tour of the public institutions of Middlesex and Essex Counties, at the suggestion of my cousin Fred Tarr, it was arranged for the party to eat at the Massasoit a shore dinner cooked by Jeff.

At the last moment, the Governor's secretary telephoned the Admiral (who by that time had succumbed to that disturbing instrument) and tried to ring in a few extra political guests.

"I'll have to ask Jeff," the Admiral said, and gingerly lowered the receiver until it dangled from the cord. At first the Linden users of the telephone regarded it as a sort of independent menace, if left to its own devices. Jeff did not like to throw his weight around. He was pained, but firm. The clam

267

chowder had already been started, and he could not stretch it. Nor would it look right to serve a different soup course to some members of the official party. That was enough for Admiral Quimby, who was a Democrat from birth. He told the Republican secretary of all the Republican officials that the original number of guests was the highest he could accommodate, and keep up the standards of his hotel.

After that lunch, not a day passed for several weeks in the course of which Jeff did not receive a flattering offer to cook for some rich state politician, but he could not leave Linden or his lifelong employer or his devoted clientele. He spent many a fine day off in the colored section of Boston, either on the back of Beacon Hill or over toward Lafayette Street, and knew how city life was, how gay and how diverse, how filled with enjoyment and temptation. But he felt as much a part of Linden as the granite quarry or the depot. He had grown up with the place, and was accepted there, because not once, from babyhood to dignified old age, did Jeff ever express any desire to marry some white man's sister. For that matter, he never looked too long at any black man's sister, either. He thought woman's place was in someone else's home, and as far from the kitchen as possible.

Jeff had one of his moments of triumph when a group of Malden boys, high school athletes, gave a dinner to honor their new coach, an all-American end from Dartmouth, named Bullock, who had trained them to victory over their traditional rivals, Medford High, in the annual Thanksgiving game. Bullock was taller than Jeff, quite lean and angular, and approximately the same shade of black, somewhere between *lignum vitae* and mahogany. The boys urged Jeff to sit with them and Bullock at the table, which, of course, Jeff would not do. His duties were too pressing. But he joined them all for coffee and cigars.

No member of the Linden Improvement Association would have sold a house or lot to a Negro, quite certainly, although the offer to purchase was never made by any of them until after World War I. I doubt if at any time in its history, Linden has had more than six Negro residents. The only families capable of supporting hired girls or servants of any kind, the Partridges, Dawson Freeman, and Deacon Clapp, hired Scandinavian and Irish girls, alternately, and tried between-times to decide which kind had the fewer drawbacks.

There is no denying that the Linden Protestants were clannish and somewhat smug, in racial matters, and that the regional feeling between them and the Irish Catholics was such that social intercourse was limited. That did not mean they could not be neighbors, or could not do business together. The younger ones mixed on the athletic fields and back lots, generally speaking, on the merit system. Good ball-players were fairly numerous, but outstanding ones had a special rating, wherever they appeared. Race discrimination and segregation reached its height in the high school, where fraternity members felt superior to nonfraternity members and the latter, for the most part, felt a loss of caste and humiliation that varied with individual temperaments. No high school fraternity in Malden then invited either Catholics, Jews or Negroes to join. The national or international bylaws of all the fraternities then prescribed, as part of the initiation ceremony, that each new member must affirm that he was "of the Caucasian race."

Jeff Lee's baked beans were soaked all Friday night. On Saturday morning, about seven, the water was poured off and the beans, acceptably swelled, but not cracked, were sorted carefully. One tiny pebble, overlooked, might mean a broken tooth. But that was not the reason Jeff sorted them with care.

269

They would taste better if his clients could attack them with freedom.

Soaked and sorted, the beans were placed in a large earthen bean pot, salted in layers, and morsels of fat salt pork about one inch by one and a quarter by one and a quarter (which would shrink in baking about thirty percent by volume) were tucked in. The beans and pork were then covered with fresh cool water which had no unpleasant mineral taste, and were flavored with black molasses, covered, and the pot was slid into the oven, which was moderate, not more than three hundred degrees If, because of other things being baked in the course of the day, the oven had to be much hotter than that, the beans were taken from the oven and allowed to sit, covered, on the back of the stove near the closed damper. From time to time, a few spoonfuls of hot water were added, to take the place of that lost by evaporation. This was continued until midafternoon, when the fragrant juice of beans and pork and molasses was allowed to thicken naturally, about fifty percent.

Each time the cover of the bean pot was lifted, the ritual incense ascended, and the odor disseminating in spindrifts and invisible tendrils was caught by the household drafts, crept into nooks and corners, wavered, enticed, ennerved and invited.

Baked beans on Wednesday or Thursday, say what you will, are not exactly beans on Saturday evening. They taste good, but they have a way of throwing a man off his stride, of working havoc with his subconscious.

Of the several kinds of beans that may be raised, purchased or imported, Jeff favored the northern pea bean and the red kidney bean, two-thirds of the white and one-third of the latter. Crude black molasses from the barrel is better than the refined stuff sold in bottles. There should be plenty of fat pork, with a faint streak of lean in each piece, and the beans must be cooked until they are "done," but never until they are soft or mushy. Each individual bean, golden-brown and shining in modest resurrection, contributes according to its quality and perfection to the ensemble. Ideal communism of the comestible. Democracy of the delicious. Free men's food.

For sheer visual beauty, it is hard to beat a steaming plate of beans, juicy golden-brown, shaped and heaped by divine engineering, the tones of topaz, garnet, old gold and mahogany, set off by the blue and white patterns of Spode, with which New England then abounded. The tactile contrasts of smooth, well-cooked beans and pork with the intermediate texture of the steamed brown bread, generously buttered, yield nuances which are gustatory, sensual, aesthetic, social and spiritual. A man who wolfs his plate of beans, and cannot tell the difference between good and vile ones, is not to be recommended as an acquaintance, employee, employer, friend, lover, counsellor or teacher.

Linden people, back in the days when each man knew his neighbors and was careful at first about strangers, were inclined to view with suspicion anyone who was careless about food, either in raising it, buying it, transporting it, cooking it, serving it, or eating it. It is safe to say today, of the United States in general, that with the best and most abundant supply of foodstuffs in the world, the highest purchasing power, the most ingenious and practical utensils, devices, and machines for cooking, and the most leisure for eating, the nation is deplorably fed, with a standard of cooking as low as can be found anywhere on this planet, save possibly in England. That could not have been said about Linden, at the turn of the century. If it ranked below Rouen or Toulouse, it was miles above New York or Los Angeles, today.

CHAPTER SEVENTEEN

The Barbershop

PROBABLY the first woman I knew well in Linden who might have been called a "feminist" was my grandmother, who died in 1902, overlapping the new century by two years and extending by the same span the Biblical allotment of three-score years and ten. And her principal interest was not merely in securing rights for women but defending what she called "common sense." In her day, that had not been easy. I shall leave it to the reader as to what extent it is, or is not easier today.

The old tintypes indicate that she had been handsome, as a young woman, and in middle age. My own memory holds her image as a regal and dignified old lady, who wore styles that were becoming, carried herself erectly, and spoke out firmly in support of her beliefs and opinions. Her limited means and the valvular heart trouble that restrained her, but not too rigidly, made it impractical for her to take an active part in the current crusades, but she followed the women who did with her logic and approval.

She was one of the first on Cape Ann to ridicule the doctrine of infant damnation and to reject the then-popular conception of a Hell of fire and brimstone. She had joined the Unitarian Church, to the horror of her family of Congregationalists. That did not prevent her from preferring the works of Thoreau to those of Ralph Waldo Emerson. I have already mentioned that she was the mainstay of one of her sisters who got a divorce. She thought it was nonsensical for men to learn what they knew from women schoolteachers and at the same time deny women the vote. She called Carrie Nation a crackpot and fanatic, and Mary Baker Eddy a fraud. She admired the young women who rode horses astride, and rode bicycles, and the few who played lawn tennis in Linden she encouraged to modify their corsets and skirts in order to have the requisite freedom of motion.

When Mary Stoddard went to work in an office, in preference to being a schoolteacher or a librarian, my grandmother applauded her decision, and I think she envied Dr. Mary Walker, who got a degree in medicine, attended soldiers at the front and finally had her hair cut short and wore men's clothes, the latter by sanction of an act of Congress.

Just before my grandmother died, one of her last expressions of indignation was occasioned by a newspaper report that a New York policeman had threatened to arrest a woman on Fifth Avenue because she was smoking a cigarette.

"Whose business is it, if a woman wants to smoke?" she asked. "Probably that same officer has a mother in Ireland who smokes a pipe."

On the other hand, my grandmother had little patience with the younger women who let themselves be led into all kinds of absurdities by the arbiters of styles. When she saw a hat with an enormous brim, laden with plumes, birds' heads, wings and feathers, clusters of artificial grapes, plums and cherries, she would warn us to keep away from it, so we would not catch fleas or hen lice, or get bitten by hornets. The long clumsy skirts that were dragged through mud and dust, the hefty bosoms that protruded in front and the bustles that stuck out behind, with a wasp waist in between, brought forth her caustic comments.

"Women have been placed in such a ridiculous position that they act like clowns, and dress like nightmares. There's nothing left for them to do except make fools of themselves," she said.

"Let 'em go far enough, and the men'll get scared, and make believe that women have some sense, for a change," said Daisy Hoyt, one of my grandmother's favorite companions, although Daisy was thirty years younger.

My grandmother was vexed when my older brother, Charles, decided to run for city councilman, as she was when Fred Tarr, her favorite nephew, went into politics. She and Miss Stoddard were alone in condemning the way Henry Cabot Lodge and Teddy Roosevelt forced the war upon Spain and slandered Grover Cleveland. Of McKinley, she said:

"All he's good for is to pee whenever Mark Hanna eats asparagus."

All this was painful to Charles, who from adolescence to the day of his death was the most loyal and sincere Republican in the country. Charles prided himself on his balanced mind and considered judgment, and rightly. He would have been as fair a judge as he was reliable as a civil engineer. He permitted himself only two out-and-out enthusiasms among the leaders of the party, Teddy Roosevelt in his youth, and Herbert Hoover years later.

Whenever the newspaper contained an item that riled the feminists, my grandmother was likely to have callers that day—Mathilda Stowe, Mary Stoddard, and Ruth Coffee. A female wrestler was arrested at Crescent Beach, where she had offered to take on all comers, men or women, catch-as-catch-can. I was sent to Malden with Grandmother's bank book, to draw out some money so she could help pay the Amazon's fine.

Mathilda, my grandmother particularly admired, because

she did as she pleased, in such a way that no one could interfere, and when Mathilda appealed to her to ask Charles, as Linden's councilman, to take steps to make the city health department remove the public drinking ladle from the fountain in Linden Square, my grandmother agreed. Both women knew that if Dr. Moody took the initiative, he would be thought of as a crank, and his practice, what there was of it, would suffer.

It was not easy to get rid of that public ladle on a chain. Most of the men around the Square, and others who frequently refreshed themselves at the fountain, made violent objections. Charles, who had been working with the Metropolitan Water Works and knew something, technically, of the dangers of contagion, was willing to make the motion, but Dawson Freeman, who already had pegged Charles as Linden's first governor of the commonwealth, tried to talk Charles out of it.

"Let somebody else do the things that are unpopular," was Dawson's advice.

That was a little shocking to Charles, who went right ahead, resolved to do his duty as he saw it. That evoked from Dawson even greater admiration, and Dawson went all over Malden telling the story and saying that, at last, Linden had a councilman who had the courage of his convictions.

Actually, the drinking ladle was not removed until three years later, when some drunk yanked it off, accidentally, and threw it down the drain. It was never replaced.

After Grandmother died, Ruth Coffee ran across a drawing of Dr. Mary Walker in *Harper's Weekly*. The sketch showed the style of Dr. Walker's haircut, which was a moderate bob. That fascinated Ruth. She would look at the magazine, again and again, and stand before her mirror, trying to visualize what she would look like, bobbed that way.

"Won't it make you conspicuous, *Tuan*?" asked Alice, who was enjoying their privacy and relative seclusion so profoundly that she was reluctant for Ruth to do anything that might ruffle the calm.

"Folks would soon get used to it," Ruth said.

"But where would you go?" Alice asked.

"To the barbershop. Why not?" Ruth said. The impulse was growing.

"You wouldn't," Alice said, actually trembling at the thought of entering that den of ribald masculinity. As a matter of fact, she was not far wrong.

Webb Higginson, the Linden barber, was a tartar. He was a nervous, disagreeable little man, about the size of Dud Shultz, with freckles all over and sparse auburn hair he kept plastered down with petroleum jelly and combed with microscopic exactness in the least becoming way. His rust-colored moustaches were limp, so he had to use a moustache cup to keep the fringe out of his coffee, which he drank intermittently, all day long.

"Don't that stuff keep you awake?" Doc Moody asked.

"It helps," snapped the cocky little barber, in his squeaky, rasping voice.

Webb had opinions, on any and all questions, but on certain subjects he was as violent and voluble as a terrier. His best customers—the Admiral, Uncle Reuben, J. J. Markham, Packard, George Sampson, Henry Laws, Luke Harrigan, all the men around the Square—went daily to Webb to be shaved, as much to get him going on his pet obsessions as to avoid what now is called a "five-o'clock shadow." They all had individual shaving mugs, lettered with their names or initials, in a rack on the wall.

When race meetings were in progress at any of the distant tracks—Old Saugus and Reading were near enough so that all the men attended—it was difficult to get a shave or haircut without Webb's being interrupted by a telegraph boy from the depot. The telegrams were addressed to Webb Higginson, tonsorial artist, but without opening them he took them across the street to Eben Kennedy's poolroom. Even in those early days, the reformers were busy, trying to make it difficult and hazardous for citizens to back their judgment or try their luck on the sport of kings. Western Union, which then operated mostly in the railroad stations, had made a rule, as a concession to the *unco guid,* that telegrams would not be accepted for or delivered to poolrooms, where the wicked bookies flourished. I suppose there never has been a period in history when some people have not been trying to keep other people from betting.

Webb had fixed ideas about that. "A man's got a right to make a God-blamed fool of himself if he wants to," Webb said. "We all know every race is crooked. . . ."

"Not every race," Uncle Reuben would say.

Webb would flare up like a torch in a tunnel.

"Every last one of 'em. There isn't a single solitary race that isn't fixed. No, sir!" the barber would say, snapping his scissors like the bill of an angry stork and tapping the floor with his dainty patent leather boots, the smallest size.

"I saw a man lose five dollars on the Ben Hur Chariot Race, the other night at Mechanic's Hall," the Admiral said.

"Who'd be fool enough to bet against Ben Hur?" asked J. J. Markham. "That's one race that's fixed, all right, and everybody knows it."

"This fellow bet on Ben. He and his friend from down in Maine matched quarters to see who'd get which chariot, and the loser drew Ben. Something went wrong with the turntable and the other driver came in first," said the Admiral.

"You see?" said Webb Higginson, grimly. "You can't depend on nothin'."

Webb's definition of a thoroughgoing son-of-a-bitch was a man who asked for a haircut on a Saturday night. Haircuts were a quarter, shaves a dime.

Of the sporting events I heard argued back and forth in and around Webb's shop, two stand out in my mind. First, the Jeffries-Fitzsimmons fight, in which Lanky Bob from Australia was knocked out by the California boiler-maker in eleven rounds. This contest resulted in a number of fights among the boys in Linden, because Jeffries, up against the trickiest boxer then known to the ring, had adopted a crouch that no one seemed to understand, but all the boys who fancied themselves as scrappers had to try out.

The other event that lingers in my memory was the race in which the trotter, Croesus, broke the world's record, doing the mile in two minutes, flat. There was a similarity in those two contests, because Fitzsimmons, more freckled than Webb Higginson, with abnormally broad shoulders tapering down to a slim waist and legs that had nothing but length, was a freak in appearance. And Croesus, champion of trotters, had a head like my Great-Uncle Lije's Zach, shaped like a jug, with ill-matched ears and an ultra-roguish eye. I have always been drawn to freaks and monsters, and extreme ugliness and distorted shapes have excited me as much or more than conventional form and beauty.

Webb was one of the first in Linden to install gas lights, but his shop continued to smell of Ed. Pinaud's hair tonic, bay rum, tobacco smoke, hair and lather, and kerosene. He used kerosene in the small stove on which he kept his coffee hot.

"It's a wonder you wouldn't put gas lights in that old disorderly house of yourn," Webb said to the Admiral.

"Not on your tintype," said the Admiral. "I see in the papers every day where some hayseed wanders up to Boston, gets him a room, then blows out the gas."

That was true. Every hotel room had conspicuous signs: "Don't blow out the gas," and the house detectives made the rounds many times each night, not to interrupt the guests' pleasure, but to sniff for leaking gas. If some jay blew it out and died, the detective got fired.

On Saturdays or before holidays, Webb hired Rad Yarbor-ough to help him. The barber did this, not so much for the convenience of his customers, as to make Rad suffer and defer to him. Webb knew that Rad hated him, so passionately that it drove Rad almost to desperation, and still, Rad had to eat, and barbering was his only trade. Between-times, Rad hung around with the gang at the blacksmith shop. He was a lean, hard-faced alcoholic who spent most of his days "on the wagon" in order to keep out of jail. He was one of the most violent men in Linden, by nature, also one of the most repressed and restrained. Whenever either Webb or Rad sharpened a razor, he thought longingly of the other's tender throat.

"Some day I'm goin' to kill a man," Rad would say, over and over again, sometimes to himself, again to whomever was lis-tening. When drunk, he would say this gleefully, with a de-moniacal gleam in his merry slate-blue eyes. When he was sober his eyes were cold and his manner listless, but he knew his trade, and never took a drop while he was working or showed up in the shop with liquor on his breath.

"I'll come to see you fry in the chair," Webb said to Rad.

"Mebbe so, mebbe not," was Rad's reply.

Webb Higginson lived over on Elm Street, in one of the muddiest stretches, so he did not walk home at lunchtime. In-stead, his old Danish mother put up a lunch for him and he ate it in the shop, whenever there was a lull. Rad worked only on busy days, when there was no time for lunch. He had no taste or appetite for solid food. Webb would work deftly, paus-ing every moment to carry on his vehement arguments. After talking at the top of his voice several minutes, Webb would turn to the other chair.

"Isn't that right, Rad?" Webb would ask.

Very incisively and coldly, Rad would answer, "No," and go on stropping or clipping or shaving. Rad's hatred could be felt, could be cut with a razor, and also Webb's perverse satisfaction. There were not many he could bully and irritate. His old mother, his subdued red-headed daughter Emily, and, because Rad had to have a little money, his helper.

One of the remarkable things about Webb Higginson was his consummate skill. He might get angry, curse and shuffle and choke, because Mrs. Vanderbilt or Mrs. Astor had watered a horse from a solid gold pail, or women had swooned and stampeded at a New York cathedral when an American girl had married a title. Between spasms, he would turn to his customer in the chair, and his dual personality, that of master-craftsman and hysteric, would assert each facet in turn. Barbers who cut a man while shaving him, did not charge for the job. None of Webb's customers complained. Rad Yarborough was quite skillful, but not as fast or as sure.

It was on a Friday before Labor Day that Ruth Coffee took the plunge, and showed up at the barbershop to have her hair bobbed. Knowing how Webb detested women, and took it out on them whenever he got a chance, Ruth made sure that a few good friends of hers were on hand. Mr. Wing, who patronized the barber on the days his valet was drinking, my Uncle Reuben, Luke Harrigan, and the Admiral all were there, and all knew what was coming off. So did all the gang around the Square.

Ruth came down the street, waving comradely greetings to the clerks and proprietors of the stores, and the customers, opened the barbershop door, was greeted casually by the men in whom she had confided, and took a vacant chair to wait her turn. Everyone acted as if nothing unusual were happening, except Webb, who began to turn all colors, to grit his teeth, narrow his eyes, and show what looked like symptoms of apoplexy.

"Was there something you wanted, ma'am?" he asked, after a pause. It was unwritten law that no women, except mothers with young children, ever entered the premises.

"I'm not in a hurry," Ruth said.

All the men rose, with elaborate politeness.

"Please take my turn," each one said.

"What is this?" demanded Webb, shaking with anger.

Ruth took from her breast pocket the clipping from *Harper's Weekly* and showed the sketch of Dr. Walker to Webb.

"I want my hair cut like that," she said.

"This ain't no penitentiary," said the irate little barber.

Rad Yarborough, who was from Tennessee, suddenly reverted to type.

"I'd be proud to cut your hair, madam," he said, with a bow and a flourish.

"Thanks, Rad," said Ruth, and got into his chair.

While the men watched, with covert glee, and Webb glared and chewed his moustaches, Ruth's haircut proceeded. She had a well-shaped head, quite noble, and when Rad had finished and she looked at herself, before and behind, in the mirror and hand glass, all the customers outdid themselves in admiring the result. The only time in anyone's memory, Webb Higginson, stropping a razor furiously, cut his best strap clean in two. Ruth paid her quarter, added a dime for a tip, which Rad graciously accepted, said: "So long, everybody," and departed.

When the last customer had gone away that night, and they were closing the shop, Webb said, his reddish-brown eyes smouldering:

"I won't be needing you here any more."

Rad smiled his most dangerous smile. "Oh yes, you will, you little runt," he said.

"Who's boss around here?" demanded Webb.

"The one who's been covering up for Kennedy with the racing results," said Rad.

The two barbers looked at each other with venom, one calm and collected, the other flushed and mad. Webb dropped his eyes, and the next day, Saturday, Rad came in to work as usual and nothing more was said.

The only young man in Linden who took a fancy to Emily, Webb's daughter, and wanted to marry her, was Dick Evans, the second clerk in Markham's store. Evans was frugal and thrifty, and never patronized the barbershop. While he was courting Emily, he called at Webb's house every Wednesday evening and Sunday afternoon, and Webb and his taciturn old mother did everything possible to make the young folks uncomfortable. Webb let this go on for a year or two, waiting, and when Evans, according to the custom then prevailing, had a private talk with the father and asked for Emily's hand, Webb glared with satisfaction.

"Where do you get shaved?" Webb asked.

"I shave myself," Evans stammered.

"In that case," said Webb, "you might as well be your own bride."

So the courtship ended abruptly and Emily left Linden to go into training as a nurse in the Peter Bent Brigham hospital in Boston. She never came to Linden to see her father and grandmother again.

CHAPTER EIGHTEEN

Law and Order

THE Linden Improvement Association was organized, primarily, to keep foreigners out of Linden. The President was an Englishman named Newcomb, who lived at the crest of the Salem Street hill, not far from Great-Uncle Lije's place, and the Treasurer was a newcomer, a young man named Ashley, who had letters from a New Hampshire congregation and joined the Congregational Church right away. Naturally, the most influential member, who held no office, was Norman Partridge, the local rich man. My brother Charles was active in the Association before he went away. My relatives belonged. All the Protestant deacons who were landowners attended the meetings, and by some very tactful diplomacy on the part of J. J. Markham, the few well-to-do Irishmen who had property interests in Linden were persuaded to join.

There were few women members, because not many women owned land or houses in Linden and most of those were timid widows who never would speak out in meeting and trusted their male neighbors to advise and protect them. The exception was Mary Stoddard, whose old mother, when she died, had left Mary the house and lot almost across from ours, on Beach Street. This house had been rented to Henry Laws, the English cobbler, who also belonged to the Association.

Beginning with the year our house burned down, there was quite a building boom in Linden and this, added to Faulk-

283

ner's predicament with a Jewish influx that amounted to a flood, and the ragged but happy Italian peasants who were settling across the Linden line in Revere, prompted the public-spirited Linden residents to a burst of activity that was new to the community, and somewhat incongruous.

The old wooden schoolhouse was destroyed by fire, which no one regretted, and another one of brick, with a dome about the size of a large maple sugar kettle, the color of Roquefort cheese, was put up two blocks west, on Oliver Street. Linden now had acquired a firehouse of its own. Four or five two-family houses had been put up on vacant lots, for investment, and had been rented promptly. Then Norman Partridge decided to build a warehouse, on the edge of the marsh by the Saugus Branch tracks, just beyond the Lynn Street grade crossing. It was Linden's first modern building, in industrial style.

The Partridge warehouse was built of corrugated metal, with a cement floor and a tar-paper roof, that was almost flat and was supported from within by pillars made of iron pipe filled with concrete, and steel girders. It was about fifty yards square, and twenty feet high, and because of its location it acted as a windbreak for the northeast blizzards and piled up drifts as high as the roof itself, so that children playing there frequently dropped clean out of sight and narrowly escaped suffocation. An elaborate wire fence was built around the area, with metal gates for the admission of wagons and pedestrians. All in all, it looked like the forerunner of a modern death house and concentration camp. Besides, when a long freight train tried to switch a car or two of leather onto the Partridge side track, it puffed and wheezed back and forth for hours, blocking all traffic through Linden by way of Beach Street and Lynn Street. As if this were not enough, Jim Puffer, whose grocery had failed for the third time, was removed from local

284

commerce by Mr. Partridge and placed in charge of the warehouse, with easygoing Irv Walker for an assistant.

The metal walls, in hot weather, radiated heat like an oven, and the tar paper on the roof smelled a mile. Inside there was such a freak echo that men shouting instructions back and forth could not understand one another, and with practically every carload that came in, some kind of accident to the help occurred. The inexpert locomotive engineers and firemen sent to Linden by the Boston and Maine were always developing hotboxes or knocking down the bumpers at the end of the side tracks. In short, Linden's first venture into the industrial field, like so many other aspects of our town, was predominantly a comedy value.

The general meetings of the Linden Improvement Association were held in Associate Hall, unless the weather was too cold and the Hall furnace had broken down, in which case the members stepped over the line into Revere and accepted the hospitality of the Massasoit House banquet room. In either case, there were enterprising boys who followed the debates from hidden points of vantage, and seldom were they sorry they had come.

The growing Italian colony on the edge of the marsh, within sight of Linden, was troubling the leading spirits of the Improvement Association no end, for Italians, in large numbers, depressed real estate values as low as the Jews did, and the Linden women did not relish the strong smell of garlic on the trolley cars. There was no way to prevent Senator Mangini from arranging the purchase by his countrymen of lots in Revere, or making effective protests because of the nature of the ramshackle buildings they put up. But one of the members of the executive committee of the Association had been reminded by his wife that most of the work done by the Italian homesteaders was performed on Sunday, which was against the law. Each Sunday, swarms of immigrants, in full view of the Linden churchgoers, worked with old boards, tar paper, second-hand window frames and doors, hammer and nails, pick and shovel, building and gardening from dawn until dark.

At the meeting when the subject was introduced, Mr. Newcomb was the first speaker, and he complained that the array of shacks, privies, and impromptu fences, jerry-built and overcrowded, was an eyesore.

Miss Stoddard arose, and the organizers who had planned a smooth course for their resolution, sighed and shuffled nervously.

"Mr. Chairman," Miss Stoddard said. "May I ask the last speaker a question?"

The Chairman, little Mr. Ashley, could think of no reason why a question would be out of order.

"If the gentleman wishes to answer," Ashley said, glancing uneasily at Mr. Newcomb.

Newcomb rose. "Certainly. Certainly," he said, and looked as if he expected the worst. No man had ever tangled with Miss Stoddard and come out with the long end of the stick.

Miss Stoddard's homely face wreathed itself in a most disarming smile. Mr. Wing, the Admiral, Luke Harrigan, and my Uncle Reuben sat up straight, glanced expectantly at one another and waited.

"The last speaker," said Miss Stoddard, "has objected to the houses of our prospective new citizens in Revere on aesthetic grounds."

"Pitch 'em a little lower, Mary," whispered Uncle Reuben. "That went over their heads."

She smiled again. "On account of their appearance," she said.

"Does the lady wish to ask a question?" the Chair asked timidly.

"I should like to ask the gentleman, through the Chair, if he is charmed and uplifted by the sight of the warehouse within the Linden limits, put up by one of our leading citizens who can afford the best?"

Heads turned and faces with pained expressions glanced at Norman Partridge, who was sitting about four rows in front of where Miss Stoddard was standing. She went on, warming to her subject.

"I should like to ask, while we are objecting to the blights on our landscape, if the former speaker has ever seen a building, erected for any purpose whatsoever, with more unsightly proportions, more incongruous materials, more utter disregard for Linden's appearance, not to mention convenience. I should like to inquire if the gentleman has ever sat on his heels, an hour or two, in order to cross the tracks on Beach Street, our main thoroughfare, because of the situation of the said warehouse? I hope the gentleman will not object if I move to include in any resolution condemning as eyesores any building or buildings, in or outside of Linden, the warehouse I have mentioned."

Miss Stoddard sat down, and the silence was tense. Mr. Newcomb was uncertain as to what he ought to say. Some men were grinning, others frowning. Norman Partridge was motionless, and not resentful, but he was dismayed and astonished. It was plain that he had never thought about the looks of the warehouse before, and that, now he thought of it, it seemed to him atrocious. It was the temporary chairman who saved the situation.

"The suggested amendment," Mr. Ashley said, "is out of order, being outside the scope of the original motion."

Miss Stoddard did not press the matter further. As the committee had planned, a delegation of three was appointed to call upon the selectmen of the town of Revere, and to send written protests against open violation of the Sunday laws to the representatives and senators from the district in the General Court.

Senator Joseph Mangini, of Revere, was also chairman of the board of selectmen. He was genial, energetic and popular, and one of his pet projects was the removal of Italians from the slums of Boston into "God's fresh air" where they could live in health and happiness and vote directly for him. In this endeavor he had the full cooperation of the Democratic machine in Boston, because in those years Italian citizens voted the Republican ticket.

The Senator's law offices were on Tremont Street, in Boston, and every prosperous legal firm in that city had associates representing all the racial elements of the population, so that if a presiding judge were a Yankee, the firm could send a Yankee lawyer to plead the case; or if the jury were predominantly Irish or Jewish, the counsel was Irish or Jewish, as the case might be. On Mangini's outer door, the following names were stencilled neatly on the clouded glass pane:

> Giuseppe Antonio Mangini
> Aloysius J. O'Rourke
> Elisha Feinstein
> Charles Sumner Frothingham

Senator Mangini received the Linden delegation, listened carefully to what they had to say, and returned soft answers. His constituents were poor men who worked hard all the week, and only on Sunday could they find the time to build their homes. Mr. Newcomb explained that his Association did not wish to be unreasonable, that it was really the appearance of the buildings that troubled the Linden real estate men and property owners, not so much the Blue Law violations.

"You mean, gentlemen, that you would wink at my friends' breaking the laws, if they would spend more money on their houses and sustain your real estate values?" the Senator asked.

Mr. Newcomb and the others hesitated, uneasily. Senator Mangini became more suave and agreeable.

"Let's all enforce the laws," he said, and the next Saturday evening, he had a formidable array of banjo torches set up around the busy little colony and precisely at midnight they were extinguished in unison and all work stopped. Sunday dawned, and although the Italians feasted and drank, and played music all day, not a stroke of a hammer or a drone of a saw was heard. Senator Mangini and some of his aides drove out to the marsh, in a magnificent shining black carriage, and passed from shack to shack, joining the festivities and partaking of the hospitality.

From the windows, porches and broad lawns of the Massasoit House, the regulars watched with glee, the news spread westward over Linden, and a feeling hung in the air that something was about to happen.

The junior associate of Mangini, O'Rourke, Feinstein and Frothingham was a product of Groton and Harvard, with uncles on State Street and aunts in Louisburg Square. He was a presentable young man, tall but not too tall, well built without being crudely athletic, conventionally dressed, but immaculately, and had a friendly manner, correct and reserved but not snobbish. When he got off the streetcar that Sunday afternoon, with a fine new camera and a pair of field glasses strapped over his shoulder, no one knew who he was, or what were his connections or intent.

It happened that Norman Partridge and his mousy, red-faced little wife liked to have their children interest themselves in gardening. So that certain of the flower beds that beautified the Partridge estate were not planted and tended by the gar-

dener, but belonged to one or another of the Partridge children, who were sixteen, thirteen, and eleven, respectively.

Theodora, the younger sister, thirteen, had a fine bed of
pansies in the front yard, near the corner of Lawrence and
Beach Streets. She was a studious girl, intelligent, rather shy,
never popular with boys, but her homework kept her busy
through the week and on the Sunday when young Mr. Frothingham chanced to be in town and the weather was ideal for
amateur photography, Theodora was weeding her pansies,
kneeling on a piece of sailcloth to protect her long cotton stockings and modest Sunday dress. Her father, the benevolent shoe
manufacturer, was kneeling by her side, helping her.

Having taken several snapshots of Mr. Partridge and Theodora busily at work, young Frothingham tracked down Spike
Dodge, the cop, and asked him to arrest Mr. Partridge for violation of the Lord's Day statutes. Theodora, being a minor,
could not be charged directly on that count, but her parents,
according to another old Massachusetts law, were responsible
for her Sunday conduct and unless Mr. Partridge could establish that the weeding of that particular bed of pansies was
"necessary," as the word had been interpreted by the early
Massachusetts courts, he was liable to fine or imprisonment,
or both.

"Look, Ferdy," Spike said. "You see that field of cabbages
over there?"

"There's no one working on the cabbages," young Frothingham said, not getting the point.

"I tell you what," Spike continued. "Why don't you count
'em. And if yuh find one missing, just stay there."

"Am I to understand that you decline to arrest Mr. Norman
Partridge?" young Frothingham asked, ignoring the persiflage.

"You're smarter than I took you for, mate," agreed Spike,
and sauntered away.

By the time Spike had reached Black Ann's Corner, the Harvard lawyer caught up with him again, and this time Frothingham had with him two witnesses, both of whom had seen Mr. Partridge and Theodora weeding the pansies and were willing to swear to it. This time Spike was more respectful, because one witness was Tim Curtin, the one-armed hero of the Cuban campaign, and the other Steve O'Shaugnessy, who was studying to be a priest.

"Have a heart, Steve," Spike said. "Can't you and Tim explain to this young fellow who Norman Partridge is? Besides, who cares about a few pansies being weeded?"

"It's the law," said young Frothingham. "And the law is no respecter of persons."

"I haven't seen a thing," said Spike. "And if you gents want to make a complaint, why don't you go up to the station, and leave me alone."

Young Frothingham now was making copious notes of all the conversation. His next call was on Alderman Trumbull, who lived across from Weeks' field, on Salem Street. The alderman was a choleric, excitable old gentleman who was completely upset by any new idea, sprung on him suddenly, and who talked and spluttered as if he had a hot potato in his mouth. He came out on his front porch in his shirtsleeves, still half-dazed by the awakening from his Sunday afternoon nap.

"What's this? What's this?" asked Mr. Trumbull, after Frothingham had begun to state his case.

"You are an alderman of the city of Malden, are you not?" asked Frothingham.

"Of course. Of course. What of it?" said Mr. Trumbull, impatiently.

"I have complained of a flagrant violation of the law, in your precinct. I have brought the matter to the attention of your local police officer. He informs me that a Mr. Norman Partridge, because of his affluence and social position, is not subject to arrest," said Frothingham.

"Arrest Norman Partridge? You're crazy, young man. What for?" spluttered Mr. Trumbull.

"Weeding pansies," Frothingham said calmly.

The alderman, not believing he had heard correctly leaned forward and cupped his ear.

"Weeding pansies," Frothingham repeated.

Mr. Trumbull turned red and purple. "You mean to say there's any fool law against weeding pansies? Young man, whoever you are, go away. I say, go away."

"The law does not specifically mention pansies. It forbids any kind of work on the Lord's Day, unless the work is necessary and cannot be accomplished on another day," young Frothingham explained.

"Most confounded nonsense I ever heard in my life," said the alderman.

"Would you repeat that, please?" asked young Frothingham, writing in his notebook.

"I've got a good mind to chuck you down the steps," Mr. Trumbull said, his anger rising. "Coming out here to raise up a mess. Mind your business. Go back where you came from."

"By what right would you throw me downstairs?" young Frothingham said, taking off his glasses. Unluckily for everyone, one of Trumbull's five sons, all of whom were famous halfbacks, had been listening from inside. It was Walton, and he promptly rushed young Frothingham down the steps to the sidewalk and blacked his eye.

"Sorry I haven't time for a fight, just now. We'll settle this another day," the young Harvard man said, calmly, as he dusted himself off and started out to find Spike Dodge again. The cop, not expecting to be bothered twice on the same afternoon, was in a cool grape arbor in a corner of the Calkins yard with Maive Bagley, and when Frothingham found Spike, having been tipped off by the Spanish War veteran who disliked everybody, the officer was not wearing his belt, holster or night stick, and had shed his helmet and uniform coat.

The candidate for the priesthood, who again was accompanying Frothingham, looked at Maive reproachfully and she blushed all over, where anyone could see. The urbane young Harvard lawyer raised his hat.

"I am sorry, ma'am, to intrude, and if Mr. Dodge will accompany me, to arrest the son of Alderman Trumbull, who has assaulted me, there will be no need to mention this charming little respite from his duty," Frothingham said.

Spike was not too quick on the trigger, but he got that one, all right, and had to go with Frothingham back to the Trumbull residence. This time a sizeable crowd, men and boys who had heard something of what was afoot, went right along behind the Harvard man. The terrible-tempered alderman stormed out to meet them on the sidewalk.

"I'm responsible for what happened. Not my son. Arrest me. I demand it," Mr. Trumbull said. "We'll go get Norman, too. We'll see if this young whippersnapper from Harvard can play fast and loose with the people around here. We'll get to the bottom of this."

When Norman Partridge was informed of what had taken place, and that he was being charged with violation of the Sunday laws, he took the matter very gravely. If he, thoughtlessly, had been at fault, he must set a proper example. He was the last man who wanted any special favors, because of his money or position. Unescorted, Mr. Partridge drove all the way to the police station in Malden Center to give himself up.

CHAPTER NINETEEN

The Rich and the Needle's Eye

◆

VERY early in life I grasped the fact that being the richest man in the community had its drawbacks. Too much was expected of Mr. Partridge in the way of good examples and patriotic and Christian behavior. With a practically unlimited bank account to draw on, he could not spend his money, and think about the wisdom of it afterwards, as Dawson Freeman or Uncle Reuben did. He could not frankly make pleasure and high living his goal, like Mr. Wing.

Mr. Partridge was quiet, quite diffident in manner. He was good-looking, too, in an inconspicuous way. As the principal pillar of the Congregational Church, he had to make up deficits and pay off mortgages unostentatiously. Even in his wife's simple and ordinary neighborly charities, Mrs. Partridge had to be especially tactful and many kind acts she performed were productive of resentment which, if unexpressed, was perceptible. The children, Millicent, Theodora and Leroy, had the toughest time of all. Their father was a member of the school committee, so their unquestionably high scholarship was always being covertly questioned. Leroy provided the footballs, baseballs, mitts, masks and gloves. His father had a basketball court laid out, and a tennis court, so Leroy's friends could have the best equipment with which to play. The boy was about my age, and, as classmates, we skipped every other grade in the grammar school. Leroy was not strong, but he was game.

He was not an outstanding athlete, but felt obliged to knock himself out, in competition with faster and heavier playmates. Not a day passed in the course of which Leroy, somehow, did not have to take a lot of unjust and self-inflicted punishment merely for being the son of the man who was his father.

The girls were brilliant, intelligent, charming, but local boys were wary about going with girls who had brains, and the Partridge girls both resembled, physically, their homely mother and not their handsome father.

I suppose Mr. Partridge spent about twenty thousand dollars a year on his family and household, not an enormous sum, but almost astronomical according to Linden standards. He must have been a good businessman, because his shoe business increased in size and importance.

Mr. Partridge's house was not elaborate and showy, nor even good architecture. The design was stuffy and without distinction, but the place was large and comfortable. The furnishings were likewise inartistic, in a Victorian way, but they were luxurious and practical, and nothing was lacking in what then was known as modern convenience. The whole house, from concrete cellar to finished attic was heated by steam, with radiators that were noiseless and tractable, and responded to the handles of their valves. And reliable steam heat, when it was needed, would be one of the first requisites of heaven in the minds of the average Lindener.

It was said of Mr. Partridge that he treated his help well and fairly, and all Linden knew how good he was to his relatives and in-laws. There were few Linden houses that had not felt the touch of his generosity and kindness, still I could not escape the feeling that Mr. Partridge's good deeds gave him more embarrassment than simple pleasure. He loved horses and drove smart ones, but they were fonder of the stable man than of him. He had no intimate friends among the men, although they all liked him. He did not hunt or fish, drink or smoke, philander or gamble. The front he presented in Linden was the measure of the man. His health was not bad, and not rugged. Actually, Norman Partridge was very much the kind of man my brother Charles turned out to be, only Charles had many friends and associates and neighbors in Dayton who were as prosperous, or more so, than he. And Charles had no children. My point is that both of them had an authentic quiet worth, and orderly instincts amounting almost to nobility, and all their virtues and talents were more noticeable than their ability to have fun.

Imagine such a man as Norman Partridge, in the Malden police station, aware that he had desecrated the Lord's Day and broken the laws of the Commonwealth of Massachusetts. The scene, that Sunday afternoon, was a memorable one.

Alderman Trumbull, in the course of the three-mile ride on the streetcar, from Linden to Malden Center, had had time to cool off a little, and to wonder even more dazedly just what the whole thing was about. As he glared at young Frothingham, who was seated across the way, trying to make conversation with the disgusted Spike, the alderman could not quite see a Malden police chief or a judge paying serious attention to anything the young dude might say. What was he saying, anyway? Mr. Trumbull did not pretend to understand, but he knew he had lost his temper, that his son, Walton, had committed a pardonable indiscretion, and that it would be best for all concerned if, somehow, the matter could be patched up, or let drop and be forgotten. The alderman, therefore, was further disconcerted when he encountered Norman Partridge in the Malden station, the Partridge carriage horses having far outstripped the conveyance furnished by the Malden and Lynn Street Railway Company. Mr. Partridge was not trying for a quiet, peaceful settlement. He had already told the

Malden chief of police that he had done wrong and must face the consequences, like any ordinary citizen. At that stage of the game, Mr. Partridge did not know that the Trumbull family was involved, to the extent of assault and battery.

Charles Sumner Frothingham, III, was as calm as if he had been practicing several generations. He presented his card, and the police chief, who had instantly had the impulse to have him thrown bodily out of the station, on general principles, caught his breath. On the card the young Harvard whipper-snapper's name appeared as the associate of Senator Mangini, and the Chief, who had been placed in his good job by the Republican politicians of Malden, knew well that his backers would as soon offend the Angel Gabriel as the powerful Italian senator from Revere, who was then in the act of removing in wholesale lots from Democratic Boston where their votes were lost in the landslide, brand-new Republican voters who would be most useful in the voting districts of which Malden and Revere formed a part.

"Now, gentlemen," said the Chief. "This is all a misunderstanding. Let's not be hasty. Supposing I call Senator Mangini, and see if we can't smooth the whole thing over."

Alderman Trumbull bubbled enthusiasm for that suggestion, his torrent of words piling up over one another's dead bodies, like victims in a theatre disaster. Young Frothingham, however, had his eye on Norman Partridge, who, at the idea that law-breaking could be condoned by political chicanery, had turned pale and even more grave than before.

"Naturally, I should defer to the opinion of my associate, the Senator from Revere," the Harvard man said, "but Mr. Partridge would be placed in an embarrassing position. Unfortunately, his neighbors throughout Linden all know what has occurred, and if he is not booked, and goes scot-free, it would be remembered against him by his fellow townsmen who hold him in such high regard. They would be forced to the conclusion that wealth and influence outweighed common justice. Am I stating your position correctly, Mr. Partridge?"

"I ask no special consideration," Mr. Partridge said.

"Mr. Partridge feels that the citizens whose antecedents have been in America from the first, should be especially scrupulous about obeying the law, and not plead ignorance of it as an excuse," Frothingham continued.

"Never mind what Mr. Partridge feels. He's right here. Let him speak for himself," the Chief said, grinding his teeth.

"Have I misstated your position, sir?" young Frothingham asked Mr. Partridge.

"I stated my position before you arrived, young man," said Mr. Partridge. "If I have violated the law, I should be charged. . . ."

"What kind of a charge is weeding pansies?" growled the Chief.

"If you'll pardon me," said young Frothingham. He took from a shelf on a wall that was covered with law books the last volume of the Revised Laws of Massachusetts, flipped it open, and showed the Chief the statute, passed in 1800.

The young Harvard lawyer, overjoyed because of Mr. Partridge's naïve cooperation, took advantage of every angle of the situation. He did not want the alderman or the alderman's son, on a charge of assault and battery. The bigger game had already come within range.

"I am willing to forget the attack upon my person," the young lawyer said. "I quite understand that the alderman was annoyed. His nap was interrupted. His son acted in good faith, without grasping the circumstances. Why not book Mr. Partridge, as he wishes, let him post a nominal sum for bail. . . ."

The Chief narrowed his eyes and clenched his fists.

"I'm running this station," he said. "Mr. Partridge don't have to put up any bail. He's free on his own recognizance."

"Quite," said young Frothingham. "But you haven't booked him yet."

"I'd like to book you, on the other side of your kisser," the Chief said, and went through the formalities of booking Mr. Partridge, who signed his name, wrote his address in the book, blotted the words carefully.

"I'm sorry, sir," the Chief said. "This isn't my idea. Who isn't ignorant of the law, I'd like to know? Why just last week the City Council and the Board of Aldermen passed that basketful of ordinances" (the Chief indicated a wire basket loaded to the brim) "that I haven't had a minute to read yet. And not only those. The County Commissioners turn out a batch, whenever they feel like it. And the State Legislature . . ."

"The Commonwealth. . . . General Court," prompted young Frothingham.

"Don't tell me what to say!" said the Chief, turning on the young lawyer so violently that he tipped over the inkwell and forgot what he was saying.

Young Frothingham turned to Mr. Partridge, as man-to-man. "The original statute, taken in Colonial times from the English common law, would have made it necessary to expose you in the stocks, sir. Now it's only a fine, or imprisonment, or both," he said.

At the mention of the stocks, Mr. Partridge winced and looked at the floor.

"They must have thought up these fool laws about the time they chartered Harvard College," said the Chief. "The stocks!"

The young Harvard man smiled again. "Ah, yes. And don't forget the ducking stool. . . . But that was mostly for women. Elderly women," he said.

299

"Look, Portia," the Chief said, rising. "I don't have to take any more guff from you."

"I was just going," said young Frothingham, amiably. He held out his hand to Alderman Trumbull, courteously, and the irate old man was trapped by a reflex action into grasping it, then dropping it like a hoptoad. Frothingham bowed to Mr. Partridge and extended his hand to him, and, after hesitating, Mr. Partridge could think of no reason for refusing it.

"Sorry to have made all this work for you, Spike," the young man said to Dodge. "And you, Chief! You might give me a ring whenever you're in doubt about the law. Glad to oblige."

With that, young Mr. Frothingham bowed himself out of the room. The Chief glared at Spike, trying hard to think of a pretext to fire him off the force. Mr. Partridge went out to where his horses were hitched and drove back to Linden, after offering the alderman a ride. Alderman Trumbull had other ideas. He had escaped a personal disaster, and if he could hush up Mr. Partridge's predicament, as far as the press was concerned, no one would be hurt too much. So while Mr. Partridge was on his way home, the alderman sought out a Malden editor, influential in Republican politics and all Malden affairs. I think that was the evening that Mr. Trumbull decided that those of his sons who could get through high school should attend, not Harvard, but Tufts.

The Malden editor shall remain nameless, but he readily agreed that not a word concerning Mr. Partridge's arrest should appear in his paper, and volunteered to see Senator Mangini that same evening, and arrange with him to call off his fresh young associate. So the editor took a streetcar over to Revere, found Senator Mangini in the midst of an Italian wedding feast, in the course of which he had already consumed about a dollar's worth of the finest imported Chianti. Chianti, that year, sold for fifty cents a gallon, wholesale.

"Don't give it a thought," the Senator said to the editor. He knew about the editor's influence in Malden, and thought he would get more out of him than he could gain by harassing Norman Partridge, in the interest of the West Revere proletariat. Senator Mangini ordinarily kept his word, quite scrupulously, but that evening he was having a fine Italian-American time and by the time he tried to send word to Charles Sumner Frothingham, III, to suspend his crusade for the Blue Laws, the young man was not to be found.

Young Frothingham was relaxing, at Jake Wirths in Boston, after what seemed to him a fruitful day. The Blue Laws assignment, in Linden, was the first chance he had had to distinguish himself in an office to which he had been admitted more on account of his name than his ability. With Frothingham, also celebrating, in terms of the wonderful Würzburger beer that Wirth kept on tap, was a reporter on one of the Boston dailies, another Harvard man. Harvard graduates were plentiful in Boston, and it seemed to the working newspapermen that the number of Harvard boys who were willing to work without wages, just for the experience in what they called "journalism," always ran above four figures. The reporter, having been given the Blue Laws story as an exclusive, had earned some kind words from the night city editor, who had already started a cartoonist drawing the Partridges among the pansies in Linden, from photographs Frothingham had provided. But it was the policy of that newspaper, whenever a prominent man was charged with anything, or attacked, to give the victim a chance to make a statement, if possible in the same issue in which the story was printed. My boys, there were newspapers then.

The Boston daily had no representative in Linden. In fact, the night city editor up to that time had never heard of such a place. His local reporter in Malden had no telephone. So he tried Lynn. In Lynn, the paper was represented by a conscientious and careful reporter named Charley Archer, who worked on the Lynn *Item*. Charley was respectable, presentable, meticulous—about forty years of age. He felt the dignity of his calling, and would take no nonsense from anyone who disdained the press. Charley was definitely an old-school reporter, who abhorred slang and sensationalism, denounced the typewriter as a clattering nuisance that clogged the flow of thought, and doggedly verified all names, dates and places before he turned in his copy. Charley was respectably married, had bought a house in Lynn, and was already firmly set in his ways, but, like most good reporters of that era, he loved dearly to drink. His wife, a singer who earned as high as twenty-five dollars a Sunday in some of the more prosperous Greater-Boston churches, and who had social and professional ambitions, was stern, almost rabid in her opposition to alcohol. Their vital disagreement on this point made life somewhat difficult for both of them. Charley loved and admired Viola, and felt guilty about having restricted her prospects. She had known when she married him that newspapermen were scandalously underpaid, but she thought they had influence with the right people, and an entrée everywhere.

It had been agreed between them that Charley could drink a decorous amount, in line of duty, on weekdays, but on his day off, which was Sunday, the understanding was that he would be abstemious and devote himself to her. In order not to let it appear to her that he wasted too much of his substance on drink, Charley had never disclosed to Viola that he did occasional assignments in Lynn and vicinity for the Boston paper, and thus was able to spend what he earned on space-rates without her audit. The Sunday of which I am writing was about like other Sundays, for Charley. Viola had turned in a creditable "Face to Face" and "The Palms" at a morning service in the Salem Baptist Church, and was attending a rehearsal of the local branch of the Handel and Haydn Society that evening. Charley, at the time the copy boy from the *Item* had found him, and given him the message from Boston, was listening drowsily to a dozen mixed voices singing snatches of "The Messiah," with unorthodox starts and stops. He was thinking very wistfully of whiskey, rum and ale.

When Charley had to deceive Viola, ever so slightly, it made him nervous and self-conscious, and his manner, when he told her he had a hurry call from his paper was such that she was sweetly skeptical.

"Shall I wait up for you, darling?" she asked, in a way that made him certain that she would. Viola had a nose that could pick up through an olfactory fog of cloves a zephyr of booze that an ant would muff.

"Please don't, dear. I've got to go to Linden," he said.

"Whatever for?" asked, in mock horror, the choirmaster who had overheard. Outsiders were likely to speak that way of Linden, when they mentioned it at all.

Charley made his way to the *Item* office, and, with much grumbling and protesting, got the Boston city editor on the telephone. He disliked and distrusted telephones more than he did typewriters. Having in mind that Viola would have to see something tangible, to justify his long absence, Charley asked the Boston editor if he could cover the *Item* on the story, too. Since the *Item* was an afternoon paper, there was no objection.

More light-heartedly, Charley headed for a livery stable. This was not the epoch of press cars with sirens, the drivers of which kept the motors running at the curb in case an emergency arose. But by nine-thirty, in a city like Lynn (if there is another like it), the horses and buggies for hire had been well weeded out. The horse Charley got had a spring halt, harness sores, and no impulses to hurry. The buggy was spattered with mud from the last rainstorm, and had not recently been greased. Charley bought a pint from the livery stable man, since the saloons in Lynn were closed on Sunday, and bottled goods could not be procured in the ordinary way. Liquor by the glass, to be consumed on the premises, was available in restaurants if food was served. This was the law in most Massachusetts cities that countenanced liquor at all. The result was that in hundreds of taverns, including the Massasoit, a property fried egg, made of rubber and skillfully colored, was attached by means of a large pin to the center of the tables around which customers were drinking. That covered the letter, if not the spirit, of the statutes.

Norman Partridge went to bed about ten o'clock each evening, and was sleeping steadily before the reporter from Lynn had got five miles on his way. The girls and Leroy, all were studying. About the time Millicent, the oldest, had reached high school, she had become persuasive and logical enough to convince her pious father that improving the mind was a proper activity for the Sabbath. All the Partridge children liked to study.

About eleven o'clock, Charley Archer, having consumed the pint and tried his best to urge the hired horse along, rounded Black Ann's Corner. Outside the stone crusher he saw a group of men, one in police uniform, and heard them disputing violently. He pulled up his nag, wound the reins around the whip in the socket, and got out of the buggy. The men who were reviling the cop, all Irish and well oiled up, were so intent that no one noticed the stranger on the sidelines.

From what was being said, Charley quickly understood that the four Irishmen, who worked weekdays at the quarry, had been playing cards in the office, by the light of the watchman's lantern. The reporter was delighted, since the incident was in line with his assignment. Spike Dodge, after warning the card players, had intended, quite naturally, to go on about his business, but when Charley stepped up, presented his card as a Boston reporter—all roving reporters carried engraved cards indicating that they represented the *Boston Evening Transcript*—and asked if the men who had been playing cards on the Sabbath were to go scot-free, Spike was on another spot. Spike's task was not simplified by the attitude of the drunken Irish quarrymen, who tipped over Charley's buggy and were determined to throw him, clothes and all, into the nearby creek. In the free-for-all that ensued, Spike had to make use of his billy, and was lucky to come out with his life. He had only one set of cuffs, which he used on Chuck O'Riordan, the night watchman. The other three, Luke McGann, Pie-Face O'Day, and Terry Haigenny, deployed in as many directions. Terry started for Cliftondale under the misapprehension that he was going the other way, toward home. Pie-Face O'Day, who was an exponent of direct action, staggered into the woods toward the underground storehouse to get a stick of dynamite. Luke, leaning forward at such an angle that he had to run to keep from falling flat on his face, headed for the south side of the tracks for reinforcements. Meanwhile, the unlucky Spike had to call for the wagon, while the handcuffed watchman tried to kick and bite him as he phoned in the tiny little office.

All this was meat for Charley, who came out of the affray only slightly dishevelled, but midnight was the deadline, he had not yet interviewed Mr. Partridge, so he had to leave Spike to his own devices, and, after taking down the names and addresses of the card players and roisterers, he and a few bystanders righted the buggy, adjusted the harness and awakened the horse, who had dropped off to sleep in spite of the commotion.

The reporter found the Partridge residence, hitched his horse to the ornate iron post, mounted the steps and pushed

305

the bell. Leroy opened the door. It was eleven-thirty by that time, and no callers had ever arrived as late as that, but the appearance of Charley Archer and his neatly engraved card counteracted any misgivings that the faint odor of bay rum, cloves and whiskey had aroused in the boy.

"I'm sorry to disturb you," Charley said. "My editor is most anxious to give Mr. Partridge the opportunity to make a statement, about the charges against him."

"Papa is abed," Leroy said, but Millicent and Theodora appeared at the head of the stairway and decided that their father would want to be awakened, under the circumstances. When, a few minutes later, Charley interviewed the bewildered head of the house, all the children sat in. Millicent, who had a sharp sense of satire and of humor, was especially intent.

Mr. Partridge gave his simple version of what had happened, not sparing himself.

"You believe in one day's rest in seven?" Charley asked.

"I do," said Mr. Partridge.

"Do you think our immigration laws are likely to bring about a Continental Sabbath?" Charley asked.

"Those who come here should benefit by our customs," said Mr. Partridge.

"Do you believe in Sunday sports, like baseball, for instance?"

"Emphatically not."

"Do you go driving?"

"To visit the sick."

"I notice your son was studying," Charley said.

Mr. Partridge looked uncomfortable, but Millicent spoke up.

"It is always proper to improve one's mind," she said.

"Do you approve of Sunday card games?" Charley asked.

"Certainly not. Card playing is never necessary."

306

"Is card playing in Linden on the Sabbath generally disapproved?"

"I think so," Mr. Partridge said. "I sincerely hope so."

"If men defied the law and played cards openly on the Lord's Day, would you be in favor of having them prosecuted?"

"To the full extent of the law," Mr. Partridge said.

Charley thanked him, bowed to Millicent and Theodora, shook hands with the boy, and got ready to depart. "By the way," he asked disarmingly. "Are you a member of the Linden Improvement Association?"

"A charter member," Mr. Partridge said.

"Your association excludes certain races from the Linden area?"

"Careful, Papa," said the wary Millicent. Mr. Partridge looked at her in surprise.

"I have nothing to hide," he said to his daughter. Then he turned back to Charley, who was at the doorway, and whose manner was most casual.

"It's the same in Lynn. Jews and Poles have ruined property values," he said. "My own house and lot have depreciated fifty percent."

"That's the unfortunate effect of an influx of foreigners," said Mr. Partridge. "Our association has no prejudice."

Charley smiled, sympathetically.

"You believe, then, that it's all right to admit Jews to the country, but not to Linden," he suggested.

"Father," warned Millicent. But Mr. Partridge was determined to be honest.

"That is not inconsistent," he said. "There are many persons to whom we would not wish to deny the rights and privileges of American citizenship, and whom we would not select as neighbors or companions."

"Many thanks. You've been most kind. Good night," said Charley. But he had a few more questions.

"Do you employ any Jews, Mr. Partridge?" he asked.

"I think not," Mr. Partridge said.

"Any Irish?"

"Probably a few. I'd have to look it up," he said, and a shadow passed over his earnest, troubled face. "There was a time when the head of Partridge and Company knew by name and appearance every man who worked for us. Sometimes I think I liked things better, then. Business, lately, has become impersonal, almost out of individual control."

"Do you approve of unions?"

"Please, Father," begged Millicent.

"Our men have no complaints. We do our best for them," Mr. Partridge said, serenely. "When there's no disease, no cure is needed."

This time Charley made his getaway, warm with inner satisfaction. As he opened the door, the clang of the Malden patrol wagon, which had not been heard in Linden for years, if ever before, was arousing Beach Street more thoroughly than the Minute Men were stirred years before by Paul Revere.

At the Massasoit bar that Sunday evening, the talk had revolved around the advent of young Mr. Frothingham, the pansy-weeding episode, and Senator Mangini's campaign for law and order. When a reporter came in, just before midnight, and started telephoning a Boston paper, everyone in the Massasoit gathered within earshot, to hear what was reported. Charley fussed and snorted, shouting at the top of his voice to the rewrite man, and the drinkers of Linden were regaled with Norman Partridge's views and the arrest and detention of the four Irishmen—O'Riordan, O'Day, McGann and Haigenny—for gaming and rioting at the quarry. When Charley assured the rewrite man that Mr. Partridge, free from a charge of Sabbath-breaking on his own recognizance, advocated the utmost penalties for the four working men who had been caught playing cards, the Admiral, Mr. Wing, Uncle Reuben, and all the others grinned and pricked up their ears. It was apparent that Linden would be on the lips of hundreds of thousands the next morning who had never heard of it before, and that Mr. Norman Partridge was getting the works, at the hands of a coterie of experts.

There was a halt in the telephone conversation. Charley Archer covered the transmitter and turned to the Admiral.

"The editor wants to know, Mr. Quimby, if there are prominent citizens in Linden who do not agree with Mr. Partridge, who favor a more liberal Sabbath, for instance?" Charley asked.

"May I give him some names," said the Admiral, reaching for the phone. Expansively, the Admiral introduced himself, then reeled off a list of his friends who would be glad to be quoted, against class or race discrimination, or fanatic Blue Laws that interfered unreasonably with a citizen's pleasure. To each Linden name, the Admiral, in his element, attached a high-sounding title: Miss Ruth Coffee, eminent feminist; Christopher Van Volkenburgh Wing, Manhattan society leader with property interests in Linden; Patrick G. McSweeney, street railway official; Jefferson Madison Lee, internationally famous *chef de cuisine;* Herr Doktors Pehr and Paavo Wallenius, of Helsingfors and Linden, well-known sculptors; Walter Grosvenor Packard, student and practitioner of mesmerism; Jonathan Cheever, sanitary inspector (the Linden swill man); Alexander Graydon, descendant of the financier-patriot; Elbridge Gerry, lineal descendant of the signer of the Declaration of Independence by that name.

"You may quote Mr. Gerry as follows," said the Admiral. "My ancestors did not visualize a nation that would nurture bigotry and prejudice, with one rule for the rich and another for the poor."

"Are all these people willing to go on record?" the editor asked.

"I give you my word. I will vouch for each and every one of them," continued the Admiral. "Miss Mary Stoddard, of the staff of Photo Era. Her principal reason for advocating votes for women, sir, is her belief that women will repudiate the Blue Laws, so that on the one day a man and his wife may be together, they may enjoy legitimate entertainment and work together and improve their modest little plots of ground."

By the time Charley Archer got back on the phone, the Boston editor realized that he had a sensational story, on which he was beating the world. He offered Charley on the spot what the latter had always desired, a steady job on the Boston daily, beginning that moment, and he asked Charley to stick close to Linden until further notice, with headquarters at the Massasoit House. Instantly Charley was received into the fold with the traditional Massasoit hospitality, with the initial result that, some time about dawn, my Uncle Reuben drove the hired horse back to Lynn, with Charley snoring on the seat beside him. Having been told about Mrs. Archer's aversion to drinkers, my uncle tried to smooth things over for his new friend. He found the address, saw a light in the window, and when, as he was helping Charley out of the buggy, Mrs. Archer appeared in the doorway, my uncle drew himself up and said:

"You must not think your husband has been drinking to excess. He has sustained a severe electric shock, in the line of duty, while he was using a defective telephone."

Mrs. Archer unbent, to the extent of helping my uncle get Charley upstairs, but the effect was spoiled when, on the topmost stair, my uncle caught his heel on the brass rim of the stair carpet, lost his balance, and fell backward down to the lower hallway, taking with him a section of the banister rail.

It took a lot to put Uncle Reuben out of commission, so he got up, made his exit with what dignity he could, and found his way to the Saugus Branch station, to get the first train back to Linden. The tired horse, who had slipped my uncle's mind, along with the buggy, wandered disconsolately around Lynn for a couple of hours and finally showed up, driverless, in the livery stable.

CHAPTER TWENTY

Of Public Entertainment

SAMUEL BUTLER defined happiness as a state in which one was not actively aware of being miserable. The great novelist might have been thinking of Linden. From the high ground of Salem Street to the flats where the Irish were regaled with piggery odors from over the Everett line, from the head of Beach Street to Black Ann's Corner and the Square, there was usually a comforting absence of tension and struggle that has not been enjoyed anywhere on this planet in recent years. When an event shot up a fresh stalk and bloomed like the fabulous century plant, such as the Blue Laws episode, involving the technical arrest of Norman Partridge, and nation-wide publicity that was Linden's own, the quiet relish of living, the matter-of-fact acceptance of the daily routine, was suffused with glee. Pulses beat faster, people tingled and liked each other and were willing to take chances. Acquaintances became friends, and friends became inseparable. Ginger ran his streetcar more recklessly, fiercely clanging his gong. Horses that all their lifetime had stood without hitching suddenly took it into their heads to have one coltish fling, and ran wild, scattering goods and wagon parts, and giving someone a chance to be a hero by stopping them, when the horses were about ready.

There were three men of Linden I have not yet mentioned who, when the community was stimulated and unified by participation in a rare experience, knew what folks were doing and saying from one end of town to the other. They were: Roger Kaulbach, the letter carrier; and the huge, good-natured brothers, Fat and Randy Clarke, who owned the ice company, each driving a wagon.

Roger made the rounds twice daily, and knew all the front doorways. The icemen were familiar with each and every back door, back porch, and kitchen.

Everybody called Roger Kaulbach by his first name, and quite a few Linden people who had known him well for years could not have told you his last name. He was never in too much of a hurry, and talked aloud to himself almost continually, either reproaching himself for being behind-time, or the correspondents of his clients for sending too much or too little mail. He had a little niece somewhere who was a passionate collector of stamps, so that when, for instance, my brother Charles was getting quite a few letters from Frank Weymouth, an engineer who was then in Nicaragua, Roger would wait expectantly, taking off his uniform cap and wiping his forehead with a bandanna, while Mother tore off the corner of the envelope on which was the foreign stamp. His gratitude when Mary Stoddard, after her mother's death, gave him an almost complete set of the first United States issues, was so profound that it kept Roger skipping and hopping and doing sudden pantomimes for days.

Roger's disconcerting habit of assuming a ballet posture and circling a lamppost with mincing dancing steps two or three times, when he was absolutely alone on an uninhabited stretch of one of Linden's sparsely populated streets, led some unthinking people to hint that he was slightly crazy. That was far from the truth. He was completely crazy, but as harmless as a hassock and extremely useful. Now and then he would cry, for no reason at all, and when anyone would ask him what was the matter, he would insist that he was mourning for his wife's first husband. His wife, Vernona, was Linden's only Christian Scientist, and there had been some talk when her first husband died, because she had refused to call a doctor until his jaw, which was frightfully swollen, had burst of its own accord.

It was well known throughout Linden that Roger and Verny, as Vernona was called, had not spoken to each other directly for years. Instead, they kept a wheezy pug dog and addressed to him what each wanted the other to overhear. Not only did they not converse, but each one bought provisions and cooked his or her own meals, eating them at separate tables, Roger's in the kitchen, and Verny's in the dining room. Their house was high on the rocky lane that led from Salem Street through the woods to the Pike, and Roger had laid out his mail route so he could have lunch at the Massasoit.

Getting mail delivered by Roger was like being an umpire when Nick Altrock was clowning. Roger would mount the front steps and ring the bell. Then he would start rummaging through his large leather sack, as the door was opened.

"Mmmm. Now let me see. Ah. Mmmmmm," he would murmur, frowning and sometimes letting his feet execute a dance step or a shuffle. "What have we here? An advertisement from Jordan's. A bargain sale, ma'am. Don't go. Don't believe them figures. When it says 'Marked down from a dollar to ninety-nine cents' it means the moths have got into the stuff so they're marking it up from fifty cents to ninety-nine. And Mrs. Paul. Don't be fooled about them pennies, either. Every penny you save costs you more than a dime. I can prove it. Good day, ma'am. I'll prove it next Thursday. Today, I'm five minutes behind."

314

On the following Thursday, Roger would remember, and would insist that pennies wore out pocketbooks and pockets, carried serious infections, smelled like crowded streetcars, and made a man feel rich, by their weight, when he had not enough to buy a pot to cook in.

"Ah. Mmmmm. Now then. I thought I had something here," Roger would begin. He would shuffle a while, and then hand over the letter. "From Charles," Roger would say. "You're fortunate, ma'am, to have a son like that. Fine, honest young man, Charles. He'll make some good woman a husband, one of these days."

Roger would take back the letter and glance at the postmark again. "Still in Philadelphia, I see. Thought I heard he was goin' out West. When you write him, tell him that's where the money is. Out West. They don't bother with pennies out there. No, *ma'am*. Don't forget."

And Roger would trip lightly down the steps, as if he were holding a lady's long train. While the roots of the Balm of Gilead were still bulging over the sidewalk, Roger would always pretend to trip, and when he felt extra good, he would actually fall, and beg the tree's pardon.

Roger had served in the National Guard during the Spanish War, but he would not permit anyone to call him a veteran because he only got as far as Chickamauga. As a matter of fact, Roger had provided so much spontaneous relief and amusement for the troops that were shuddering with malaria and burning with yellow fever that no officer would have escaped lynching if Roger had been transferred elsewhere. Besides, Roger was a phenomenal penman. He could write, with free-arm motion, embellishing his letters with scrolls, birds, fishes and animals. His Major at Chickamauga had disliked writing letters, so Roger had opened, read and answered all the anxious and passionate letters that arrived with each mail sack from the Major's doting wife.

"That," Roger explained, "was why I couldn't go and get my head shot off."

Sometimes he would pretend to cry about it, and now and then got to weeping in earnest. Nearly every day, at dinner-time (noon), Roger and Tim Curtin would get into an argument as to which was worse, San Juan Hill or Chickamauga. But it was on the strength of his army service that Roger got his job.

When Roger would see Dick Lanier pottering in his small garden, he would yell:

"What yuh doin', Dick?"

"Manurin' my strawberries," Dick would say.

"I'm peculiar. I like cream on mine," Roger would retort.

This routine was just as good with other farmers, about gravy on potatoes, or butter on green corn. Often Ginger would stop the car, so his passengers could hear what Roger said. Then Roger would sit on the track, and have to be dragged off by main force.

Roger thought the greatest man in the world was Harry Lauder, and would sing "Oh She's My Daisy" when he met an old woman or an old maid on the street, enacting one of his vivid pantomimes until the woman in question would wish she could drop through the ground. But no one was really offended.

The Linden icemen did not carry out the conventional iceman's role, by cuckolding all the Linden husbands. They both were too big and heavy, and had too much else to do, even if the women had found them irresistible. Actually, they had nothing whatever to do with women, and in spite of their bulk and strength and capacity for overexertion, their voices had never changed and were high-pitched and incongruously boyish.

"Fat!" his brother Randy would say. "Some day I shall forget myself and strike that horse. He's gone and eaten all of Mrs. Plummer's moss roses."

"Plague take him," Fat would say, and look at the horse so reprovingly, his huge moon face aquiver with emotion, that it seemed as if any beast would be touched, and would instantly reform. Actually, the iceman's horses were extraordinarily dependable and intelligent. They were as deliberate and slow as the fire horses were eager and fast, but were fine, well-kept geldings, all four of them chestnut brown.

The Clarke brothers lived on the edge of Pickle Pond, so named because of its shape, and their father had built the ice house, with its derricks and long wooden chute. They had always been bashful and awkward, too big for the largest seats and desks provided in the Linden school. Their father had died when they were in their middle teens, they had always worked hard, and their old mother had beaten them with switches when they were running the business and three times her size. They were so good to her that they pretended to suffer and would beg for mercy when she felt like whaling them.

"Now, Ma," Randy would say, according to my Great-Aunt Elizabeth, one of the few women old Mrs. Clarke would have anything to do with. "Now, Ma! Don't you thrash Fat. It's my turn today."

"It isn't, either. Go on, Ma. Randy got it last time," the brother would insist.

"I got a good mind to lash both of you till the blood runs," the old lady would say. "I saw what he did to that calf."

"Please, Ma. Don't yell. What if other folks hear you?" the boys would say, squirming with shame and embarrassment.

" 'Twould serve you right. Take down your pants!"

"Now, Ma. We're busy today."

By the time I was entrusted with watching the icebox and putting the card in the window, the Clarke boys were thirty and thirty-one years old, and their mother was dead. One of her last acts had been to throw a mug of porridge all over Randy because Fat had forgotten to put molasses in it.

It may seem inhuman, but one of the standing amusements in Linden was to stuff the Clarke boys with food, the hotter the weather the better, to see how much they could hold without getting what was called "a sunstroke."

"Randy. You've got to taste that lemon pie," Daisy Hoyt would say, showing the iceman a sample of her cooking that fairly blossomed with meringue. "Some folks don't know that it's better, made with duck eggs."

Wherever they would go, they would be tempted with sandwiches, pastry, puddings and cake, and their appetites were colossal. They could not refuse, and when the humidity was at its worst they knew all too well what the consequences would be. Not a day went by that the Clarke boys did not drink a dozen bottles of beer, apiece, and when they collapsed in somebody's back yard or on their wagons, five or six men would stretch them out in the shade, pack loose ice around them and pry open their mouths to pour in a bracer of coffee or whiskey. No one knows how they stood it, but they always came out of it all right, if severely shaken.

Either one of the Clarke boys could have covered Linden in a single day, but they had customers in Broadway, Everett, and Cliftondale, and no one wanted ice delivered after eleven o'clock in the morning. By that time, half the heat of the day was gone. So Fat and Randy each drove a wagon, from six in the morning until nearly noon, and in the afternoons they did their housework, including sewing and embroidery, and slept. Sometimes in the spring or the fall, when the weather was too pert for them to sell much ice, and not pert enough to freeze the pond so they could cut it, they slept twenty hours or more each day, and all the time they were up they were eating.

Like many of the connoisseurs in Linden, who had never known the word, the Clarke boys got their cider from the postman, Roger Kaulbach. Roger made superb cider, and bought apples and ran a little mill on the side. The only person in Linden who would not drink Roger's cider was Vernona, who made a barrel of her own and would never let her husband even sample it. Vernona once left Roger, and stayed with a sister in Swampscott for a week, because Roger took their sick pug to a vet in Cliftondale.

"God is good, you stupid lunkhead. More than that we cannot ask," she muttered, glaring at the dog who was in the throes of what seemed to be asthma, then at her husband.

The Clarkes were Roger's best customers for cider, and they delivered the cider he made to his other clients.

Those of you who started out in life with Frigidaires and Quiet Mays will not remember how important it used to be not to forget the ice card. On a hot muggy day in Linden, the ice melted so fast in those old-fashioned iceboxes that you could hear it dripping in a kind of mocking telegraphy into the pan that was set underneath. Remembering to keep the pan there was important, too. Otherwise you ruined the oilcloth on the floor.

The Clarkes' ice cards could be turned four ways. They were conspicuously oblong, and colored half red and half yellow on

319

each side, with large black figures on the yellow, and large white figures on the red, so by placing it in the front window, flat side down, with the figure "5" on top, you could inform the iceman that you needed a five-cent piece that day. The same card, reversed with the flat side still down, and the "10" upper-most, meant a ten-cent piece. With the narrow edge down, the other side of the card would indicate a fifteen-cent or a twenty-five-cent piece. For a quarter the Clarkes brought in about two hundred pounds.

All summer they kept their ice stored in sawdust, which they bought from the carpenter, Mr. Carlson. The ice was put away, and loaded into the wagons, in two-hundred-pound chunks, and was skillfully trimmed with pick and ice tongs to the requisite measure. The Clarke boys knew every icebox in Linden, its shape and capacity, and shaped the ice they brought in so on hot days the chest would hold the maximum amount and the food would not spoil. They felt ashamed and quite apologetic if their ice melted too quickly, or contained a little fish in a state of suspended animation.

In winter, all the boys would go to Pickle Pond to watch when the Clarke brothers cut the ice, with large two-man saws, and hoisted it into the ice house, by block and tackle up the chute. They laid the pieces in sawdust and built up their piles as carefully as the Finns laid stones on a walk. They had handled ice since they were able to stand, had lived within its chill and knew the patterns of the frost, the stratification and crystallization, the translucence and the mystery, its virtues and its perversities. And they were the last of the Clarkes to live as Clarkes always had. For even while they were toiling and collapsing, trenchering, guzzling, and carrying loads on their backs that would stagger a mule, twentieth-century prac-tical science, at which their countrymen were most adept, was making them obsolete, like the coopers, the blacksmiths, the livery stable proprietors, the bicycle dealers, the whalers, the motor men, and other good men and true who were likewise unaware of what was happening.

I shall never forget Roger's antics on the Monday morning that Linden, the Blue Laws, the pansies, the Protestants and the Irish were all over the front page of the Boston paper. Of course, by afternoon, all the Boston papers had picked up the story, and the Associated Press had telegraphed it to New York, Philadelphia, Washington, Chicago, and all points West and South. When he got off the streetcar, leather sack on his back, he had a newspaper spread in his outstretched hands. While all the neighbors watched and chuckled, Roger sat on the curbstone and pretended to read. He rose, clutched his forehead, electrified by what he had seen in print. Daintily he plucked a little flower, and started tripping away, like Oscar Wilde. Then he became the cop, by stretching to his full height, reversing his cap and taking up a stick. Acting one part, then the other, he threatened, protested, and led himself off to jail by the ear.

At every front door, Roger had a laugh with some housewife, and the Clarkes, fitting ice into ice chests, clucked and shook their heads in sympathy as their customers made their comments. In a few of the houses where the church people lived strictly, there was indignation against the Italians and their politician, and that insufferable young Harvard man. Everyone suspected that Linden would see much more of him. Roger, in fact, reported that Frothingham had been on the steps of City Hall when the doors were opened that morning, in order to bail out the four Irish quarrymen who had been kept in jail overnight. There the young lawyer had met Mr. Partridge who, when he had seen the paper and read his own horrifying

opinions, as interpreted by the newspapermen, had decided
not to go to his office that morning until he had paid the Irishman's fines. The meeting between Mr. Partridge and young
Frothingham had been a very cool one, on Mr. Partridge's part,
while the Harvard lawyer had assured his victim that no one
from the Senator's office had been responsible for the word-
ing of the newspaper accounts or the editorial opinions expressed.

The first headlines, accompanied by an effective cartoon
four columns wide, read like this:

LINDEN'S TOP BRAHMIN
SHATTERS SABBATH LAW

Norman Partridge, Rich Shoe Man,
Church Deacon, Local Leader,
Admits Weeding Pansies;
Freed Without Bail

FOUR COMMON LABORERS
DETAINED IN JAIL

Malden's Anti-Jewish Suburb
Split Into Hostile Camps
By Blue Laws Crusade

FOES OF PURITANISM
DENOUNCE DISCRIMINATION

In the text of the story, prominently displayed, was the inter-
view with Charley Archer, that Mr. Partridge read with some-

thing approaching consternation, since his own words had been used in such a way that he could not deny them.

The accused shoe magnate said that immigrants should learn American ways, and not import loose customs from Europe.

After admitting that he was an active member of an organization consecrated to keeping Jews out of Linden, the wealthy defendant said:

"It is not inconsistent to admit Jews into the United States, and exclude them from Linden. There are plenty of citizens with whom one prefers not to associate."

"Do you employ any Irish immigrants?"

"I'm not sure," said Mr. Partridge.

"Any Jews in your plant?"

"None that I know about," the manufacturer said.

Mr. Partridge does not believe in unions, holding that just employers give the workers no cause for complaint.

In answer to a question, Mr. Partridge admitted that he had voted for a resolution at a meeting of the Linden Improvement Association protesting Lord's Day violation on the part of Italians in nearby Revere.

"Did you know that your committee had tried to make a trade, offering to condone violations of the Sunday laws if the new residents of Revere would cooperate in sustaining Linden's real estate values?" Mr. Partridge was asked.

"That was done without my knowledge," the accused man insisted.

"But you heard about it afterward?" the reporter asked.

"Yes. But I did not approve," was the reply. Under further questioning he admitted that he had made no formal protest.

"Any Italians employed in your factory?" he was asked.

"None. The Poles are larger, stronger men," the manufacturer said.

"Any Poles in Linden?"

After consultation with his older daughter, the shoe magnate replied that he thought there might be a few. Evidently he had not met the Linden Poles socially, or the Italians, the Jews or the Irish.

There was much more, equally true and equally misleading. Nearly everyone felt sorry for Mr. Partridge, and at the same time they were highly amused.

The subsequent proceedings in the courtroom were over in less than ten minutes, but the place was jammed, with a huge overflow crowd outside, and the visiting newspapermen and sketch artists swarmed over Malden Center like locusts and were taken to Linden on a special trolley car, to view the pansy bed marked "X," the Partridge estate, and the scene of the crime at Black Ann's Corner. Mr. Partridge was convicted and fined, at his own insistence, and so were O'Riordan, Mc-Gann, O'Day, and Haigenny, but the courtroom was thrown into hysterics by the plea, in behalf of the Irish defendants, by Charles Sumner Frothingham.

"In this country, men are free and equal before the law, if not in Linden drawing rooms," the young lawyer said.

"There are no Linden drawing rooms," the judge said. "What you call drawing rooms in Back Bay are called sitting rooms here."

"I stand corrected," Frothingham said. The four Irishmen were proud of having their names and pictures in the papers, knew all their expenses were being paid by someone they would like to shake by the hand, if they knew who he was, and had been given a few stiff drinks by their Harvard attorney, who, in spite of his pronunciation of words like "raazberries" and "eyether," was turning out to be a fine lad, after all.

"My clients, although they are poor working men, with only rudimentary education and only the natural social graces inherent in free men everywhere, are nevertheless sensitive and proud. Mr. O'Day, I believe, is the most recent arrival from the Old Country, having been only two hundred and eighty years behind the *Mayflower,* a span of years that will diminish in impressiveness as the centuries roll on."

"Let us permit the centuries to roll on, and get this case disposed of," said the judge.

"I could start back in tracing the ancestry of these four gentlemen with Brian Boru; and the eminent authority, Mr. Geoffry Keating, contends that all Irishmen are the descendants of a son of Noah who left the Ark before the advent of the Dove of Peace, by means of a raft on which he took with him all the beautiful women who had survived the deluge. The raft drifted to the shores of Ireland. . . ."

"Hurrah!" yelled Pie-Face O'Day, who was drinking in with

rapture every word. The judge forgot himself and threatened to have him ejected from the courtroom.

"Your Honor," said Frothingham, blandly, "we could scarcely proceed without the defendants."

The judge turned beet-red and swore under his breath.

"The point!" the judge said. "The point!"

"My point is that these honest men, so pure in heart that they were not aware a friendly card game was wicked, do not wish to be outdone by Mr. Norman Partridge. They request, your honor, to be fined as much as he was . . . apiece, that is to say."

"Granted," the judge said, and finally got the next case under way. The rest of Frothingham's carefully prepared statement was handed to the reporters, however, with enough copies to go around. The photographers outdid themselves in taking plate after plate of the Irishmen digging into their pockets and paying their fines in nickels, dimes and even pennies.

Again the newspapers had a field day. Mr. Partridge's money was refused by his codefendants, and that was enough for more headlines.

On the following Sunday, the entire membership of the Wenepoykin Bicycle Club of Linden, of which Charles had been an enthusiastic founder, was arrested on the marsh road leading through Revere to the seashore, not only for performing what was termed "unnecessary work" on the Sabbath, but for riding on the sidewalks, the road having been doused with the entire contents of the Revere water wagon to make it all but impassable. It was a lucky coincidence for Charley Archer that he and his photographer chanced to be in the bushes by the roadside just in time to cover the arrest.

The day, on the whole, was a bleak one for Charley, because his wife, determined that he should not be debauched into a hopeless drunkard by his vicious new friends at the Massasoit, had closed the house in Lynn, appeared with her trunks at the hotel, and said she would stay there and share his room until he had finished the assignment.

A stranger to Massachusetts might take it for granted that the *reductio ad absurdum* of Lord's Day observances would have resulted in prompt repeal of the Blue Laws, or a tacit understanding that they would not be enforced beyond reasonable limits. Actually, the whole history of that quaint commonwealth is replete with examples to the contrary. The more absurd a law or a method of official procedure in Massachusetts appears to the liberals of the outside world, the more frantically will the leaders of the old Bay State rally around, to prove that they are right and the outsiders are wrong. One could cite the witchcraft trials; the destruction of the first American Maypole; the Red Flag Law of World War I that caused the arrest of Harvard students by the score, Harvard's color being vivid crimson; the law illegalizing "parodies" of "The Star-Spangled Banner" which, until it was hastily amended, prevented instrumental renditions of the national anthem by soloists, bands and orchestras, because it had been originally written as a four-part song; the execution of Sacco and Vanzetti, on evidence that would have been laughed out of court in the Fiji Islands, or by an Eskimo tribe; and the suppression of the works of many of the reputable and talented contemporary authors who elsewhere are read by young and old.

Before the ink was dry on Norman Partridge's court record, various Protestant organizations in Boston and throughout the commonwealth held special meetings, to defend the Blue Laws to the letter, and oppose any relaxation of the Puritan Sabbath. The Watch and Ward Society of Boston took the lead. President Eliot of Harvard, who in the course of his forty years as head of that institution and many more as President *emeritus* seldom overlooked a chance to make himself conspicuous, advised extreme caution in tampering with the wisdom of the Founding Fathers. Nearly all the Boston Protestant clergy fell into line, with some brilliant exceptions which included the Reverend Edward Estlin Cummings, of the Arlington Street Church.

Against this array of conservatives, Senator Giuseppe Mangini took up the gauntlet, with the help of our friends who hung around the Massasoit, and a fair share of the Fourth Estate, not to mention bicycle manufacturers, seed merchants, and sportsmen, generally.

In Linden, where the spark was ignited, things settled back to normal, and were quiet for a while, but not for long.

CHAPTER TWENTY-ONE

Church Fair

ONE of the reasons why Linden was such a satisfactory birthplace is because folks there, as a rule, were not ambitious. Whether this was due to the widespread and continuous emphasis of the teachings of Christ, I cannot say. Modern psychologists would say that most of the Linden people were very "well adjusted." The girls wanted to get married, and their mothers sometimes tried to help them, as the literature of the period will testify, but a change had come over the young people, rightly or wrongly, and they had begun to feel that times were different and that they should not pay too much attention to the wisdom of their parents.

So the romantic dreams were, in terms of Linden life, a job that was pleasant and paid fairly well, a small house financed by the Improvement Association, children who were not maimed by firecrackers on the Fourth of July and would be thrilled by what one could afford to give them for Christmas, a healthy stretch of what Joyce described as "father's pants will soon fit Willy," and lastly, "Silver Threads Among The Gold."

Of course, anyone who was troubled with a consuming ambition left Linden, and the advantage was mutual.

Boys did not like to be considered too smart. I still remember with shame and horror that while I was in the fifth grade, the principal of the school came into our classroom one afternoon, had a whispered consultation with the teacher, and I was asked to go with him into the hall. Naturally, a number of reasons why my superiors might want to punish me ran through my mind. Instead of being shaken or rattaned, however, I was escorted to the eighth-grade room and what I saw there got me really worried.

Billy Thole, of the family in Wing's block that had the world-famous puppets, one of the larger boys I had always especially liked and admired, was standing, flushed and sullen, at the blackboard. Billy knew more about the world than his teachers did, but he was not apt at arithmetic. The atmosphere of the classroom was bristling with hostility toward the principal, the teacher, and me.

I glanced at the figures on the board. The problem was not beyond my scope, in fact, seemed quite easy, although a little complicated.

"Elliot. Will you show Billy how to solve that problem?" the principal asked.

Billy looked down at me and turned away disgustedly.

I have always been easily confused, in public, and it took me several seconds to get the inspiration that saved me from grave unpopularity.

"Certainly," I said, and the expressions on the faces of Billy's classmates hardened.

Feeling numb and helpless, I began to work on the black-board, and suddenly I realized that I was not obliged to accommodate our persecutors. After I chalked up my first mistake, and felt the atmosphere clearing and the principal freezing, I made an epic hash of the rest. It came to me, and I have tried ever since not to let it slip my mind, that I was not put on earth to set other people right. So the principal had done better than he knew, as far as I was concerned. I had learned a lesson quite beyond the range of arithmetic.

My vanity, I regret to say, was such that after school that day, I showed Billy Thole and the others that I could solve the problem, but they forgave me for that.

Not many of the young men in Linden had horses and buggies, nor could they afford to hire them from the livery stable in Maplewood. Lovers knew where to find countless quiet nooks and corners—empty sheds, grape arbors, haylofts, porches of the churches and public buildings, natural shelters afforded by stone walls and bushes, shady lanes, haymows, spaces under railroad platforms. One of the favorite rendezvous for spooning (now called "necking") was the long carriage shed alongside the Congregational Church, well shaded by a thick hedge on the adjoining property. I think it is safe to say that as many new lives were started there as there were funeral services inside.

In the winter, arrangements were not so easy. Even if the older people wanted to be considerate, there were not many houses that were heated all through, and everybody had to huddle together in the rooms where the hot air registers worked best.

"Our Heavenly Father is no blamed fool," Uncle Reuben said, once. "He knows it's easier for sinners in the summer, and for married folks in wintertime."

My uncle had interesting theories about summer and winter. One day at the Massasoit, when Frieda, Dawson Freeman's large, blonde, husky, slow-moving hired girl walked by, the Admiral remarked that she would be fine for the winter.

"That's where you're off your base," my uncle said. "In the heat of summer, you want one of those great big lazy girls. Their skin keeps cooler. Now for the winter, I'll take one of the little dark restless kind. One of them could heat up Associate Hall."

The telephone did much to diminish the practice of writing love letters, as lovers formerly did although they might see each other every day. The first horseless carriages were not designed for dalliance, and made too much trouble anyway. Electric lights were either on or off, and could not be turned low, as in "Just A Song At Twilight." In the winter, the girls who could play the piano or melodeon began to learn popular songs, not of the old-fashioned variety like "In The Gloaming," but a new strain of music, for better or for worse, that came from Tin Pan Alley.

The first ragtime arrived in Linden with the century, not the genuine Negro music that was sprouting in New Orleans, but a vaudeville or white man's version which, although inadequate and unjust to the original, gave those of us who are built that way a tremendous kick. The first ragtime song I remember was restrained, indeed, in its syncopation, and was inspired by the advent, or increased popularity, of the telephone.

The most popular two-step was "Red Wing," and the arrangement contained only the three basic chords, no more. Dancing was tolerated, but not encouraged by the Congregationalists, condemned by the Methodists, while the Episcopalians permitted dancing in the Parish House, and charged admission. The Catholics danced when and where they pleased, but never in church.

There were many Linden parents who believed that the playing of popular songs and the new ragtime unfitted a child for a creditable rendering of "The Happy Farmer," "Valse Bleue," "Star Of The Sea," and the other "classical" pieces favored by the local music teachers. I sought to disprove this theory by beating out as solid a "Soldiers' Chorus" from *Faust* and "Pilgrim's Chorus" from *Tannhäuser* as could be found in the countryside.

At church socials Charles went in for serious numbers, like

331

"Asleep In The Deep," "When The Bell In The Old Tower Rings," "Forgotten," or "I Hear You Calling Me." The last-named song I had to transpose two full notes downward from the John McCormack key, and then risk a fuzzy high note on Charles' part. He was much better on the low notes, at the bottom of "Asleep In The Deep" and "Jedidiah."

One could not attend a church social in those days without hearing some bass sing "Cousin Jedidiah."

> *There's Aunt Sophia,*
> *And Hezikiah,*
> *Maria,*
> *Josiah,*
> *And Cousin JEDIDI*
> *I*
> *I*
> *I*
> *A*
> *A*
> *H.*
> *Oh won't we have a jolly time*
> *Oh won't we have a jolly time*
> *Go, Polly, put the kettle on,*
> *We'll all have tea!*

There was sure to be a girl graduate from the Emerson School of Oratory, where Delsarte gestures were *de rigueur*. She would do a dude monologue like: "I cawn't thee why fellowth wide in twolley carth," or a "Wynken, Blynken and Nod" that made boys want to kick over baby carriages.

Early in the fall each year, the Kickapoo Indian Show would make Linden, stopping first in the Square, then on Beach Street under our big tree, then around to Black Ann's Corner. The performers were Negroes dressed as Indians and the barker came from a circus, was extra white and pale, and wore a stovepipe hat and frock coat. They sang songs, war-whooped and did Indian dances, and tricks of sleight-of-hand. The show bored me, but I liked to hear the barker, and to see who fell for his spiel and bought the Snake Oil, at fifty cents a bottle.

I was a member of a little orchestra that played for the church entertainments and other Linden shows, and we really got hold of "Smoky Mokes" and the "Maple Leaf Rag" and never let them up till they were hollering. Of course, we did not then have the benefit of the Dixieland Jazz records, but we did the best we could. Our hillbilly numbers were far superior to the sickly whining of store cowboys today, for we had Uncle Reuben, Mr. Daley, Mr. Wing and a number of old-time chorders and fiddlers. When we played "The Arkansaw Traveller" or "Turkey In The Straw," the customers sometimes stamped the church until it threatened to come down. One spoonful of that kind of music in a bathtub of tepid water is what one hears on the radio today.

My mother, as I have already made clear, was a timid, unaggressive woman, who did more than her share of the church work, but liked to keep herself in the background. It had to be her luck to accept the chairmanship of the committee to stage the Congregational Church Fair on the year it was held in Associate Hall, and nearly was the Fair to end all Fairs, bringing down upon Linden another deluge of excitement and publicity. I had expansive ideas about production and entertainment that I had never been able to give their full scope, and Mother, being busy with other details, incautiously listened to me. I wanted it to be the most varied and lively show the town had ever seen, and I think it was, in ways quite unforeseen.

In the first place, Ruth Coffee's immense energy and dynamic personality were enlisted, and her ideas of production dwarfed mine. At any stage of life, Ruth would have been as likely to go into a bear's cage as a church, but since Alice had been with her, Ruth had persuaded her to spend Sundays with her folks and to go to church with them, as she did before the break. Alice was chosen, with Mrs. McNeir, to act on the committee with my mother, so Ruth rolled up her shirt sleeves and took hold.

By now Ruth wondered how she had endured living alone so long and Alice, sometimes when she woke up in the night, shuddered to think of what existence had been when she was exposed to the buffets of fate and the scramble for survival. Her mother, baking for Cobb, Bates and Yerxa, also felt a stiffening of her spine and held her head high, but neither she nor Elvira could bear the mention of Ruth's name.

Ruth and Alice were busy from morning until night, and no longer did Ruth accompany the men on their shooting trips on the marsh, or linger with them at the Massasoit bar. Alice worried too much, if Ruth were away, with a shotgun, and was timid about staying alone in the cottage after dark. She was careful not to stay too long in the hot sun, or expose herself to the winter's cold. If she felt the least bit dizzy she used smelling salts, and Ruth personally saw to it that on frosty days she was wrapped up snug and warm, had a soapstone in her bed, and stayed under the covers in the morning until Ruth had stirred up the fire and had a warm breakfast ready in the kitchen.

The Newcombs next door had an unused barn, near the boundary between the two lots and this Ruth bought to use as an antique shop, with the land around it for an out-of-door display. Pehr and Paavo built a new stone walk to the Salem Street sidewalk.

The barn had solid oak timbers, and a chestnut floor, with

two-inch planks a foot wide. Ruth stripped off the old boards, reinforced the walls with two-by-fours, and nailed on clapboards in a way that drew a grunt of appreciation from the gruff Swede carpenter, Carlson, from whom she bought the lumber. The roof was freshly shingled, the stalls were converted into show places for old furniture. Slowly the barn was filled with McIntyre eagles, old Windsor chairs and rockers, butterfly tables, Duncan Phyfe tables, Lafayette benches, framed chromos of George and Martha Washington, Miles Standish, John Alden and Priscilla, and sturdy New England relics, with quite a few choice Sheraton, Chippendale and period pieces from France and England, sets of dishes, pewter ware, Indian wampum and Colonial coins, stamps, buttons, wooden salad bowls, carved whale's teeth, whalebone canes, old colored engravings, and Colonial pottery, odd rolls of Early-American wallpaper, daguerreotype albums, family Bibles, spinning wheels, hooked rugs and rag rugs, patchwork quilts, and other treasures from the years gone by.

The acquisition of each article was for Ruth and Alice an adventure, from which the maximum of delight was wrung, and customers began to come from far and wide. Alice polished the old silver and pewter, and became very skillful in mending dishes and pottery. Ruth repaired the broken furniture, and never passed off a piece that had been retouched for a hundred percent original. The bric-à-brac was displayed as tastefully and carefully on the shelves as the teas were served in late afternoon. Not one cross word ever passed between the partners.

Pehr and Paavo, as Ruth began to have more and more calls to help refurnish old houses, were drawn into the orbit and spent less time carving names and inscriptions on gravestones. No matter what he did in the daytime, Pehr lit out, as usual, for the Massasoit bar when he was through, but Paavo gradually gave up reading Swedenborg and spent part of each evening sitting with "Miss Cough-fee and Miss Toonsund." Ruth noticed, with some misgivings, that Paavo's honest eyes were fixed on Alice whenever Alice was in sight, that the big Finn watched every birdlike movement of Alice's hands, was thrilled at the sound of her voice, and picked up whatever she dropped before it fairly touched the ground.

Mother was a little dismayed when I talked to her about having a different entertainment program each evening, from Monday until Saturday, but she let me go ahead. The members of the Wenepoykin Bicycle Club agreed to give a blackface minstrel show with an olio featuring a prize cakewalk after intermission. That was scheduled for the opening night. On Tuesday, the members and friends of the Eagle baseball club, on whose team Leslie was catcher and I was the shortstop, were to perform a melodrama, coached by Luke Harrigan. Mr. Wing took over Wednesday evening, for a program of folk dances. On Thursday evening, we got up a concert program, at which Mrs. Archer and other professional church singers agreed to sing, and all the music teachers and their best pupils were signed up to play piano solos and duets, selections on the violin, cornet, clarinet and 'cello. It was Friday evening I was most excited about. The renowned Thole family consented, for the first and only time in Linden, to donate their services and present a puppet show. On Saturday, we settled for a sumptuous bean supper, to be followed by an auction when all the wares, goods and art objects unsold were to be disposed of, with Dawson Freeman as auctioneer.

Linden got into the spirit of the occasion, and denominational lines were cut to shreds. Catholics, Episcopalians and even Methodists joined with the Congregationalists, and the hardened sinners of the Massasoit worked harder for the Fair's success than the deacons and their wives. For before the days when canned entertainment on the air, phonograph records, and the screen was everywhere, those who had the instinct to perform were as eager as those who wished to enjoy the show from out in front. The magnitude of the plans and arrangements already had my mother dazed and filled with foreboding, but Ruth Coffee, Dawson Freeman, Uncle Reuben, and other cohorts went vigorously ahead. Every Linden merchant, shopkeeper, or tradesman donated what he could afford, and the housewives cooked and delivered their specialties.

Ruth, from the stock of the antique shop, loaned and set up typical New England rooms in which the various articles for sale could be displayed to the best advantage. There were counters, each in charge of a subcommittee, which were piled high with groceries, provisions, pies, cakes, homemade candy, embroidery, dry goods, hardware, second-hand books, fruit, tea cosies, hassocks, pin cushions, glassware, toys and Indian sweet-grass baskets. Beside those, there were special booths for sweet corn dipped in hot melted butter, popcorn with molasses, fish and clam chowder, baked beans and brown bread, hot boiled lobsters, fried oysters and clams, oysters and clams on the half-shell, jellies and preserves, jams, pickled pears and candied watermelon rind, hams, fancy sausages, pickled pig's feet, corned beef, smoked lamb, smoked fish, wild ducks, woodcock, venison, fresh salmon and trout, sea snails, walnuts, chestnuts, butternuts, nigger-toes, almonds and castanas, sarsaparilla and root beer, grape juice, sweet cider, perry and lemonade. All the booths were festooned with colored bunting and evergreen boughs.

As the opening day drew nearer, the work to get things ready at the Hall got faster and more furious, and lasted far into the nights. It seemed to Ruth and the others, when Saturday came around, that they would not be able to make the grade. They worked all morning, and in the afternoon more men

who were free a half-day on Saturdays joined them. But someone slipped into the Hall while everyone was out for supper
and by tampering with the pendulums, slowed down both
banjo clocks. No one thought about the hour.

When the Hall clocks indicated the hour of eleven-thirty,
outside it was a quarter past twelve, and well into the forbid-
den Lord's Day. Ruth, Alice and Paavo, and even Pehr, were
putting the finishing touches to Ruth's decor when in came
the cop, Spike Dodge, flanked by Charles Sumner Frothingham, III, and a flock of witnesses the lawyer had collected. Of
course, Charley Archer and some other reporters brought up
the rear guard.

"Sorry, Miss Coffee, Miss Townsend," said Frothingham,
showing them his watch. Paavo, understanding imperfectly
what was going on, stood by, but when he saw that Spike was
about to lay hands on Alice, the gentle, honest Finn became
a madman, as suddenly as a geyser shoots up toward the sky.
Near to his hand, unluckily, was an antique pestle, and before
anyone realized what was happening, Paavo had floored Spike
Dodge with a blow that would have jarred an elephant, and
had started for Charles Sumner Frothingham, III. That young
man, who had run the quarter-mile for Harvard, made a flying
start, but he ran square into the arms of Pehr, who was amiably
drunk, but not *hors de combat.* In an instant, two Finns and a
Frothingham were spinning like a giant pinwheel. Alice saw
that Spike was bleeding and unconscious and promptly fainted.
The reporters hovered on the sidelines.

Frothingham would have liked to call the whole thing off,
but more police came, and Paavo was arrested for assaulting an
officer with a dangerous weapon, in pursuance of his duty, so
Ruth and Alice decided to go along, and plead guilty to another Lord's Day violation, in order to help the Finns, if they
could. Pehr and Paavo both had said farewell to reason. It

took eight men to get them into the wagon, and even more, when they arrived in Malden Center, to get them out again.

Dr. Moody, as soon as he had examined Spike's injury, sent a hurry-call for an ambulance to take him to the Malden hospital, and in less than two hours it appeared. Meanwhile, the doctor had told the reporters that Spike's skull had been fractured and that he was suffering from concussion of the brain.

If a prevailing mood of gaiety and *gemütlichkeit* could be built up in Linden in preparation for a church fair, a sudden tragedy or disaster could plunge the community into gloom, so that chipper little men like J. J. Markham, who ordinarily darted and chuckled around his grocery store like a pet bird, slackened his pace, became morose and was continually forgetting behind which ear he had stuck his pencil.

The Congregational Church bell started clanging at nine-thirty, hours after the early Catholics had dribbled past our house bound for Maplewood. But Deacon Parker did not put his weight on the rope with his customary zest. From all points of the compass, along Linden's streets, the worshippers converged, but none of them were sprightly or self-satisfied. My mother, dressed for church, looked as apprehensive and remorseful as if she had clouted Spike Dodge herself, after starting all the fracas. I was blackly depressed, myself. I did not want the cop to die, or Paavo to be strapped in the electric chair. And I was ashamed of myself for not being able to keep those two possibilities uppermost in my mind, when actually I could not forget the five shows that were coming along, one evening after another. In all of them I had some part to play, either as accompanist or, as in the melodrama, the villain's role, the Count de Courville.

The Reverend K. Gregory Powys, whatever his faults, was not the man to haul in his neck after having wrestled with him self, asked God's advice on his knees, and decided on the text of a sermon. Again the subject was an unfortunate one. The Congregationalist preacher, sturdy little Welshman that he was, had believed it his duty to speak out, plainly, on the Lord's Day controversy. None of his parishioners knew that, and none of the other Linden folks who went to the other Protestant churches, or the Congregational Church that morning would have had standing room only.

Eleven oclock arrived. The last bell stopped clanging. The regulars were all in place, in their pews, with a fairly good crowd of occasional churchgoers, like my Uncle Reuben, Dawson Freeman and Roger, the mail man, who did it to infuriate his Christian Science wife.

Mrs. Ford played the organ. She had had a busy week rehearsing singers, pupils and dance acts for the Fair, so she stuck to the tried and true selections she could play with her eyes closed. The mixed quartet sang "Softly appear, over the mountain, the feet of those who preach," etc. Of all the quartet numbers, this puzzled me the most, because, as I visualized the action, the preachers coming over the mountain would have to be walking on their hands. On that Sunday morning, however, I felt an emptiness in my stomach when I smiled to myself. Spike Dodge, I repeated grimly, must not die. The Sunday papers I had seen at Dawson Freeman's had mentioned that the wife of the stricken police officer was prostrate at the bedside, and one Boston daily, whose copyreaders had never heard of a Protestant cop, had a priest administering extreme unction. I shuddered at the words, only dimly knowing what they meant.

As always on Sunday morning, the moment arrived when the Reverend Powys squared off, straightened his lapels, took two paces forward to the podium and flung himself upon the enormous Book. When I heard his resonant voice bawl out the text, I felt gooseflesh all over. It was Mark II, 27.

"And he said unto them. The sabbath was made for man, and not man for the sabbath."

Of course, Norman Partridge, his wife, two daughters and one son, were only five rows from the front, on the aisle, stage-right. And Mrs. Townsend, with Elvira and Alice, who was out on bail, and worried sick about the Finn, were seven rows back, stage left.

The Reverend Powys began his sermon, and thirty seconds afterward his flock discovered that he was not lined up with the Watch and Ward Society, President Charles W. Eliot, or the die-hard Yankees who would not read a Sunday paper. He favored the views of the unregenerate black sheep who menaced the peace and morals of Linden from that sink of iniquity, the Massasoit House.

"No man putteth new wine into old bottles: else the new wine doth burst the bottles, and the wine is spilled, and the bottles will be marred," the preacher quoted.

"The Massachusetts B . . . the B . . . . the Blue . . . the Blllllllue Laws, wrrrrrritten in an age of darkness and superstition . . . . b-b-b-b-borrowed from England from which Americans had fled . . . . are not fit to contain the wine of present-day life," he said.

"Our Lord Jesus, one day, went through the cornfields with His disciples, and as they went, the disciples began to pluck the ears of corn. Do you not think that, by going a little farther, they could have found some cuh . . . . some cu-cu-cu-corn already plucked?

"And the Pharisees said unto Jesus, 'Behold, why do they on the sabbath-day that which is not lawful?'"

The Reverend Powys laid down his sermon and stepped clear of the podium, rotating his right index finger raised aloft. He was vibrating like an overcharged boiler. His eyes glared and his moustaches trembled.

"Did our Lord say to the Pharisees, 'Arrest us? Fine us? In future we will obey the letter of a foolish law?' Or did He put the Pharisees in their place?

" 'The sabbath was made for man, and not man for the sabbath.'

"Jesus did not say He and His disciples would wait for revision of the statutes. He did not suggest that He would apply to the Low Priests, so that they in turn could consult the High Priest, who would talk it over with the t-, with the t-, with the tttttttttttyrants of Rrrrrrome, with the result that, perhaps, years later, after our Lord had died, been buried and after three days had risen again, he outmoded laws would be corrected. With his other Divine qualities, our Lord had common sense.

"I know it is claimed, by the Pharisees of today that men should wait and tarry, until, after due process, a bad law is amended. I say, 'You are doing no service to the cause of law, by prolonging ancient follies.' There are times to turn the other cheek, and times to protest, as the life of our Saviour indicates. Each man's conscience is his own, but he should think as long and pray for guidance as meekly before clinging to old errors as he would hesitate before committing new ones.

"Let us pray!

"Oh God in Heaven, who has lent His children, as well as hands and hearts, a mind, help them to go forward, not backward, in the light of reason. Aid those of us, we pray Thee, who enjoy the blessings of government of the people, not to be the servile victims of government by other people, but to take the lead.

"Have mercy on those who are passing through the valley of the shadow of death, and those, who in a sudden burst of temper, upset the fruits of a lifetime of toil."

I understood that the peppery little Welshman not only was putting in a word for Spike, but for the Finn as well, and that Norman Partridge, who paid nine-tenths of the bills, had been told off, and no mistake. I thought my poor mother was going to dissolve in apprehension. When the meeting was over, I intercepted Lincoln Freeman, in whose house there was a telephone, and learned that Spike was still unconscious. No change. I had four rehearsals to attend that afternoon, and each one went worse than the one preceding. My mother's Fair, I felt sure, was already a flop and I wanted, if not to die, to go to sleep like an enchanted prince for fifty years or more, when the mess we were in probably would have blown over.

Pehr, the older Finn, who had assaulted only young Frothingham and eighteen assorted cops, without permanently or gravely maiming any of them, had been freed on bail, which Frothingham furnished. The lonely mason had walked straight from Malden Center to the Massasoit, and had stood morosely at the bar, about twelve consecutive hours, after which the Admiral and Jeff Lee had lugged him upstairs and put him to bed.

Monday was a terrible day. Spike still was dead to the world, and the doctors had decided that an operation was the only thing that would save him, if anything would. Pehr slept until six p.m., and then started drinking again. At that same hour, the Fair was officially opened. An hour before, my mother, Ruth Coffee and a dozen faithful men and women had gathered fearfully in Associate Hall, not knowing what else to do. Among them was Jeweller Drown, who noticed that the banjo clocks were slow and readjusted them.

About half-past five, groups of Linden people began moving toward the Square, and from every trolley car and Saugus Branch train, throngs of curious outsiders, attracted by the wave of publicity, arrived. Before the Fair had been open fifteen minutes, the Hall was filled to capacity, but no one had bought anything excepting slices of cake and pieces of pie, fudge, taffy and chocolate drops, bananas and oranges, sweet

corn with butter, popcorn and molasses, fish and clam chowder,
ham and chicken sandwiches, pickled pigs feet, and quantities
of other edibles. Up to that day, I had never heard of a buffet
supper, but, in retrospect, I realize that Linden and her guests
had an almost historic one that Monday night. Some of the
booths were cleaned out before it was time to herd the customers into various niches and corners in order to place the
settees on the floor for the minstrel show. The Hall had a balcony that had permanent benches and would seat seventy-five
persons. Usually, not more than twenty sat up there. That
evening we packed in one hundred and ten.

I must not give the impression that the opening was gay. It
was funereal and ominous. My mother and others were on pins
and needles to see if Norman Partridge would come, after the
attack on him from the pulpit the day before. When Mr. Partridge showed up, with his family and in-laws, they found other
matters to worry about. But none of them was more worried
than I was. Backstage, in the small drafty dressing rooms,
pantry and kitchen, with an overflow down in the coal cellar,
the members and associates of the Wenepoykin Bicycle Club
were blacking up and dressing. Among them was the most
promising of the end men, from Boston, who at rehearsals had
kept everyone in stitches: Charles Sumner Frothingham, III.
Not only did he play a diabolical banjo. He was to sing a solo,
"You're a good old engine, but you done broke down," and
I could not help wondering what would happen if, before we
got that far, the news we all were dreading, about Spike, had
been announced. In the olio, Frothingham's act was not so
topical. He impersonated a blackface dude, with the traditional lisp and broad "a," who had worked as a waiter in a
Harvard mess hall and was trying to train the cheering section
of the newly established Negro college down South.

"Now you'all, when we'unth team appeahth, we'unth mutht

give three wouthing cheeahth, not tho boithterouth ath to be obnothiuth, yet with prethithion."

Those are a few lines I still remember. The whole monologue was a knockout.

Ordinarily I should not have taken such a load on my conscience. I had the faculty of watching and relishing harmless fiascoes with the best of them. But my mother was chairman and my orchestra—I thought of it as mine, although I was only eleven years old—had to sit between those kerosene footlights and the crowd.

Les Wilson, who once had trod the boards with the Ben Greet players, and now was a piano tuner and salesman who lived on Lawrence Street, was the interlocutor, stage manager and director of the minstrel show. He was a pompous little chap, with a large head, bulbous nose, and short legs holding up a normal-sized body. But he was quite a showman, and knew crowd psychology better than I did. After a huddle with Frothingham and Milly Thole, whom the Fair seemed to be bringing together in no uncertain way, Wilson amplified the rehearsed arrangements for Frothingham's coon song.

The Hall was jammed, aisles and all. If a modern fire chief had glanced in, he would have fainted. The orchestra sailed into the overture, "Smoky Mokes," but the start was as ragged as a regatta. Actually, it was not until we reached Uncle Reuben's chorus on the jew's-harp that we got together. The curtain parted, one half as it should, and the other, after being hauled with main force by a brace of volunteer stagehands. Deacon Parker refrained from coughing that night, but little Edna Prescott had swallowed a fish bone, and had to be carried out, retching and shooting her chowder, which, because of the crowded aisle, spattered more than a dozen of the customers.

Mr. Wing, from the piano, seeing my face, smiled, winked and leaned over.

345

"Weak stomach," he whispered, grinning broadly, without missing a beat. "Or are we that bad?"

His philosophical attitude cheered me, and I picked the guitar with more zest. I was to play a half-dozen different instruments before the week was over.

The next bit of audience participation came from the gallery. You all know how the old-time minstrel shows were set up, on the stage. The interlocutor, most elaborately dressed, occupied a throne, stage-center, and around him sat the blackface chorus, in tiers, so those in front did not obscure the others. The Wenepoykin Club had found six good end men, who sat near the wings, three on a side, with bone clappers, harmonicas, banios, sweet-potato whistles, and tambourines. The end men crack most of the jokes, using the interlocutor as straight man, sing most of the solos and do most of the burlesque or comedy routines. The trio on the left were: Roger, the mail man; Packard, the lady-slayer; and William Daley, Sr., the only Negro comedian extant who had a rich Irish brogue. The right wing was held down by Charles Sumner Frothingham, III; Mrs. Dud Shultz, née Big Julie Goan; and a little man no one had noticed before, until he wistfully had presented himself at rehearsal. This dark horse among the minstrels gave his name as Professor Marlowe, and then quite a few of the performers remembered having seen him around the blacksmith shop. Even fewer then recognized him as a part-time barker they had seen at Austin and Stone's, in Scollay Square.

Les Wilson had arranged the program so the numbers would contrast with one another. After the opening chorus, Roger Kaulbach, after a pantomime of trying to telephone the interlocutor, sang "Hello, My Baby," and warmed up the house. His fellow end man, Mr. Daley, knew no coon songs and seemed allergic to learning them, but he had a fine natural tenor voice, with all the Irish nostalgia in it and, as a gag, it had been arranged for him to sing, black as coal: "Ireland must be heaven, for my mother came from there."

Mr. Daley got no farther than that line when Pie-Face O'Day and his cronies from the gallery began to yell and fight. All the Irish were far enough along in liquor so that they did not recognize, under the burnt cork, their fellow Irishman and friend, Bill Daley. Dick Lanier, Ginger and a few of the cooler heads tried to shush them, and instead provoked a free-for-all. Arms, legs and heads tangled and the nest of outraged Irish and those who had been drawn into the *mêlée* rolled squealing, kicking, gouging and biting down the stairs, out the back entrance and into the little railroad park, from which the sound of it competed with the show for a while.

Still, the show was not going over. The harder the talent worked, on the stage, the less resonance the audience seemed to afford. The moment for young Frothingham's solo was getting closer and closer, and the rumors I had heard that the Trumbull boys were planning to rush the stage were disconcerting. Not only on account of art for art's sake, but because whoever rushed the stage had to go over the orchestra pit, in which there were several valuable instruments, as well as musicians of both sexes, ranging in age from sixty to eleven.

While Big Julie was singing "The Old-Time Religion" with a voluptuous shimmy as part of the accompaniment, the young Harvard man slipped from the stage. Evidently he was going to make a more elaborate entrance than most of the soloists did, who simply rose from their places when summoned by the interlocutor, and took the stage front and center.

As Big Julie finished, and before the scant applause died down, Dawson Freeman, unblacked but jubilant, rushed onstage and silenced the bewildered audience by holding up his hand.

347

"Ladies and gentlemen," Fred announced. Even the Rev. K. Gregory Powys peered in from the wings. "I am overjoyed to announce, and I knew each and every mother's son of you will be as glad to hear, that Officer Clarence Spencer Dodge has been declared by the attending physicians out of danger."

Everyone got up and started cheering, and most of the women started to cry. Dawson checked them for another moment.

"The operation was entirely successful and the officer is now fully conscious and has spoken with his wife. The prayers of Linden have been answered."

Then Paavo was not a murderer. What else they might find against him was trivial, after that. For an instant, I came about as near believing in God as I ever did. The instant passed. I reminded myself, in time, that God, if he existed, could have rewritten the whole scene in advance, but I had a brief thrill, as who did not who was then in Associate Hall. Fred, smiling and waving, reluctantly went off-stage. We of the orchestra struck the chord of G-major, one short, one long, and went into the vamp for Frothingham's song. The interlocutor rose, and to an audience that had been inspired and aroused in one split second, announced that Mr. Banjo was going to sing "You're a good old engine, but you done broke down."

Again the crowd stood up and yelled, and even my mother, for the first time in days, laughed aloud. For Charles Sumner Frothingham, III, the blackest member of a very black troupe, came in wearing a cop's helmet and uniform, and holding a large pewter club which bent, absurdly, whenever he leaned on it or turned it in his hands, and which he deformed and straightened as he sang, in a way that illustrated picaresquely faint ribald implications of the lyrics, although he had dry-cleaned them resolutely for the occasion.

It seemed to be fate's intention, that amid such general relief and rejoicing, my bashful and powerful Great-Uncle Lije should be the fall guy. After I cannot tell you how much persuasion on the part of his male and female friends and relatives, Lije had consented to be blacked up, to wear a long curly wig with ringlets, to be introduced as Professor Samson, and do a strong-man act. After the intermission, when the olio was half over, Lije came onstage, to a torrent of applause Our orchestra had Remick's folio for incidental music on the stands, and turned to the appropriate numbers, for suspense in dangerous acts. Lije picked up a standard anvil, raised it high above his head, let it down behind his neck, straightened his arms to the limit again and set it softly down on the stage, without raising a sweat. Instead of making the stunts look hard, honest Great-Uncle Lije was doing them with the greatest of ease. He had to exert himself, however, to tear in two a Montgomery Ward catalogue. He straightened out a horseshoe, lifted both of the Clarke boys at once, and as a climax of his performance, undertook to break a tennis ball with his hands, by compression.

The stage manager, to give variety to Lije's act, had coached him to do the tennis-ball-crushing routine in profile, turning first to one side of the audience, then the other. I do not quite know how to explain what occurred, except that the silence was profound and the audience's attention highly concentrated. The incidental music was suspended, so that we could come in with full chords to swell the applause after Lije was successful. I do not know whether it was caused by something he had eaten, or by his anxiety because the tennis-ball trick was the hardest of all, but he strained, turned, strained, grunted, reversed, his muscles swelled, his veins protruded. And then, before the seams of the ball gave way, a sharp yet fuzzy report, like the tearing of cloth, resounded through Associate Hall, from the stage. Lije, in a panic, dropped the tennis ball and

349

plunged offstage, and the yells, shrieks, whoops and guffaws shook the building. No one could help laughing, excepting a few women who, trying to be prim, were all the more conspicuous.

It was a full ten minutes before the show could proceed, without Great-Uncle Lije, it goes without saying. He never tried a feat of strength again, and only one man, who paid dearly for his lack of caution, ever asked him to.

When the opening night was all over, and Mother, as committee chairman, with a few of her faithful helpers, was making ready to let Tommy Craven lock up the Hall, I noticed she was looking as troubled as over, while the rest of us were all elated. The night's receipts were being counted, and the higher they mounted, the more panic-stricken Mother became.

"Why, Rena. Two hundred and sixteen dollars . . . More? That's impossible. What shall I do?" Mother said, to Mrs. McNeir.

Usually, the Fair netted the church about twenty-five dollars a night, when all expenses were paid.

Benjamin McNeir, Rena's husband, volunteered to walk over with the cash to the Massasoit House, to ask the Admiral to lock up the money in his safe. That relieved Mother's mind. She would not have slept a wink with all that money in the house. As it was, Rena McNeir was the wakeful one, since Benjamin did not show up at home, after his errand, until half-past three. Benjamin seldom got a chance at the Massasoit, and made the best of it. My Uncle Reuben, who took Benjamin home, increased his already stupendous unpopularity with his friends' wives.

On Thursday evening, the night of the serious concert, which most of us feared secretly would be a frost, the enigmatic little Professor Marlowe saved the occasion. His burnt cork removed, his silver hair, cut long, and his expressive silver eyebrows, the hurt look around his mouth and his great glowing eyes proclaimed him as an actor, and moreover, a tragedian. The modern movies would have us believe that whenever good fellows got together, in pioneer or olden days, some broken-down actor would deliver the soliloquy from *Hamlet*. Not Professor Marlowe. His big number was "The Ballad of Reading Gaol."

Before staging his "Ballad," the intense little man, a stranger to Linden, consulted with Mr. Wing, who put his purse at the Professor's disposal for costumes and properties. So after Mrs. Archer had sung "I know a place where the sun is like gold, and the daffodils dance with spring," the stage lights were dimmed, that is to say, half of them were blown out. Before the curtains parted, the shuffling of feet and the murmuring of voices were heard. As the stage was exposed, the audience saw a circle of men (mostly bums from the blacksmith shop) in convict's stripes, caps, and heavy hob-nailed boots, tramping around and around in a circle, in lock step, one hand on the shoulder of the man ahead, the other holding a tin cup by the handle. Round they went, and as they trod more softly, the Professor, in convict's garb, stepped out of line and into the spotlight, baring his silver head. The martyred Wilde should have been there.

The Professor scarcely looked up at the audience as he began:

> *He did not wear his scarlet coat,*
> *For blood and wine are red,*
> *And blood and wine were on his hands*
> *When they found him with the dead.*

You could have heard a caterpillar drop.

I shall not regale you with an account of the Fair *in toto*, but Friday evening, with the Tholes, was one I could never forget. Their puppet play, which they had written and prepared to use on the road, in the Sunday evening "concerts" which were permitted in vaudeville houses, minus dance acts, was entitled "The Prodigal Son." Every man, woman and child in Linden was familiar with the Bible story, if a little confused about the moral it conveyed. Before the play was over, Mattie Freeman had to be helped out into the hallway, laughing so hard that tears streamed down her cheeks; her corset-strings gave way with a snap, and actually she could not stand up, without support of two or three strong men.

Unquestionably, the puppet shows conceived by the Tholes and their talented contemporaries were the forerunners of the animated cartoons in Technicolor so popular now.

Heroic measures had been taken throughout the week to replenish the stocks at the Fair, which were drained by such an unexpected demand. By Saturday night, there was nothing left for Dawson Freeman to auction off, and another of Mother's advisers persuaded her to substitute a flapjack-eating contest.

There were only three entries: Fat Clarke, Randy Clarke, and Mrs. Loomis from the rooming house in the Square. I would not dare to estimate the amount of money that was put up, with the stakeholder, Admiral Quimby, at the Massasoit. Jeff Lee was to officiate at the Associate Hall kitchen range, measuring the batter for each flapjack, and allowing one spoonful of pure maple syrup per cake.

This crowning event was the one that came nearest to being a flop, but everyone was satisfied. When the two icemen and the mountainous Juno, who together grossed a third of a ton, got as far as their sixtieth flapjack apiece and were sweating and blowing like porpoises, Dr. Moody put his foot down and stopped the contest, refusing to be a party to triple manslaughter, so all bets were off. It was just as well, for after the fiftieth round, some of the impressionable and dainty women among the spectators were stifling screams as each mouthful was swallowed.

Thus ended that memorable Congregational Fair, and Mother slept soundly that night.

While she was sleeping, Charles Sumner Frothingham, III, unfastened his Phi Beta Kappa key, at the Massasoit bar, and bestowed it on Pie-Face O'Day.

CHAPTER TWENTY-TWO

The Professor and the Stonecutter

PLANTAIN weeds spring up in a New England yard, appearing in one corner as fast as they are dug out of the grass in another. So it was with Linden's wellspring of energy that was cloaked under a deceptive mantle of inertia and tranquillity. If there were nothing doing south of the tracks, something broke out on Beach Street. During a dull few moments in the Square, mild excitement would be brewing at Black Ann's Corner. When there were no feuds in the Girls' Friendly Society of the Episcopal Church, dissent was popping in the Ladies' Social Circle. If all the ministers were at peace with their flocks, then some overzealous patron of the Massasoit was getting himself on the temporary black list by whacking at snakes that were not there. The seasons brought comedy and tragedy, and the coming events sometimes cast their shadows before, and frequently did not. Many, many of the footprints left on the sands of time by Linden folks were soon washed away. One can safely say that Linden life was real, if not earnest, and while the grave seemed to be the goal, there was plenty of scrimmaging around the center of the field.

Everyone felt sorry when Paavo Wallenius was sentenced to four years in the Charlestown State Prison for assaulting an officer with a dangerous weapon. Spike Dodge was sorriest of all. All the politicians, including Senator Mangini, tried to get him off, but nothing could be done.

Paavo, in the prison, worked steadily twisting rope, and be-tween-times read Swedenborg and dreamed about Alice, who, with Pehr and Ruth, was faithful about calling on visiting days. The Finn seemed to have found, in his cell, the peace that passeth all understanding. As long as Pehr had promised to work every day, and only drink at night, the younger brother was satisfied. Just what he expected, in connection with Alice Townsend, it was impossible to understand. With so much time on his hands, Paavo had scrambled the physical with the metaphysical so intricately that no one hoped to untangle them for him again. He had identified Sweet Alice with an angel whose name, so she had told him, was Rhama, and both Rhama and Alice were to meet him at the Last Judgment, hand in hand, and would take their places on the right of the Throne.

Then, again, alone with Pehr, Paavo would begin to lecture his brother on what one of them should do, if the other got married, how they should stay together, as their mother had wished, and all concerned would be safe and happy.

"I can't make him out," the warden said to Ruth one day, apropos of the Finn.

"If ever you do, call me," Ruth said, heartily, but she was worried, just the same, and so was Alice. Already they were dreading the day when Paavo would be unrestrained again. Both women, and Brother Pehr, although the latter never talked about it, knew that Paavo was madly in love, and get-ting farther from reality, day by day.

Faithful to his promise to his brother, Pehr straightened himself out, moved back into the house and shop, and worked, all by himself, each day. Pehr was the one seen daily in Linden, and whose lonely persistent figure, at work or in silence at the bar, wrung their sympathetic hearts. But Pehr was as un-approachable as he was proud and determined. No one knew what to do for him, until one morning, the silver-haired Professor Marlowe, who, seedy and restless as a captive animal, was pacing back and forth in front of the blacksmith shop, registered the making of a decision, faced right, and walked deliberately across Lynn Street to Pehr's stone yard, as if he were going onstage.

"Good morning," the Professor said, in his sonorous, well-modulated voice. "I trust I am not intruding."

"Gude morning. I'm busy," Pehr said, but not unkindly.

The Professor sat carefully on a blank gravestone of convenient height, as if he were stage-center and the audience sat between them and the Saugus Branch embankment.

"You are fortunate, sir," the Professor said, weighing his words, "to have an honorable profession which depends, not on the caprice of scheming publicans and impresarios, and the fickle public, but on the other hand is remunerative and healthful, eternal and dependable. No man looks at you askance. No landlord dogs your footsteps like Uriah Heep."

"I knew two fellows, cousins, by name Heep," Pehr said politely. "One was Irish fellow, the other worked on the railroad."

The Professor ignored the interruption, rose and struck an attitude. "We followers of Thespis, alas, are not the darlings, but the stepchildren of fate. One day we are smothered with public acclaim, with laurel on our brows; the next, impoverished and despised; our services scorned, our triumphs forgotten."

Pehr, trying to catch the Professor's drift, was concentrating, his chisel ready, his mallet poised. Across the street, a dozen of the bums were watching covertly, wondering how it would all end.

"Continue with your work," the Professor said. "Continue, I beg of you, sir. I shall meditate."

The Professor sat down on the stone again, face toward the

expanse of marsh, over which a thin restless mist was gathering.

"If you'll excuse me," Pehr said, and resumed carving the granite.

A few minutes later, Ruth came over from the cottage with a dish in her hands covered with a napkin.

"Hello, Pehr. 'Lo Professor," Ruth said, and to Pehr: "I brought you some gingerbread, for your dessert."

Pehr thanked her, shyly, and watched her as she carried her gift into the house. He listened, guiltily, as if he expected an outburst. He was not disappointed. Ruth strode out of the house and up to Pehr, arms akimbo, trying to make him look her in the eyes.

"What did you have for breakfast, you big chump?" she demanded.

"I had some coffee," said Pehr, sheepishly. Miss Coffee was the only thing on two feet that could buffalo him.

"Cold?" Ruth snapped.

"Brother used to make the fire," Pehr said. "For me, it's too much trouble."

"Last night you ate at the Admiral's free lunch, I suppose," she went on.

"Like always," agreed Pehr.

"And what about today's lunch?"

"I'll read the paper," Pehr said. "I don't get hungry now."

The Professor rose. "I was about to suggest," he said, "that while Mr. Wallenius's brother is, let us say, the guest of the commonwealth, and unavoidably absent, that perhaps I might be of service."

"You?" Ruth said, in astonishment.

"I am not unacquainted with the culinary art," said the Professor.

"How much. . . ." Ruth began.

The little silver-haired actor looked pained. He held up his hand, bowed his head, and shuddered in a way that would have carried to the highest balcony.

"Madam. Prate not of filthy ducats. Nothing was farther from my mind. To share the repast I had prepared, that would be within the bounds of fellowship. But honorariums! Fees! Emoluments! Fah!" The Professor raised his head while Ruth apologized.

"I'll help you clean up the dump," she said. Then, to Pehr: "Keep right on working, squarehead. I've got another job for you, the minute you get done. A stone porch in Swampscott."

The Professor looked at Pehr admiringly. "I have always envied those who have an aptitude for work. Toil brings its own relief, methinks."

The little old man and Ruth entered the shop, and hurried through into the living rooms behind. They paused, gasped and looked at each other.

"Confusion now hath made his masterpiece," the Professor said.

Together they set to work, and before many minutes had passed, Ruth was wondering why she had passed that little man and overlooked him so many times. He was humming softly and happily, bringing order out of chaos in a gentle, quite delicate way.

"A diamond in the rough. An *enfant terrible!*" the Professor exclaimed, softly, with an indulgent shrug toward the yard where Pehr was working.

Ruth saw the fishman coming along Salem Street and, standing in the doorway, bellowed and beckoned. A little later, Mr. Stowe pulled up his cart in front of the doorway. The Professor, now wearing an apron tied up under his armpits, and an improvised dust cap fashioned from a napkin, went out to the tail of the cart, cocking his noble head from side to side as he looked over the fish display. Ruth watched, amused and fascinated. The bums across the street were moving like hens in a crate, trying to miss nothing of the spectacle, but awed by the presence of big Ruth and the terrible Finn.

The Professor built a fire in the range, grilled the mackerel he had selected, boiled some beets and baked some potatoes, made coffee, using an eggshell to settle the grounds, and hurried over to Weeks' barn to get fresh cream and whip it for the gingerbread.

"I'll be damned," was all Ruth could say. She stayed for lunch, and while Pehr worked that afternoon, the Professor stretched himself luxuriously on Paavo's empty bunk, dozing, reading from his pocket Shakespeare, and rehearsing a few recitations he had delivered in former years, as he expressed it, "with phenomenal success." When it came time for the six o'clock blast, he put on his hat and patched frock coat and went out into the yard, standing beside Pehr as if the spectacle they were about to witness was on a par with the attack on Fort Sumter or the stoning of the woman taken in adultery.

The warning whistle blew, the men with red flags hurried along the car tracks, to warn vehicles and pedestrians. High on the face of the ledge, the granite pattern wavered, rose in fragments, disintegrated into dust, slid and plummeted down to the level of the pit. Black smoke, shot with white and sulphur, billowed and churned. Around them dropped flying chips of stone.

"I think we better get a drink," Pehr said.

"If I were in funds. . . ." the Professor said, regretfully.

"I'll pay," Pehr said.

"That I could not countenance," said the Professor. "While I have lost much and suffered cruel reverses, I am not a leech."

Pehr shrugged. He had done his best, and was not good at persuasion. The Professor hastily changed his tone.

"Nevertheless and notwithstanding," he said, "I know from

sad experience how bleak it is to drink alone. And bleaker still, to drink not at all. Perhaps our good host, Admiral Quimby, could find it in his heart to extend me temporary credit. . . ."

By that time he was walking along at Pehr's side, across the fields toward the Massasoit. Thereafter, he and Pehr were inseparable, and Linden was thankful for having been relieved of the spectacle of Pehr's loneliness.

It was incredible how the little actor bloomed, with his new feeling of comradeship and security. He kept house for Pehr, and it was a toss-up as to which one took the other home at midnight. Professor Marlowe held the bottle-companions spellbound with the Porter's soliloquy from *Macbeth,* whole scenes from *Lear,* in which he was, in turn, the fool, the king, and the treacherous daughters. The Professor's "Barbara Frietchie" could not have been excelled by the original cast. He got his trunk out of hock, and moved it into Pehr's house. In it were odds and ends that fascinated Ruth and Alice whenever they spent an afternoon with the Professor.

Odd bits of costumes or properties were among the Professor's relics, along with yellowed theatre programs, from the West Coast, and the South, and along the Mississippi and the Ohio rivers. The little actor had been around, but seemed to have missed New York, Chicago and London. He had a visored Confederate cap from some Civil War play. He borrowed a sunbonnet from Alice. When anything was done at the Massasoit, it was done thoroughly and well, so Elbridge Gerry, at the Admiral's request, spent hours of an afternoon taking the duck shot from some shotgun shells. So that when, in the course of the Professor's recitation, the rebel soldiers fired and shattered Barbara's flagstaff, the old actor, with the visored cap on his head, could fire the gun, filling the barroom with thunderous sound and smoke, and startling the daylights out of any newcomer who chanced to be present. "Barbara Frietchie," complete with sunbonnet, flag and pole, Stonewall Jackson, and the shotgun, became one of the Massasoit's features, and the quality of it, along with the fame of Jeff's shore dinners, was praised from the Berkshires to the tip of Cape Ann, and farther Down East than Bangor, Maine.

The early fall in Linden began the magic season when the weather was predictable for a while, bright enough to be encouraging, sharp enough to be stimulating, not too windy or too calm, days not long enough to be wearisome, nights not too short and inadequate. Perhaps too much has been written about New England and the autumn leaves, perhaps not enough. It is useless to pretend that one has seen color, unless one has witnessed that startling and progressive transformation of the orchards, groves and hillsides. It was as if some divine hand had lifted out the blue from all the warm and radiant hues, so that the sky was pure, aloft, and the earth displayed all vegetable and mineral tints and shades, vivid and subtle, stark and sensitive, rigid and moving, buff and coral, russet and sienna, ochre, chrome, purple and indigo, flame, ruby, vermilion, scarlet, black and gold.

One autumn morning none of the bums at the Linden blacksmith shop on Lynn Street was saying much, and the devil knows what they were seeing, of the larger perspective. Pehr was working in his yard, the loafers were playing mumblety-peg. Their faces were twisted between glee and depravity when, with suppressed grimaces and lewd remarks, *sotto voce,* they saw the Professor, wearing an apron and a boudoir cap he had crocheted himself, emerge with a well-loaded basket to hang Pehr's clothes on the line, and his own, more flimsy and refined. They fluttered, those damp garments, white and colored, as if cloth colors in rowboats had sighted the unexplored continent of colors on the northern hills and were signalling in a puny way, to see if the mainland were inhabited.

Soon all hands were intrigued by the approach of a light spring wagon, drawn by a sorrel horse, and containing three men strange to Linden. The rig pulled up, not at Pehr's stone yard or the blacksmith shop, but alongside a swampy vacant field that stretched from the Finns' place toward Lawrence Street. The three men got out and unloaded wooden cases containing surveyors' instruments, a transit, a level, a chain and a rod.

The gang around the blacksmith shop watched the surveyors skeptically, not being able to guess what anybody would want with that particular lot. The Finns, next door, had built up theirs on a foundation of tin cans and ashes, covered with crushed stone, sand and loam, so that it stood four feet higher than the neighboring ground. The Linden boys began to assemble, attracted by the mysterious instruments and the cryptic signals and measurements the surveyors made. The surveyors replied good-naturedly but noncommittally to all questions, enjoying the avid curiosity and conjecture their work inspired. Before the day was over, they had driven corner stakes south of the Finns' southern boundary line to a depth of one hundred and fifty feet on a frontage of one hundred feet.

My Uncle Reuben threw a scare into Bart and the blacksmith shop crowd by saying that the new lot was being bought by the Salvation Army, which intended to put up a meeting house and save the whole gang.

Ginger McSweeney, who spent long periods of waiting on the turnout nearby, assured the bums that Mother Shannon, from Saugus, was going to put up a branch cat-house, to give her Saugus trollops a change of scenery.

Mr. Newcomb, of the Improvement Association, insisted that the land did not belong to any member of the Association, but to a party named Knowland, John Jacob Knowland, who lived in Winthrop. The officers of the Association had been intending to get in touch with him, but had procrastinated because the land was unpromising.

"Jacob, eh?" asked the Admiral, significantly. "A Jew, maybe?"

"John Knowland doesn't sound Jewish," Mr. Newcomb said, but he was troubled, just the same.

He was more troubled after the investigator for the Association reported that while Knowland had been an Aryan while he lived, he was dead, and that his heirs had recently sold the entire strip, from the Finns' down to Lawrence Street, to Senator Mangini. An emergency meeting was called, and there were rather sharp recriminations. Someone had slipped up badly. The Jewish question in Linden had come to public notice again, when the Reverend K. Gregory Powys was eased out of his pulpit, having stated in the press that he was categorically opposed to racial discrimination, as being exactly contrary to the teachings of Christ.

My Uncle Reuben, the Admiral and Mr. Wing, all members of the Association, took the floor at the emergency meeting and spoke, not unkindly, but indignantly, reproaching the committee for a lapse that might well cost Linden its one hundred percent non-Jewishness. After the meeting, the trio got into the Admiral's rig and drove southeastward across the marshes.

At the bar that evening, Pehr and the Professor did not have a dull moment. The regulars insisted that they knew the secret of who their new neighbors would be. This, they both denied.

A few days after, a string of six dumpcarts drove to Lynn Street, from Cliftondale, loaded with empty cans and ashes, and started filling in the swampy ground. The drivers had been hired to load the dumpcarts from the Cliftondale town dump, and spread the ashes between the stakes on the Lynn Street property. That was all they could say.

Day after day, dumpcarts filled with ashes drove in, loaded, the tailboard was let down and the body of the cart tipped backwards. The whoosh and thud of falling ashes and the rattle of cans were accompanied by a cloud of dust that drifted across Lynn Street and dimmed the crowd of loafers for a while.

By the time the snow fell, the new lot had been brought up to the level of the Finns' land, and the ashes had been covered with a layer of crushed stone from the quarry nearby.

But when, from the Atlantic, the first northeaster blew, covering Linden with a blanket of snow, all construction and local animosities were suspended. In winter, it was hard for the most frantic xenophobes to fret about something that could not happen before spring.

CHAPTER TWENTY-THREE

Nomads and Dilettantes and Music

OUR yard was a small one, about sixty feet by one hundred, but because in those days there were few houses to obstruct the view, it seemed as if all of us had unlimited space. Weeks' field lay in front of our porch, and beyond it, the woods. By turning east by north, we could see all the way to the ocean. I had brought woodbine and ferns from the woods and transplanted them, training the vines on a trellis to shade the front doorway and setting out the ferns in shady corners where the grass did not flourish for lack of sun. Woodbine is one of the first vines to show the autumn colors, and is one of the most brilliant, hardy and rapid of growth. Around the linden tree that had been planted to reconcile me, grew tall English violets. Farther back, Mother had a bed of cinnamon pinks, pure white, and rose bushes marked the borders between our yard and the adjoining ones. We had a small fir balsam tree in the back that stubbornly refused either to grow more than ten feet high or to perish. The struggle went on a decade or more and when the balsam gave up, it died a lingering death through five or six more years. In a town and a country made for trees, that stunted fir of ours was the least promising that could be found, and still I would never cut it down.

From the damp days of spring, before all the patches of snow had left the woods, until the leaves turned and were blown from their branches, Linden was drenched and surrounded with flowers. In the woods, anemones, purple, white and yellow violets, lady's-slippers, columbines, crocuses, gentians, and jacks-in-the-pulpit grew in silence; rich and delicate points and color tones, alternately, in profound shade and dazzling sunshine, enlivening without insistence the greenness that tinged the atmosphere, from treetops to rocks and black soil, and the carpets of pine needles. The wild fruit trees, apple, plum, and cherry, all had their time to bloom and suddenly from unnoticed corners asserted in blossoms their exquisite shapes, which at other seasons were blended into the background. The berry bushes flowered, bore fruit, then subsided: wild blackberries, raspberries, checkerberries flat on the rocks, elderberries with heavy drunken fragrance, huckleberries, wild strawberries, and barberries, Chinese vermilion. It was enough to see them and touch them, without fretting too much about their names.

In the swamps stood blue, white and yellow fleur-de-lys, cat-o'-nine-tails, skunk cabbages, and the red-winged blackbirds and bobolinks swayed. The bobolink, among all the reed birds, had an undeserved lack of popularity with New England boys, because of the jingles William Cullen Bryant had written, under the title: "Robert of Lincoln."

> *Merrily swinging on briar and weed,*
> *Near to the nest of his little dame,*
> *Over the mountain-side or mead,*
> *Robert of Lincoln is telling his name:*
> *Bob-o'-link, bob-o'-link,*
> *Spink, spank, spink.*

After having been forced to memorize eight stanzas of that kind of eyewash, Linden schoolboys who at heart were sound and kind, would start out hunting bobolinks with slingshots, being unable to get at the bard directly. It was a pity, on both counts.

I have often wished that the bobolinks had been able to quote to Mr. Bryant and his devotees a line from "The Love Song of J. Alfred Prufrock," by T. S. Eliot, another New England poet, but a truly gifted one. The line is:

> *That is not what I meant at all;*
> *That is not it, at all.*

On the Linden ponds, frogs' eggs, turtles, pond lilies with flat leaves, not shaped like plates, or hearts or anything else in nature: shaped like leaves. One could feel a rising excitement, as if something wonderful were about to happen, just thinking of the shapes of leaves, the oaks, maples, elms, sassafras, birch, beech, poplar, willows, horse chestnuts.

In summer, milkweed and Queen Ann's lace, the meadows and fields were swept and steeped with color. Buttercups, daisies, dandelions; and later, goldenrod and wild asters. Sunflowers against the barns, wild roses along the stone walls. It did not seem possible that Linden had room for so many. One could walk the length of Beach Street in ten minutes, but not without seeing thistles and tansy at the corner, water lilies along the creek, white and yellow in profusion all over Weeks' field, and Partridge's field, besides the flower beds in all the front yards.

When the sap started running, a few of us went to Sugar Pond with jackknives and lard pails. The ice between the sugar maples would hold sometimes, and other times, not, but if we got wet feet, or got in up to our waists, we simply built a fire and dried ourselves and our clothes. From willow branches, easily whittled into shape and bored with a spike we heated for the purpose, spigots were made, and holes were bored in the maple trees, a few feet from their base, with a one-inch bit and brace. The lard pails were hung on the spigots, and each day we went back to collect and store the sap. I do not know to this day who owned those miles of woods, or the marshlands. The question never was raised. Each man, in Linden, had a vast estate. He was important. He was lord of all he surveyed. Shapes, hues, patterns, odors or colors were spread over immeasurable areas for him.

We have visited briefly a few of the houses in the Irish and Italian colony of Linden, Mario Bacigalupo's and Tom Bagley's. The Irish outnumbered the Italians at least fifty to one, and made up about one-quarter of Linden's population. Behind their houses were level fields, rather soggy underfoot, and a piggery, not a model one like the pork packer's in Revere, but a porcine circle of Hell where pig souls wallowed in mire, got only the inferior grades of Linden swill, from the poorer houses, and in revenge for their shabby treatment, sent out clouds and quintessences of stink that was so vile it was also comical. One inhaled it, shuddered, and laughed like a loon. A cacophony of olfactory sensations passed over Linden when the wind blew from the south, but some of the Linden Irish near the border could smell it when there was no wind at all. Nothing could be done about it, because the piggery was technically a remote part of the township of Everett, which cared not a tinker's damn whether Linden stank or not.

Between the Irish houses and Holy Cross Cemetery stood a detached grove of trees where each year a band of Gypsies camped. Why the Gypsies chose that spot, with so many miles of better woods available to them, I never understood, or asked. But I learned, in talking with them and watching them, quite a few things about Gypsies, why they live as they do, what they like, what they avoid, and what leaves them indifferent. I think, like the actors on a Chinese stage, they "make their own scene" with themselves, their trappings, and their costumes. They are not more sensitive than other people to the beauties and wonders of nature. In ways they are less so. What they want is self-determination and lack of restraint from the outside. Actually, the discipline in the tribe of Gypsies that camped in Linden was stricter than any other discipline in the town.

I do not mean that the leader of the Gypsies was harsh or cruel, that he cracked his blacksnake whip and, like Ben Bolt, caused the Gypsy girls to tremble at his frown. He was a pleasant, easygoing man, large, tall, and handsome, in spite of smallpox scars, and his name was Andreas. By outsiders, he was addressed as Andy. His wife was broad and capable, with a thrilling husky voice. Her name was Marie.

Before any of the Gypsy women left camp to go to Everett, Maplewood or Linden, they checked with Andreas or Marie for permission. The leaders liked to know where all their tribesmen were and what was going on. Neither Packard nor Dick Lanier, nor any of the Linden wolves could ever get close to one of the Gypsy girls, or talk with her alone. This the young men regretted infinitely, but stopped trying, after years and years.

The girls were handsome, in a dark, mysterious way, with flashing eyes and white teeth, and a dangerous smile. They seemed to enjoy flirting, but that was the end of it. This band of Gypsies was so clean that cleanliness seemed sometimes to be their principal occupation. There were two tents set apart as bathing tents, one for women and young children, the other for men. They were continually in use. The Gypsies built fires in the open, heated stones among the coals, and used the hot stones to heat their bath water. They wore gay colored scarfs, shawls, bodices and skirts, with dozens of petticoats, long stockings and slippers. All of these articles of clothing, and others more intimate, like long ruffled drawers and complicated underwear, not on the modern dainty side, were continually being washed. The men's clothes were washable, too. The Gypsies were traders. The men traded horses, saddles, harnesses, horse blankets, and Gypsy salve and liniment that my two sporting relatives, Lawyer Birch and Uncle Luther, swore by. The women traded or sold colored cloth, scarfs and shawls, peasant jewelry and ornamental slippers.

I introduced Ruth and Alice to Marie, the head Gypsy's wife, and they bought out the tribal supply of wrought silver bangles, clasps and bracelets, and many of the gay colored scarfs. After the first season, Ruth made an arrangement with Marie to buy all the jewelry the tribe could collect in the winter, but when the Gypsies arrived at the grove, the sale was conducted without vulgar haste. Each little article had to be displayed and admired, offered and withdrawn, and the bargaining took days and weeks which were a joy to us and to them.

Everyone else in Linden was sure that Ruth had gone crazy, and she did not advertise the fact that she and Alice each winter held a private exhibition in a swanky New York hotel and made such a handsome profit that invariably they would be ashamed to keep it all, and would buy extravagant presents for the Gypsy women in order to even things up. The whole relationship was warm and lovely, filled with mutual esteem and friendliness.

Andreas never got the worst of a horse trade, but he was firm about his technique. If a man had a horse to trade, or wanted to buy one, Andreas would ask him if he "knew about" horses. Should the man admit that he did not, Andreas would not make a deal unless his customer brought into the transaction a non-Gypsy who was willing to say that he did know about horses.

"A Gypsy will not cheat an ignorant man," he said, gravely.

It was in the Gypsy season that Mr. Wing was happiest, and our common liking for the nomads brought us into close friendship, with music as another bond.

I got my first ideas of leisure and elegance from Mr. Wing. He was a gentleman, at all times of day and night, in every season. He was never hasty, and never dull. He never had ponderous reasons for doing, or not doing this or that, and moral considerations to him were not like Indian clubs or dumbbells with which to exercise his conscience. Right and wrong were matters of politeness or rudeness with him, or questions of taste.

"*De gustibus non est disputandum,*" was a favoritie motto of Charley Archer's, but Mr. Wing always remarked that taste was one of the things worth thinking about.

"Why don't you ever stir off that broad beam-end of yours and do a day's work?" Uncle Reuben asked Mr. Wing one afternoon.

"I *have* money," replied Mr. Wing, calmly, blowing a ring of lavender cigar smoke.

The better I got to know Mr. Wing, the more money I thought he had. His investments were in real estate and some magic documents extant in those days known as "gilt-edged bonds."

"Elliot," Mr. Wing said to me one day, while his deft man, Pfeiffer, was giving his topcoat a final whisk before holding it exactly at the most convenient angle and handing Mr. Wing his pigskin gloves, "if ever I had had to work for a living, you would find me hanging around with the boys at the blacksmith shop."

That worried me a little, because I had been trying to decide what, if anything, I could ever do for a living, and how I could get some apartments and enough bonds to live as Mr. Wing did.

"You could play the piano," I suggested.

"You are not old enough yet to know where," he said, but I knew what he meant. Since Mr. Wing was so unpretentious himself, I did not let on that I knew, for I thought it would annoy him if he thought I was precocious.

The patience and consideration with which Mr. Wing spared Pfeiffer any wear and tear, during the valet's periodical drunks was equalled only by Pfeiffer's solicitude for Mr. Wing between lapses.

"You can live anywhere you want to. What made you hit on Linden?" the Admiral asked one day.

"If I lived in the city, I should become jaded," said Mr. Wing, thoughtfully. "I would not be able to relish to the full my visits to New York and London."

Mr. Wing spoke of London rather wistfully, and every other summer he went there, on a Cunard liner, taking with him one or the other of his girls. Mr. Wing was fastidious when it came to women, and was fond of only two: a petite and serious brunette named Consuelo Nuera, who taught in a Boston art school; and an ample blonde named Julieta Van Lennep, who ran a millinery business. There was no dissembling. The girls knew and seemed to like each other, but they never came to see Mr. Wing together. They visited him in Linden on alternate weeks, on Wednesday or Thursday.

"A man needs a good solid woman after one of those soulful and sorrowful kind," Hal Kingsland remarked, when he saw Mr. Wing and Julieta out driving.

Someone said that Mr. Wing had an understanding with both his women that they were never to ask him outright for anything, and that because Miss Van Lennep forgot herself and coaxed him to take her to Europe one summer, Miss Nuera was the one who made the voyage. This brought Pat Finley, the crossing tender, to the verge of a nervous breakdown. Pat, absorbed for years in the Frank Merriwell triangle, involving Elsie the blonde and the dark Inza Burrage, had identified Mr. Wing's two girls with the dime-novel rival heroines. Pat was such a passionate advocate of the big Dutch girl that he would growl like a terrier, and mutter to himself whenever he set eyes on the trim, dark Consuelo, who, secretly, was my candidate.

When the Gypsies were camped off Eastern Avenue, I would call at Mr. Wing's flat so that we could walk up to the camp together, to hear the Gypsies play and sing.

Many of the high spots in my haphazard life have occurred when I first heard a new kind of folk music, new to me, that is to say. Before my father died, he took me to Powderhorn Hill at sunset one day, to hear a brass band. The sound of those instruments and the glint of the setting sun on the bass horns and the buttons of the uniforms excited me to such a point that I ran a high fever that night, and could not sleep. I was then in my third year. Five or six years later, when I heard the Gypsies playing, on an evening in summer, I thought I should burst. I could not breathe or move or think. I wanted to run around in circles, or fly. I could not believe what I was hearing. Those dark exotic men and women plunged into their music as if it were surf, and stayed there until its ebb left them stranded again.

Andreas himself played a set of pipes of Pan. One of his cousins played the guitar. Another Gypsy called Zoltan played first violin; another played a strange kind of stringed instrument like a mandolin; a very old man with white hair played the cymbalum, with hammers that flew and bounced like drops of rain on a puddle. Marie and some of the girls danced and sang, in a language I did not understand, in words, but understood too well, in feeling.

"What's wrong with you?" my mother would ask, when I was suffering a dazed reaction. "You've been with those Gypsies again." She was afraid that intense experiences were not good for me, that they would unhinge what little practicality I had.

Wild songs! Passionate sounds! The Gypsies quietly went crazy, stopped and started unexpectedly, shaking the music as a terrier shakes a rat, brewing storms and calms; and wherever they went with their music, they carried me with them. Mr. Wing's appreciation was not as naïve or abandoned as mine. He enjoyed the music as he savoured his fine wines and cigars, with exact discrimination.

Some of the simpler melodies, and most of the poignant harmonies I was able to remember, and reproduce in a lesser way on the zither or the piano at home. I can hear them today, as I write, and see the Gypsy colors, the hues of eggplant and red and green peppers, tomatoes, summer squash. The Gypsies performed for money, infrequently, but in camp they liked to sing and play, and the only folks from Linden they liked to have listening were Ruth Coffee, Mr. Wing, Bill Daley, Senior and Junior, Uncle Reuben, Mario Bacigalupo, Olympia Di Brazzio, Professor Marlowe, Pehr, and me. Others came and stood at the edge of the grove, but they were inattentive and made fun of the clothes and the tents, and the outdoor cooking.

At all times of the day the Gypsy women seemed to be cooking, and the Gypsy children, instead of playing games, were usually at work, learning to cook or mend or train the horses and take care of them. The men did relatively little, but liked to watch what was going on, to advise and correct the efforts of the women and children. All transactions with outsiders the men, or older women, conducted.

Andreas had a distaste for law and authority that was deep-rooted and inwardly violent. Neither he nor any of his tribe got into trouble in Linden, but in Boston one winter he was arrested, and had not only to pay a fine but modify his ways. A Boston cop, walking his beat on Temple Street, up the wrong side of Beacon Hill between the State House and the North Station, was startled to see, one winter morning, the head of a horse, which was snorting and blowing out his frosty breath from an open third-floor window. Andreas and his Gypsies had not travelled south that year, with the birds, but had holed in, for some reason, in a few cheap rooms in the North End slums of Boston, had led their favorite horses up the wooden flights of stairs and stabled them in the smaller rooms.

The Gypsies did not like the cold. When the nights in Linden began to get chilly, Andreas moved them on. I did not want to be a Gypsy, or to go along with them, but I admired them.

When, before and during World War II, I heard of the unspeakable brutalities of the Nazis toward the Gypsies in Europe, I thought of Andreas, Marie and their band, and hoped they were on the safe side of the ocean. Hitler's insane jealousy of the Jews because of their intelligence was matched by his hatred of Gypsies, who, of all men who speak about freedom, need most to be free. They cannot exist otherwise, never could, and never will. It has occurred to me that while the Americans I then knew in Linden have scattered to the four winds, that band of Gypsies, those who then were children, are probably together somewhere right now. What is permanence? Which ones of us are nomads?

A word more about Mr. Wing, from his disciple. I did not start drinking heavily until after I was fifteen years old, and have enjoyed it ever since. Much of the etiquette I learned

375

from observing my old friend, whose manners were comparable with Kreisler's mastery of the violin.

"Gentlemen," he would say as he approached the bar, "let us match for the honor of paying."

"One never discusses in daylight the indiscretions of the night before." That was another of his maxims.

Let us hope that in our postwar world, now somewhat amorphous and fluid, we shall find room for men like Mr. Wing who do nothing useful except to enjoy themselves in a civilized way. Their example is instructive and inspiring to those who work hard, in the hope of having more leisure. Without them, the beneficiaries of improved social justice and economic equality would have to learn through trial and error what the gay old parties of darker ages had raised to the level of high art.

CHAPTER TWENTY-FOUR

"The Wind Blows the Water
White and Black"

IN COMPARING American life today with that of the early nineteen hundreds, without assuming that change is necessarily progress, or the contrary, which is equally untenable, the resemblances are more striking than the differences. One is inclined toward the conclusion that history is like the ocean, replenished constantly from above and all sides. If it gets saltier and shrinks, the rate of diminution is so slow as to be negligible, from the human standpoint. Our civilization does not hop from floe to floe, like Eliza crossing the ice, with the bloodhounds of evil in pursuit and salvation on the shore ahead. It is all of a piece, like Einstein's continuum of time and space—an unfinished mess or masterpiece.

Not long ago, John L. Lewis called off the most recent anthracite coal strike, which I weathered in California, breathing balmy air through open windows and enjoying the fragrance of full-blown roses from the yard. The coal strike of 1902, which marked the meteoric rise to public favor of Teddy Roosevelt, overtook our family in Linden, on which also descended, via the bleak marshlands, the first blizzards of one of the hardest winters that rugged little precinct ever saw.

For the Pauls, that was a grim period. Grandmother Dowsett had died that summer, and in cutting the rind of a squash to make pies for Thanksgiving, for Leslie and me—she did not care for them—my mother knocked a tiny bit of skin from the thumb of her right hand. A few days later she got a severe cold. Nearly everyone had a series of colds from fall to spring in Linden. But this one made Mother so ill that she had to stay in bed. That, with the housework and the meals and the fires and the mending that had to be done, was unheard of.

A few days later, she gave in, and consented to have the doctor called. He was bewildered about her temperature, which was high at one time, and below normal the next. On this third call, Mother took her swollen right hand from under the covers, and the doctor gasped and hit the ceiling. No one from Cape Ann, who had handled thousands of lobsters and all kinds of spiny fish, paid much attention to a sore and swollen hand those days. Mother was astonished to find that the slight injury to her thumb had become infected and that she was suffering from what was called "blood poisoning."

From then on until after the first of the year, the daily and nightly life at 63 Beach Street was tinged with nightmare qualities that inexorably took possession of our minds and surroundings. The doctor came twice daily, then two doctors came several times daily. Mother was moved downstairs in the sitting room. There was one operation, then two. Then I lost count of operations. I could only see Mother trying not to scream, then screaming, then unable to scream, as her smooth right arm was punctured, ripped, sliced and drained, until it bore no resemblance to anything human, and carbolic acid mixed with the smoke from kerosene lamps, and hovering death were all the smells that remained.

Leslie, with his unfailing gift for timing, went down with what they called "quinsy" sore throat, an acute form of tonsilitis most painful and dangerous. He was put to bed upstairs in the guest room, that usually was not heated in winter. It was not heated very much that winter, either. Linden had no coal. It was not a question of price, although we could not have paid a high one. The coal bins of J. J. Markham were empty, for the only time anyone could remember. He had put in his orders, but they had not yet been filled. The strike was over some time in October, but Linden being where it was, and what it was, Precinct 2 of Ward 6 got its first dabs of coal some time late in February.

Aunt Emma Noble, from Gloucester, came to us from the Cape to take charge. She brought with her, unknowingly, a bad case of German measles, and was put to bed in Charles' room, which was empty because Charles was in Philadelphia, and was above the kitchen, so the temperature was not as far below zero as it was in my room next door.

We had a trained nurse, Helen Gordon, in attendance, another of the women I have always deeply loved, and she faded away from utility like a delicate angel, and was put to bed with tonsilitis in what had been the dining room.

On the night of the most radical of the eleven operations, Mrs. Graydon, who had seen us through five or six operations before, came to help the doctors, and was holding the kerosene lamp so they could see better what they were doing and undoing, and I, the only member of the Paul family on my feet, saw the lamp waver, Mrs. Graydon turn the color of ashes and sway, and caught the burning lamp as she thudded to the floor, and the surgeon swore under his breath, and, from ever so far away, it seemed, Mother let out the echo of a scream, under chloroform.

I have before me, as I write, the chart kept by Miss Gordon. Up to 105, down to 97, that jagged line I had tried to hold steady by the force of will and desperation. It terrifies me now more than it did then, because then I was refusing, during every waking moment, to admit that it would be possible for my mother to die.

Dawson Freeman shovelled what bituminous coal he had in his cellar into a cart, and had it dumped in our cellar, and Rena McNeir, one of Mother's best friends, showed me how to use it in our stove and furnace. Meanwhile, Dawson and his large family, and all our anxious neighbors, who brought in our meals, wore heavy overcoats, mittens and mufflers in their unheated houses.

Charles got home on Christmas Day, when that chart eased up from its vicious fluctuation between 105 degrees and 95, and only hit 103½. A week later, it was wavering around normal, and each microscopic detail of living: minutes, hours, forenoons, afternoons and evenings had taken on high lights and colors, and the snow was whiter and the bare trees blacker, and one could hear each little sound, and no screaming, and the bituminous coal dust choked up the grates and warped the stove linings, but who cared.

Mother's hand and right forearm, after she was "out of danger" (fatuous phrase) looked as grotesque and useless as it had in the course of the eleven operations. It seems that my mother had talked with the doctors, who wanted, in order to save her, to amputate her arm, below the shoulder, and that she had told them she would continue living, through no matter how many operations, and had not agreed to the unanswerable one.

For months she could not use her right hand at all, and on baking days, I loaned her my hands in the kitchen and learned how to follow exact instructions. I began to think of cooking the way I formerly had thought about painting, the blending of colors and textures, the application of heat, to produce an aesthetic effect, in the realm of taste instead of sound or color. Mother learned to write with her left hand, and did so for two or three years, while massaging and manipulating her right. She would not give in, and within five years had a seventy percent use of the injured hand.

Between the time I was three and five years old, Mother taught me most of what children were supposed to learn in the grammar school. I was an uneasy child and liked to be learning something. So I entered school equipped with arithmetic, reading, writing, spelling, as much grammar as I know now, and a fair idea of geography. Grandmother Dowsett talked Mother out of attempting to teach me history, insisting there was no such thing, on paper. I have always been thankful that Mother started teaching me ahead of time, because it enabled me to skip half the grades in school and thus get out quicker. To me, attending school was a gloomy and unjust imprisonment for offenses I had not yet committed. I still think it is unfair for the authorities to assume that children are going to be so wicked that they are prepared arbitrarily for institutional life instead of activities in the open.

In Linden, as elsewhere, grief and misfortune touched all the houses, and if the fragments of Linden life I have tried to evoke seem predominantly gay, take into account that New Englanders like best to talk about amusing things, and avoid mention of what touches them most deeply or leaves scars in their minds. This is fatal, according to the present-day swamis who encourage their fellows to spill a full twenty-five dollars' worth each hour they talk of the past. I hope the pendulum swings, some day, and authors, at least, are paid corresponding rewards for refraining from talking about their personal frustrations.

I was in my middle teens before Mother came right out and told me that my father had died in the Danvers Insane Asylum. Always I had had a vague feeling that in some way we were set apart from others in town. I cannot truthfully say that I believed there was something wrong with me. I felt, quite frankly, that I was right about many things, and the others were mistaken.

My father died before I was four years old, but I have definite memories of him and of scenes in which he took part. I know he was a man who loved life, and was impractical. His dreams were bright and large, his nature optimistic, and he was alternately a successful and an unsuccessful businessman. One recollection is of a Christmas Eve when he carried me on his shoulder to see an illuminated Christmas tree in the vestry of the Congregational Church. We always had trees at home, but the one in the church must have been so much bigger and more colorful that it is the one I remember. Memory is like that, fusing smaller and less poignant items into a kind of synthesis, for the convenience of a cluttered mind.

The afternoon at twilight when he took me to Powderhorn Hill, and I heard my first band, is also very vivid. And I remember his winning an informal catboat race at Land's End, where, during his life, we had a summer cottage in Rockport. He had an argument, a very good-natured one filled with boasting and laughter, as to whether he or some other man made the best Johnnycake, and in the end, my father baked it, with a metal reflector and hot rocks. The quality of his voice was so much like that of his brothers that I have since confused the sounds of all of them.

On the wall of our sitting room, behind the old square piano on which I played hour after hour, was a tinted and enlarged reproduction of an old tintype from the family album, softened and sweetened and colored like a baby's bedroom, blue eyes and pink cheeks, soft brown hair, neatly parted, and soft brown moustache. The broad shoulders, which his brothers all had, too, and his sons all inherited, had been modified. My mother, I think, liked the picture very much, or perhaps

382

it was the best one she had. When I tried to bring her around to the subject of my father, she shied away, sadly, and mentioned that he sang in the church choir, had worked in a bank, had developed Land's End, and had owned a factory that had burned. The fire, I was given to understand, had marked the collapse of the family fortune, and my father's health.

I did not believe a line or tint of that picture, and the longer I stared at it, the more I distrusted it. Undoubtedly I should have asked my uncles what Father was like, and many times I was on the verge of doing so. I felt no impulse to ask Charles, because his standards were so different from mine.

When I was twenty-eight years old and wrote my first novel, of which the manuscript was lost, the opening scene as it came to me had to do with my father, on his knees, with other men struggling to quiet him and my mother in tears. I saw it in every detail, and when finally my mother read my description of the scene, she was shocked and dismayed. It was brutally accurate, as was another following, in which a cold black wagon drove up to the house and strange men in white coats came to take Father away. This time he was bound securely in torn strips of sheeting.

Those childhood ordeals, the terror of which I must have felt, were buried so deep in my mind that they only rose to the surface twenty-five years later. Quite a few others have arisen since, to make things clearer.

To me, my father is the unknown, intangible hero whose reality I have seldom been able to contact, and the man who, in departing this world, left practically no trail behind him that I could follow. I have never cared to hear about him from persons I considered to be poorly qualified witnesses, however dear they were to me. Too much had been told me vaguely about his sterling qualities and his virtues, but always by the kind of people who speak well of the dead, and are not the shrewdest observers of the living. I should like, sometime, to know what my father was like when he was alive. I should like to be able to reassure him that, no matter how he failed in business or in health, and was tagged to die a long and agonizing death, before we got acquainted, I consider the adventure on which he helped launch me fantastically worthwhile.

When I was thirty years old, in the throes of my first marriage, Charles, on a visit from Dayton, Ohio, where he was then City Manager, took me aside. I knew something embarrassing to him and probably both of us was coming. I had learned through the years to recognize that serious expression on his face and the way his voice thinned out and rose in pitch when he was forcing himself to a painful duty.

"Elliot," Charles said. "I hope you have not been worrying about . . . the way Father died."

I was startled into replying with the exact truth.

"I have worried about it a great deal," I said. That was true, but had not prevented me from doing whatever I felt impelled to do.

"Before I was married, I looked into the matter, and found there was nothing that could be . . . passed on to us," he said.

I mumbled my thanks, and we never referred to the subject again.

Our lack of money—I never actually thought of it as poverty —for the most part did not trouble me, because I had nearly everything I wanted badly. Once in a while, the dearth of coins became acute. One of the girls in my class in school, and one I liked and admired, was called out of the classroom one day and it was whispered around that her father had died. Any reference to anyone's father at that time caused me to shrink and try to get away, or change the subject. In those years, I was perpetually aware that I did not have one, alive, and that life for me, on that account, was not well rounded.

Late that afternoon, Leroy Partridge, who had been selected by a group of our schoolmates, called at our back door
and said that each of them was going to give a quarter toward
a wreath of flowers for Mabel's father's funeral. I went inside
and asked Mother for a quarter and she must have been especially harassed just then. She said, very sadly, that we could not
spare a quarter.

I stole soundlessly down the cellar stairs, and waited for
the bewildered Leroy to go away, and when I heard his footsteps receding down the steps and driveway, I left the house
by the cellar door, went to the Square with the blood pounding
in my temples, not knowing exactly what I should do, stole a
quarter from the cash drawer in Seymour Batt's little dry-
goods store, pretending to look for thread, hurried to the
Partridge back door, and gave the quarter to Leroy, explaining hurriedly that Mother had not been feeling well when
he called at our house, and that I was sorry to have kept him
waiting. My conscience never has troubled me concerning the
small theft. I did the best I could. But the way I felt while
Leroy Partridge was waiting and waiting on our back porch
has caught me in the strangest times and places and surroundings, twinging and throbbing like an old wound, and causing
my cheeks to grow hot and my mind to be numb for a moment,
like a limb that has "gone to sleep."

Charles, my older brother, shouldered his heavy responsibilities heroically, but without fuss. That was his way. It was
not many years before our monthly forty dollars swelled to
sixty, and more, as he made his way upward in the engineering
world. At the age of fifteen I went West and got a job that paid
handsomely, according to the standards of that year, and from
that time onward spent money faster than I could get my
hands on it, from any source whatever. That was the result, for
me, of the early years of penury, and my constant awareness

that my mother was scrimping and saving. So the same set of misfortunes and events made of Charles a truly noble character, unpretentious, restrained, and with a conservative view of the value of money and everything else. My brother Leslie, a year younger than I am, or not quite so old, if you prefer to put it that way, adjusted himself in a way not like Charles' or mine. Whatever he has had, in the way of income, which has always been close to the average but not more, he has simplified or amplified his needs accordingly, so that each day, each week and each year he comes out square with the world. Today, as I write, it is Wednesday. I venture to say that Leslie's week's pay is about two-thirds gone and he has begun to go easy until Saturday.

I sometimes felt guilty, having so much fun and action myself, thinking that Charles, with his eminence in his profession, his place as a respected leader in his chosen city, Dayton, Ohio; his wife, Camilla, who was ideally qualified to share his kind of career; and money in several banks, safely and carefully invested; was not getting enough out of life. Probably I was wrong, but I never felt that way about Leslie, who has shied away from responsible positions as fast as they were offered, content with moderate means, comparative obscurity, and not too much strain.

If I have reproached my family and relatives with over-reticence, I must admit that I am not a chatterbox myself, when it comes to revealing what has hurt or disappointed me. When I was eight years old, and had just heard Great-Uncle Lije explain how to jig for herring, I got up at dawn, having rigged up a reel and line, with hooks in series for jigging. Alone I walked miles across the mysterious marsh, among the horseshoe crabs and waterfowl, to a bridge over the Saugus, where the herring were running. I got there so early that no other fishermen had put in an appearance and, thrilled as I was with any new experience, unreeled my long line, letting the heavy sinker swing above the water.

Something happened so suddenly that at first I could not believe it. I, the descendant of fishermen and sailors, had forgotten to make fast the end of the line to the reel, so my line and tackle disappeared into the stream and I was faced with the long walk back home, empty-handed.

I was so ashamed of having done such a foolish thing that never, before today, have I told anyone about it. I was thankful that no one had been with me. I shall never forget the way that loose line looked, when it slid from the reel and wriggled into the river's surface like Balzac's "adder into a bowl of milk." I sobbed with mortification and laughed aloud, at the same time, it was so startling and comical. Everything was right and all set, but that one little failure to tie the line to the reel, before I wound it. I have thought of the way the water looked, from the bridge, of the herring that may or may not have been under the surface, of how that morning would have turned out, if I had jigged a number of herring. Nothing ever impressed me so sharply with the detestable truth that however many apples some men can pick in one day, other men will take bad falls because a pig chances to rub himself against the ladder.

When he was in funds, Uncle Reuben was generous and solicitous, and although I never remember having asked him for anything directly, he came through handsomely when he knew what I wanted. My oil colors were an example. Once he grasped the desire I had for them, he was lavish. I had explained that ultramarine blue would be all right, and was cheaper than cobalt. Result: Uncle Reuben brought me enough cobalt blue to have lasted Tintoretto a year. My bicycle was also a present from Uncle Reuben, and, while I was in high school, my first tuxedo, cut down by Moe Selib, after my uncle got too stout to wear it.

At all ages, and in all economic brackets, my tastes have been expensive, and no substitutes would ever do for what I had set my capricious mind upon. All of us had childhood problems and frustrations, or else suffered from a lack of them, due to overindulgence by parents. I do not wish to over-emphasize mine, and I cannot honestly ignore them. I have always felt somewhat cheated because I never had a religious faith to lose, or a fear of Hell to conquer.

Up to the age of fifty-six, I have seen no evidence of Divine justice operating here below, and frequently have been rather glad there was none. I studied physics, and am willing to let the physicists have their law of action and reaction. In human affairs there is luck, and I have had my share, mostly good and some atrocious.

It is impossible to mention Linden without a salute back through the decades to Luke Harrigan. His was a great poetic soul. He dressed as nattily as the late Jimmy Walker, and in better taste than James M. Curley.

Luke had no brief for politicians, whether they were Malden Republicans who gave the short end of every stick to Linden, or Boston Democrats who stole the city blind. He was an artist. With the slightest encouragement he would have worn a flowing black tie, and a broad-brimmed black felt hat. His wife, whom he adored and feared, would not let him.

Whenever boys in Linden, either Catholic or Protestant, wanted advice or help in any of their projects, large or small, they headed for Luke Harrigan's house over on Elm Street, just behind the Linden Grammar School. He helped them raise money by subscription for football gear and baseball suits, was stage manager for all their benefit entertainments, and he was one of the few Linden commuters who had a good job in the city (drawing down fifty dollars or more each week) and whose work could be seen, pointed out with pride, and inspected by any kid from Linden who made a trip to Boston. Luke was head window decorator in a Boston department store on Tremont Street, and was the Dali of his day.

The busy weeks before Christmas, his display took up most of the ground floor of the popular establishment, with lavish decorations in Santa Claus red, white cotton batting, tinsel trimmings, stars, wise men bearing tribute, sleigh bells, artificial snow and communal good cheer. Luke was the store Santa, with an uncanny way of finding out what impressionable or bashful children wanted and keeping the unruly ones within bounds. Candles never burned more brightly than in Luke Harrigan's domain, and if a branch or two of evergreens caught fire, it was promptly extinguished.

When the candles gave way to colored electric bulbs, after the Iroquois fire had made America conflagration-conscious, Luke had a way of making them high-light the multihued bangles and he burned a pot or two of candle-grease incense to heighten the illusion. It was Luke who persuaded his proprietors to import some live reindeer, from heaven knows where, who saw to it that all letters to Santa were answered, who spent his own pay in supplementing the resources of family groups who seemed to need special attention, in the interest of the holiday spirit.

In one of Luke Harrigan's windows, live little girls wore dolls' dresses, in gala costumes of all nations. His kitchenware counters had faces of Brownies and all the little people sketched on pans. His boys' department gave away puppies from the Animal Rescue League with boys' suits and shoes and rubbers. Luke first thought of "trading-stamps"; he had a Punch and Judy show in his children's book department; and a monkey who used a toothbrush in the drug department. He stationed cooks in full regalia who made flapjacks in the windows, and, when they got in burlesque arguments with the Irish dishwashers, forgot to catch the hot cakes, now and then, when they tossed them in the air. Those spilled hot cakes were charged to display advertising.

The safe and sane Fourth of July had not denatured the national independence day when Luke was in his prime, and he was the one who went to the city council and saw that Linden got a share of the appropriation for public fireworks, collected money from the men who could afford it to supplement the public funds, and when on Fourth of July evening the rockets and Roman candles, the monkey puzzles and pinwheels were set off, Luke lighted the fuses, and topped it off with a set piece depicting the American flag.

Luke Harrigan's bosom friend in Linden, outside of his brothers and cousins among the Irish, was Alec Graydon, and Alec, who seldom earned much money, was lavish with his time and the services of his old mare, Daisy, and his wagon.

In politics, Alec Graydon and Luke Harrigan had another firm bond. It was natural for Harrigan, as an Irishman, to be a Democrat, but Alec was one of the few and faithful among the Protestant Democrats, and Luke saw to it that his friend had odd jobs, driving voters to the polls, representing the minority party when votes were counted, mowing and burning vacant lots when the weather was too dry, and helping shovel out the snowplow when the going got too tough after a blizzard.

The example set by Luke Harrigan was a little trying to some of the other Linden husbands and young men who were eager to make an impression on their girls. For each Saturday, when he got off at the Linden depot from the last north-bound train, he carried under one arm a long beribboned box of flowers—violets, lilies of the valley, or American Beauty roses

—for his wife. In his other hand he had a two-pound box of chocolates, Page and Shaw's, no less. Saturday was the busiest day in the Boston department stores and Luke was on duty until late in the evening. In order to have his window displays ready for the new week on Monday, Luke had to take the streetcar into Boston Sunday evening and work with his assistants from one minute after midnight until the store opened Monday morning. Then he was free until Wednesday.

Monday afternoon he spent in the Linden barbershop, having his hair trimmed and shampooed, and enjoying, after the shave, a series of hot and cold towels that freshened his complexion and his relish of existence. His wit and logic were baffling to the Linden Republicans.

"Gentlemen," he would say. "You have most of the votes, so at least admit we have the arguments."

Luke never ranted, or raised his voice. He would shake his head, sigh deeply, and take a pitying attitude toward the standpatters who, just then, were sold on the "white man's burden," the "little brown brother" in the Philippines, the "manifest destiny" of the United States as an imperial power, the gold standard, the protective tariff, and the philanthropies of multimillionaires.

"The *Sassenach*!" Luke would say, sadly. "Now shouldn't the world be proud of John Bull. I weep when I think of the martyrdom of Ireland."

"Indeed. Are there any bleedin' 'Arps left over there?" George Hobart, the Cockney, would say. "I thought the last load 'ad just joined the Boston police force, or the 'od-carriers' union. 'Ard to say which is 'igher society."

As he spoke, Luke would absent-mindedly be taking a good cigar from his vest pocket and extending it toward the Cockney, who, still bristling, would accept it in a casual way.

391

CHAPTER TWENTY-FIVE

The Penultimate

IN THE days when Spain was free, and men were gathered at the bar, no one ever proposed a final drink. That word had too harsh and ominous a sound. They called the last drink *"La Penultima."* Thus in parting they felt no breach in the continuity of acquaintance or friendship. Writing about Linden, I feel the same way. I could never exhaust the subject. There would always be less on paper than was contained in the memories I had not touched upon. So let this chapter be the penultimate, and the reader, from his own boyhood recollections, or his curiosity as to how his fathers lived, may continue this work to an individual conclusion.

The late Gertrude Stein, a dear friend of my Paris days, said, that the immediate past seems farther away than periods more remote in point of time, since the present is made up of reactions against it, and it has not yet become historical. I repeat that what I have recorded about Linden constituted "modern life" then, as "modern" as anything taking place to-day. The present is continuous, and all we experience directly is in the present tense. We remember it that way. What we have lived is always with us, whether we are thinking about it at the moment, or not.

In the first chapter of this book I mentioned a few men who were born in Malden, near Linden, and whose names had become well known elsewhere—F. P. A., Erle Stanley Gardner, and the late Harold Stearns. Perhaps Linden's most authentic claim to fame springs from Joe Walcott, welterweight champion in 1901, and as game a fighter as ever put on gloves. Joe, black as a silk hat, with lithe legs and stocky shoulders, used to do his road work up and down Eastern Avenue. He did not exactly live in Linden, but we claimed him. He used to run from Broadway past the cemetery and through Linden Square, and invariably he would take a turn around the Massasoit House, giving it a wide berth and refusing, in pantomime, the frantic invitations from Jeff Lee and the regulars to drop in a moment and break training. Colored fighters had a hard row to hoe in those days, seven years before Jack Johnson became heavyweight champion, but Linden has always been proud of Joe Walcott, as every Malden High School alumnus thinks back with affection to Bill Bullock, our football coach, and one of the first of his race to be chosen All-American end when he played for Dartmouth.

A few years ago, the last of the Davenport heirs left her magnificent mansion and estate in Malden Center to the city, for use as an old folks' home. Her will stipulated that "nothing in the house or on the grounds should ever be changed." That is quite an order for the city fathers. One can foresee that, a thousand years from now, if a Davenport memorial toilet gets out of order, the future authorities of Malden may have to do some archeological excavation in order to find a spare part. The conditions for admission into the "home" are rather rigid. In fact, not a single living inhabitant of present-day Malden, still including Linden, has been found who qualifies. The city authorities are reluctant to contest the will, for fear that the splendid property across from the high school and next to the Public Library, on Pleasant Street, will fall into other hands.

To be admitted into the "home," an applicant must have been a resident of Malden twenty years. In a suburban city over which a metropolis is creeping, that term of residence is rare. Furthermore, the citizen seeking shelter and repose in the Davenport place must have been married thirty years, to the same person. Outside of that, he or she must be a Protestant.

I doubt if anyone from old Linden will ever be found in that institution. Hen Richards, the hermit, died before World War I, and besides, Hen never was married thirty seconds, let alone thirty years. He died quietly, in his sleep, without disturbing anyone, and all the secrets about his youth the members of the Ladies' Social Circle would have given much to know were buried with him, not in Potter's Field, but in a respectable cemetery plot his neighbors paid for. Mario Bacigalupo, who then had a fruit store of his own, put on his old clothes, dismantled Hen's old shack, cleaned up the area, and the grass of Day's field grew over it again. No one asked Mario to do this, and he consulted no one. He thought that was what Hen would have liked to have done, so he carried out the hermit's unexpressed wishes. With Hen's passing there must have been an infinitesimal readjustment of the circulation of United States' currency, for the twenty-five dollars yearly he accepted for value received, and spent mostly for flour, salt, sugar, coffee and condensed milk, without Hen to handle them, had to find other channels.

Shall we ever have an accounting machine, supersensitive as a seismograph, to mark a little dip in the curve when such losses to our economy occur?

Jerry Dineen, the industrious newsboy who everybody was sure would succeed, has done so. He is the owner and operator of a chain of filling stations north of Boston, and his wife, who was Phyllis, the red-haired Bagley girl, has lived with him more than thirty years. But they are Catholics, not Protestants, and may not darken the doors of the Davenport home, in case they lose their fortune. Jerry got his real start when Mr. Wing, up early in order to go duck shooting, stopped him one morning as Jerry was about to deliver his paper.

"Jerry," Mr. Wing said. "You may not be aware of it, but I am tremendously indebted to you."

"Why, no, Mr. Wing," Jerry replied. "Your monthly bill is paid, up to date. Mr. Pfeiffer attends to it."

Jerry called every man, including valets, "Mister."

Mr. Wing drew himself up, and inhaled the salt air.

"I am speaking, young sir, of that which is more precious than money," he said. "You have made possible for me much enjoyment of life."

"Gee. Thanks," said Jerry, groping, but receptive.

"You enter my building, I am informed, between five o'clock and six each morning, leave the appropriate papers, neatly folded, at the several doors, for the accommodation of me and my tenants," said Mr. Wing.

"I try to be quiet," said Jerry.

"That is the point. You have been considerate and noiseless each day, including Sundays, for about ten years. That means that, thanks to you, I have benefited by . . . three times three hundred and sixty-five times ten . . . you're good at figures, Jerry. . . ."

"Ten thousand nine hundred and fifty," Jerry said, with deference.

"In a weary world, where worry and fatigue press like a soiled blanket over man's dreary lot, what should you say would be the value of ten thousand nine hundred and fifty hours of blissful sleep and oblivion?" asked Mr. Wing. "In round figures, my boy."

"I've made quite a little money by not sleeping those hours," replied Jerry, quick on the trigger.

"Another item of my indebtedness," said Mr. Wing. "If there were not staunch American boys like you, unafraid of

395

honest toil and aware of its dignity, an indolent and useless member of society like me would not feel justified in taking it easy."

"Why should you work if you don't have to?" Jerry asked, kindly.

"We all have our separate gifts. I daresay you could not be idle if you tried," said Mr. Wing.

"That's the truth, Mr. Wing," said Jerry. "Two years ago my old lady made me go to York Beach, Maine, for a week's vacation. Before the first day was up, I had to get a job, washing dishes at one of the hotels, to keep from going bughouse."

"Dear me," said Mr. Wing, distressed. "Let's not pursue the subject farther. I merely wanted to ask you what you would like best to do . . . not all your life, perhaps . . . but how would you like to make your beginning? I've watched you. George Sampson could hardly get on without you. Now you can take a bicycle apart and put it back together in less time than Edgy Gerry can pump up one of the tires. This newspaper route? Of course, pennies count up, and accumulate, but a smart boy like you should not work for chicken feed. Your country has need of you, in larger ways."

"The way I look at it," Jerry said, "the bicycle is on its way out, and the coming thing is the automobile. I wish I had a bicycle repair shop of my own, built so I could convert it into an automobile repair shop and a garage, like a few I've seen in Boston."

"Can you keep a secret?" Mr. Wing asked.

"If I couldn't, lots of people on my route would be out of luck," Jerry said, sincerely. "The things I've seen, out early in the morning."

"Discretion is the better part of popularity," said Mr. Wing. "That is one talent we have in common, my boy."

To Jerry's amazement, Mr. Wing told him that he wished

to finance Jerry's plan, not as a partner, not as a philanthropist, but as a sound investment. Mr. Wing offered to loan Jerry whatever money he needed, to acquire a building site suitable for a garage and, until there was demand for automobile repairs on a large scale, a bicycle shop. Jerry was still a minor, so Mr. Wing suggested that the leases and contracts remain in his name, to be transferred to Jerry as soon as the latter could be legally responsible.

"Can I tell my mother?" Jerry asked, in a daze.

"Never tell a woman anything, young man. That's a lesson you must learn," said Mr. Wing.

"All right," Jerry said, doubtfully.

That was the underlying explanation of the high jinks, with surveyors around the mysterious lot adjacent to the Finns' near Black Ann's Corner. Actually, Senator Mangini, who was in on the joke, had not sold the land outright to Mr. Wing, because in that case the transaction would have to be recorded. The lot had been leased for ninety-nine years, only half of which have thus far passed by.

The Blue Laws controversy continued throughout the commonwealth for years and years, and has not been fully resolved even now. A bill was introduced into the General Court, as a result of the commotion in Linden, and each year the legislators had to find ways of ducking the issue, which was political dynamite.

Every bill introduced into the Massachusetts legislature in a lawful way must be read in the House or the Senate, whichever branch receives it first, be referred by the Speaker or the President to an appropriate committee, and the committee must advertise and conduct a public hearing at which any and all interested parties may be heard. Each year the Blue Laws hearing was one of the most widely attended and hotly contested. All the Puritan throwbacks and advocates of individual liberties swarmed to the State House, contradicted, ridiculed and abused one another; invariably the committee, which was composed so that it would be sure to straddle the fence, recommended that the bill be referred to the next General Court. The next year, the process was duplicated, with increasing vehemence and animosity.

Now when in Massachusetts a legislative problem becomes too troublesome and acute, and the political leaders in power stand to lose something, no matter how it is decided, they have a way of salving the proponents and opponents by appointing a joint recess committee of members of the House and Senate, with funds and the authority to hire a secretary, in order to "study" the question.

That practice is beloved by all the Boston newspapermen who cover the State House, because it is unwritten law that one of them shall get the secretaryship of the committee, and be paid $1,000, for keeping records of committee meetings and hearings and writing the committee's report. This entails not more than a dozen hours of work, as a rule, and includes all kinds of trips or junkets, at the public expense, that the secretary's imagination is capable of conceiving and making plausible.

In the year the Blue Laws fight had reached the point where it became necessary to appoint a recess committee to stall off the public another year or more, John Daniels, a good reporter and talented amateur entertainer, was given the secretaryship, in return for having used the Republican steering committee relatively easy in his Democratic paper. John convinced the senators and representatives that, in order to observe and report on how the other half lives on Sunday, they must visit New York City, in a body. The committee members, having liberal expense accounts, were nothing loath.

Daniels, a most convivial gentleman, was an inspired guide

and started out fairly early one Saturday morning in New York with the Massachusetts statesmen under his wing. The full details, and the adjective is used advisedly, of that excursion have never been revealed, but a New York reporter, at two o'clock that Sunday morning, cursing his luck because he had to work so late, strolled into the Night Court. He blinked, and gasped, unable to believe his eyes.

For lined up, looking the worse for wear, and utterly incoherent, were a bevy of gentlemen, obviously from Boston, although the names and addresses they gave were unconvincing, if not trite. The New York reporter recognized the secretary and what was left of the membership of the Massachusetts recess legislative committee to study the Blue Laws, all pleading guilty on the Sabbath to being drunk and disorderly. The women who seemed to be with them, while each one was somebody's daughter, and a few of them somebody's mother, did not look like senators' or representatives' wives. For a while, the Massachusetts Blue Laws committee backed Harry Thaw right off the front page. The report that committee made, containing recommendations for Sunday conduct, is still on file, as a public document, and may be examined at the Massachusetts State House, by anyone who cares to browse through its pages.

It was in 1922, I believe, that the Blue Laws were modified slightly in the periodical revision of the laws of Massachusetts. "Common pipers and fiddlers," who formerly had been subject to fine and imprisonment, were taken off the black list, with the approval of the musicians' union. Unnecessary work on the Sabbath, including pansy weeding, is still unlawful, although in some communities the statute is not strictly enforced.

My Great-Uncle Lije did not live to see the years of Prohibition, but his yawl, the *Petrel II,* having fallen into the service of the same group of smugglers that used to run Chinamen and dope over the Vermont border, did yeoman service between Rum Row and the Linden marsh. By that time, Frigger Bacigalupo far outranked Tom Bagley in the organization, and one of the tricks Frigger had learned by observing my Great-Uncle Lije's fine Newfoundland named Rover also helped him to keep thirsty citizens from going dry. The Italians who had settled in Revere made quantities of good red wine, and some white that was passable, too, and they kept it on the little farms which had threatened, years before, to depress Linden real estate values. Whenever strangers approached, the fierce turkeys kept by the Italians for the purpose, attacked them, and held them at bay. If the strangers in question were recognized, or had the proper password, dogs who had been trained to chase away the turkeys were let loose and the customers admitted. In case the strangers turned out suspiciously, the turkeys were left to hold the line, and always gave the Italians plenty of time in which to get rid of their illegal liquor before the government agents could effect an entrance.

Just before Paavo Wallenius was released from prison, Ruth and Alice left their little red cottage and transported their antiques to Santa Barbara, California, where they lived happily ever afterward, as the storybooks used to say. Old Professor Marlowe, who had taken such good care of Pehr while his brother was away, vanished, without a word, the day Paavo was due back home, and his body was found in the woods, near Elephant's Back, months afterward.

Ginger eventually married Little Gertie, and two of their boys, at least, drive airplanes instead of horsecars. Believe me, he brought up all his kids to be careful what they did in the snow.

The Admiral, disgusted with free men who would vote for Prohibition, closed his famous Massasoit House, took Jeff Lee and old Gimp Crich with him to Paris, and there, very happily, they died, comfortably boiled, in reverse order to that in which I have named them. The old inn burned down, and the chestnut trees were destroyed to make way for a four-lane highway that also bends around Black Ann's Corner. *Sic transeunt compotari mundi!*

The Reverend K. Gregory Powys, that sturdy Welshman with the steeple-crowned black hat, who defied his congregation on the Jewish question, was called to another church, much larger and more important, but a few years afterward, Linden was flabbergasted when he eloped with Frances Ashdown, a lovely nurse, and a sister of Rena McNeir. From reports I have heard, they have been so happy on earth that what comes later will hardly matter.

Salute, little Linden, and, for the moment, *au revoir*. What I observed among your people and mine as a child has grown upon me, as each day and each year I have been better equipped to evaluate and appreciate my memories of you. Wherever I have been, in whatever surroundings I have found myself, I have felt more like an observer than a participant.

Everyone has a birthplace, and to that locale and its inhabitants, who can say how much he owes? My real schools were the streets, woods, houses, stores and marshes of Linden, and my teachers were Linden men and women, children, and, yes, the animals. I am afraid I did little for those places or persons, in return for what they did for me. If I have resurrected a little of old Linden, so that a fragment of it may be preserved, in all its serenity and beauty, I am content.

Friends! Your glasses! *La Penultima!*